TRAVELLER'S GUIDE
TO THE

BATTLEFIELDS

OF THE ENGLISH

CIVIL WAR

TRAVELLER'S GUIDE
TO THE
BATTLEFIELDS
OF THE ENGLISH
CIVIL WAR

Martyn Bennett

Webb & Bower

FRONTISPIECE: The monument to the battle of Marston Moor

First published in Great Britain 1990 by Webb & Bower (Publishers) Limited
5 Cathedral Close, Exeter, Devon EX1 1EZ

Distributed by the Penguin Group
Penguin Books Ltd, Registered Offices: Harmondsworth, Middlesex, England
Penguin Books Australia Ltd, Ringwood, Victoria, Australia
Penguin Books Canada Ltd, 2801 John Street, Markham, Ontario,
Canada L3R 1B4
Penguin Books (NZ) Ltd, 182 – 189 Wairau Road, Auckland 10, New Zealand

Edited, designed and produced by
Robert Ditchfield Ltd
Combe Court
Kerry's Gate
Hereford HR2 0AH

Text Copyright © Martyn Bennett 1990
This edition Copyright © Robert Ditchfield Ltd 1990

Maps by David McKeown

British Library Cataloguing in Publication Data

Bennett, Martyn
    Traveller's guide to the battlefields of
    the English Civil War.
    1. Great Britain. Battlefields – Visitors'
    guides
    I. Title
    914.1'04858

    ISBN 0 – 86350 – 331 – 4

Typeset in Great Britain by Action Typesetting Ltd, Gloucester

Printed and bound in Hong Kong

Acknowledgements

No book can be undertaken as a solitary work and I am naturally indebted to several people for their help. Firstly I must thank my wife Deborah for her patient and valuable reading of the manuscript. Secondly, special thanks are due to Dr Ronald Hutton for his kindness in reading the manuscript and especially for the helpful comments he made.

Martyn Bennett

The author and producers are grateful to the following for supplying illustrations:

Colour
Martin Cavaney 174; Stephen d'Entrecassteaux 122; Department of the Environment/House of Lords 70; Colman E. Doyle 187; Grosvenor Museum, Chester 34 – 35, 166; Jerry Hardman-Jones frontispiece, 110, 111; K.J. Hoverd/Hereford City Museums 43; Museum of Oxford (by courtesy of the Earl of Dartmouth) 98 – 99; National Trust for Scotland 130 – 131; National Trust for Scotland, Haddo House (photograph by Nicholas Bogdan) 134; Newark Advertiser 86 (below); Newark Museum 86 – 87; by gracious permission of the Duke of Northumberland 30 (above); Sir Charles Rowley 151; Royal Commission on Ancient Monuments, Scotland 138; Royal Institution of Cornwall 47; Diana Saville 22 (above left), 22 – 23, 54 (below), 78, 103 (below), 126, 143, 147, 170 – 171; Scottish National Portrait Gallery 11; Jeremy Whitehouse 18 – 19, 150; Worcester City Museum 194; York City Art Gallery 63.

Black and White
Ashby-de-la-Zouch Museum 36; Ashmolean Museum, Oxford 14, 55, 56, 92, 93, 97 (above); Berrows Newspapers Limited, Worcester 196 – 197 (below); Bodleian Library (*Arch Antiq* AII 13 plate 27 of David Loggan's *Oxonia Illustrata* 1675) 97 (below); the Buccleuch Collection, Bowhill, Selkirk 188; Andrew Carpenter 160; Stephen d'Entrecassteaux 124; Dublin Public Libraries, Gilbert Library 185; East Lothian District Council 192; Grosvenor Museum, Chester 81; Hampshire County Council/Basing House 141; Hampshire County Council (Leeds City Art Gallery Collection) 148; Christopher Martin Handy (by courtesy of the 27 Foundation) 40, 127, 152 – 153; Jerry Hardman-Jones 108 – 109; reproduced by kind permission of the Harris Museum and Art Gallery, Preston 176 – 177 (above); Kenneth Hillier 36; K.J. Hoverd/Hereford City Museums 44, 94 (below); Hull City Museums 58; Hulton-Deutsch 172; Bernard Lane 48 (above and below); Lincoln County Council 16; Mansell Collection 13, 15, 41, 49, 53, 57, 60, 61, 66, 71, 73, 77, 85, 90, 105, 107, 119, 125, 139, 145, 156 – 157, 161, 175, 178, 181, 183, 190, 197 (above); Mitchell Library 137; Nantwich Chronicle 84; courtesy of the National Library of Ireland 186; National Museums of Scotland 129; National Trust for Scotland 132; Newark Advertiser 88; collection of Newbury District Museum 144; Office of Public Works, Dublin 184; Rackhams of Lichfield 42; Royal Albert Memorial Museum, Exeter 120 – 121; Royal Commission on the Historical Monuments of England 94 (above), 95; Diana Saville 21 (above), 24 (above and below), 52 (above and below), 68, 72, 76, 168; by courtesy of Sothebys 112, 149, 191; Peter J. Washbourn 65, 67 (below); Jeremy Whitehouse 117; York Castle Museum 32 – 33 (below), 100; York City Art Gallery 8, 28 – 29 (above).

For Deborah

Contents

Sir Thomas Fairfax, first Commander-in-Chief of Parliament's New Model Army.

Introduction

THE CIVIL WARS of the mid-seventeenth century were probably the most dramatic incidents in early modern Britain. Ever since they began, their causes and their effects have been, and will long continue to be, debated. But the military conflict is merely one aspect of the troubles which affected Britain in this period. Only a tiny minority of the population served in the armed forces, and only a minority witnessed large-scale military violence. Yet, the war – because it caused death, the destruction of property, a dearth of produce in agricultural areas occupied by hungry armies, and taxation imposed across the country to pay for these same armies – affected the mass of the population.

Of all these factors, it was probably taxation that brought home to most people the effects of the war. In the first Civil War, the Royalists imposed Contribution and Parliament exacted Assessment, and these were collected on a regular basis. In addition, both sides imposed excises on several goods and there was a series of minor and supplementary taxes levied at various times. At the end of the first war, the victorious Parliament maintained and even increased its taxation levels; and this continued into the next decade as the Republic sought to finance its growing standing-army.

However, this book is concerned primarily with the military action which took place between 1642 and 1651. It begins with a brief look at the skirmish at Powick Bridge, near Worcester, and ends with the battle of Worcester, some nine years later. In the eighteen chapters, a collection of actions are examined; and for the major ones, the traveller is directed to the battle-sites and to the best viewpoints and places of interest. The text is accompanied by a series of maps which complement it. Major battles are explained in detail, with appropriate references to the features which can still be discerned on the field today. The gazetteer at the end of the book gives additional tourist information connected with each of the major sites.

Inevitably a book of this type must be selective. Wales, because it saw no major battles, is only covered in sub-sections within a couple of chapters. Lancashire, which saw a good deal of minor skirmishes early in the war, is only dealt with in Chapter Sixteen, when the Scottish army was defeated there in 1648. Both Scotland and Ireland have each been dealt with in a single chapter. A separate book could be written on each of these countries, and their roles in the Civil Wars. Indeed, this underlines the misnomer of calling this conflict the English Civil War. Not all of the action involved England alone and the causes and consequences of the war concerned all of the nations which the British Isles comprise. Primarily, however, this book is a guide for those wishing to see the battle-sites of mainland Britain, but it also provides for a trip to Eire.

Each chapter has a series of subsections; these serve a number of purposes. Many simply provide background to the battles dealt with in the main sections. Thus, in Chapter Ten, the course of the war in the North, during the first six months of 1644, is covered before the battle of Marston Moor is examined. Other sections provide different forms of background detail. In Chapter One, uniforms and regimental organization are covered, and in many chapters a biographical sketch of the important participants is given. These latter studies look at the lives of leading figures like Prince Maurice and Sir William Brereton as well as the central characters like Charles I and Sir Thomas Fairfax. It is intended that these sections and the illustrations which accompany them, will round out the reader's appreciation of the Civil War period and that they will add to the picture created by the concentration on the major actions.

Two points about common perceptions need to be made. The general reader may be surprised to find that Cromwell does not merit a separate section until Chapter Seventeen. This reflects the fact that he was not the central character in the story until 1648 – 9. He first appears in Chapter Five, as a colonel, assisting with the attempts to limit the Earl of Newcastle's power in Lincolnshire and Nottinghamshire. In Chapter Ten he plays his first important role – as commander of the Parliamentarian left wing at Marston Moor. From then on his part in the war grows, but it is not until he defeats the Scottish army at Preston in 1648 and then leads the army in Ireland in 1649 – 50, that he becomes the chief actor in the drama. Therefore, the term Cromwellian as applied to soldiers, events or the period as a whole has been avoided. This was not a war between Charles I and Cromwell!

Secondly, when picturing the poor soldiers themselves, the reader should avoid the stereotypical images of a Cavalier and a Roundhead. The former did not have long curls and highly decorative clothing; nor did he face an opponent with short hair and sombre dress. (Full details of uniforms are given in the first chapter.) Indeed, the very terms Roundhead and Cavalier have been avoided. Both were terms of abuse. Cavalier was derived from the name given to the Catholic King of Spain's guards and Roundhead was a term like 'skinhead', given to young men (in this case London apprentice boys who supported Parliament) with close-cropped hair. Roundhead was a term which Parliamentarians sought to avoid, but the Royalists adopted the more romantic-sounding term Cavalier themselves.

None of the sub-sections in the text goes into much detail about the causes of the Civil War. To do so in any great detail is outside the scope of this book. Nevertheless, some form of introductory discussion is necessary in order to prevent the text from being left in a vacuum.

In 1625 Charles I ascended the throne, determined to fulfil the role of king as he saw it, and to save the souls of his subjects by altering the ethos of the English Church. From the inception of his

Charles I after Daniel Mytens

reign he began to argue with his Parliaments over the cost and direction of foreign policy, much of which was left in the hands of his incompetent favourite, the Duke of Buckingham. Charles married a Catholic princess and this was misinterpreted by a populace with an intense hatred of anything tainted with popery. Moreover, seemingly Catholic innovations were being undertaken in the Church under Charles's agent William Laud, first as Bishop of London and later as Archbishop of Canterbury. By 1629, the King had dismissed yet another Parliament after a bitter confrontation over the right to exact taxation, and Charles began to rule without one. The next eleven years, known as the Eleven Years' Tyranny or the Personal Rule, depending upon standpoint, saw government exercised by the King with the help of an enlarged Privy Council.

To raise the necessary money for government, Charles made use of a collection of obsolete or forgotten pieces of legislation. Men of a certain income, adjudged rich enough to be knighted, were fined for not having undergone the honour at the coronation. Minors who came into possession of estates, found their lands strictly administered by the Court of Wards. This was little more than exploitation of their property to the benefit of the Crown. People whose lands encroached upon Royal Forests found themselves subjected to a series of fines. The City of London was fined for not having taken sufficient care to colonize the area around Derry in Ireland, which had been renamed Londonderry for the purpose.

Probably the most famous of these fiscal measures was Ship Money. This was an extraordinary tax, levied in time of war upon coastal counties. The income was used to pay for the navy to defend the coasts. In 1636 Charles, who had levied the tax for two years, extended the collection to all the counties and made it a regular tax. Objections at first were minor ones, dealing with technical points of collection. Only in 1637 when a test case was brought about by John Hampden, did opposition really develop. Although seven of the twelve high court judges found that the King had the right to levy the tax, the narrow margin of victory indicated to many that it was a moral victory for the opponents. Opposition increased over the next couple of years, and by 1640 collection was almost at a standstill.

Whilst these events made secular government unpopular, Charles's religious policy was also causing anger. In the broadly Calvinist church which had developed after the 1558 religious settlement, there was little place for the receipt of the Holy Sacrament. The altar had been moved from its sanctum at the east end of the church, and had become a communion table in the centre. With Laud's innovations this was reversed: the table was returned to the east and railed off and the receipt of the holy bread and the blood of Christ again became an essential part of a soul's salvation. This concrete manifestation of Laudian policy became a point of conflict in the communities of England. Moreover, the seemingly lenient treatment of Catholic priests, coupled with the Queen's own popish chapel at Whitehall, contrasted with the

Archbishop William Laud.

savage treatment meted out to reformers – labelled 'puritans' –
for expressing views not thought out of place before 1625.

It was Laud's attempt to continue his reforms in Scotland which
led to disaster. He and the King were determined that the reissued
Book of Common Prayer should be enforced in Scotland. This
provoked the hostility of the Kirk and the people who pledged
themselves to defend their Presbyterian Church from Charles.
War broke out in 1639, but there was little in the way of armed
conflict and the Pacification of Berwick ended it in June. By 1640
Charles wished to renew the war, but the treasury was empty. Ship
Money could not be raised, and Coat and Conduct Money, which
paid for the army, was not coming in either.

A true and exact Relation of the
manner of his Maiefties fetting up of His
Standard at *Nottingham*, on Munday the
22. of Auguft 1642.

Firft, The forme of the Standard, as it is here figured, and who were pre-
fent at the advancing of it

Secondly, The danger of fetting up of former Standards, and the damage
which enfued thereon.

Thirdly, A relation of all the Standards that ever were fet up by any King.

Fourthly, the names of thofe Knights who are appointed to be the Kings
Standard-bearers. With the forces that are appoynted to guard it.

Fifthly, The manner of the Kings comming firft to *Coventry*.

Sixtly, The *Cavalieres* refolution and dangerous threats which they have
uttered, if the King concludes a peace without them. or hearkens unto
his great Councell the Parliament : Moreover how they have fhared
and divided *London* amongft themfelves already.

The raising of the King's standard at Nottingham.

The Parliament, which met in April, sat for only three weeks. It
would not give the King the money he wanted for nothing. It
demanded concessions from him, which he would not give, and he
dissolved it. Nevertheless, Charles embarked on the new war; his
army was heavily defeated and the Scots occupied the north of

England. Faced with this situation the King had little choice: he called a new Parliament for November 1640. This one began to remove people and organizations such as the Court of Wards, which had bolstered the Personal Rule. As he was powerless, the King had to agree. By the end of 1641, Parliament had altered the balance of power between it and the King, ensuring that Parliaments were a permanent feature of government and that they were called automatically every three years. Parliament went further and demanded a say in foreign policy to prevent a repeat of Buckingham's expensive excesses, and it also wanted a greater role in the selection of the King's ministers.

When a section of the Catholic native population of Ireland revolted in October 1641, claiming that it had the King's authority to do so, Parliament demanded the right to control England's militia – the Trained Bands. These encroachments upon the monarch's power went further than many MPs had wished to go, and a significant Royalist faction developed. By the spring of 1642, Parliament had seized control of the militia and the King had formed his court at York. Throughout the summer, Charles sought to reaffirm his traditional control over the militia, and, failing in this, he created an army. On 23 August whilst at Nottingham, he officially declared war on the Parliament before marching to Shrewsbury to link up with large numbers of recruits. By September, both sides had raised significant armies and the coming of war became a certainty.

Lincolnshire Commission of Array

1. THE BEGINNING OF WAR

SEPTEMBER – OCTOBER 1642

Many men in both armies believed and hoped that the end of the war was near. But the lessons of Edgehill were that the war was just beginning, and it had to be conducted in earnest.

THE MILITIA ORDINANCE

ONCE THE REBELLION IN IRELAND had broken out in October 1641, the question of raising an army to fight the rebels arose. However, after the King had left London in January 1642, it was felt that he could not be trusted to raise such a force without the possibility that he would use it on Parliament. Therefore the Lords and Commons attempted to get Charles to agree to them controlling the army, although it had always been the monarch's right to do so. Naturally Charles refused to accede. Eventually Parliament became so exasperated that it passed a Militia bill and put it into effect under the title of an ordinance. This was to have the authority of an act, despite not having the royal assent. Such instruments were used to govern the country whilst the monarch was absent. Indeed, they had been used during the King's visit to Scotland in 1641.

The only standing army in England was a part-time one based on county levies and under the authority of the Lords Lieutenant and their deputies. The Militia Ordinance replaced most of the present Lieutenants with men whom the Parliament felt it could trust. This was really as far as the Ordinance went. There was no immediate call to arms, despite the assertion that the law was issued for the 'safety therefore of his Majesty's person, the Parliament and kingdom in the time of imminent danger'. Nevertheless the Lords Lieutenant were to organize their deputies who 'shall have power to make colonels, captains and other officers and remove out of their places, and make others from time to time as they shall think fit'.

By the end of May, the King emphatically forbade compliance with the ordinance. Nevertheless, after it was obvious that he himself was gathering armed men about him, the Lords began to act. By early June, in Leicestershire and Lincolnshire, the

Earl of Stamford and Lord Willoughby of Parham respectively began to call out the bands in Parliament's name.

THE COMMISSIONS OF ARRAY

INITIATIVE still lay with Parliament and, by early June, the Militia Ordinance was being put into effect. In response Charles resurrected the probably obsolete legislation – the issue of Commissions of Array. This gave the right to summon the Trained Bands to a group of gentry loosely based on the justices of the peace; in this case, expelled Lords Lieutenant were included in the commission. Letters accompanying the commissions ordered the immediate mustering of the soliders, but lack of funds prevented their being on permanent call.

The commissioners were given almost identical power as the deputy lieutenants. They were empowered to collect financial help from 'such persons as have estates and are not able to bear arms'. The first commission was directed to Leicestershire where the Grey family were enacting the Militia Ordinance. The leading commissioners, the Earls of Huntingdon and Devonshire, were unwilling to commit themselves. The former's second son, Henry Hastings, who had delivered the commission, along with two colleagues as the commission required a quorum of three, began to raise the Trained Bands. This initial attempt, like so many others throughout England, failed. It soon became clear that the Trained Bands were politically divided, with probably the majority of men wishing to remain neutral. In response both sides began to issue commissions to individuals, often Militia Ordinance officials or Commissioners of Array, giving them the right to raise volunteer regiments in person. In this way England was armed for war.

SOLDIERS OF THE CIVIL WARS

FIRST, one must dispose of the old myth that Cavaliers wore flamboyant clothes and their opponents were sombrely dressed puritans. Not every Parliamentarian was a puritan and certainly not every Royalist was wealthy enough to wear delicately laced clothes. Officers on both sides needed to show only small loyalty to the regimental colours and may have expressed their tastes in clothing whilst at war. No such laxity pervaded the ranks, where the uniforms were both practical and affordable. Originally the colours were chosen by the colonels who formed the regiments, probably along the lines of their family colours. This led to much confusion as basic colours – reds, blues, greys, blacks and greens – proliferated on both sides. Only one regiment, Lord Brooke's foot, was wholly distinctive – it wore purple. There was to be no real standardization until the creation of the New Model Army in 1645 with its Venice red uniforms (and even then local armies still wore different colours). Until then armies attempted several temporary battle signs to distinguish themselves on the field of battle. These field signs took the forms of papers or sprigs of foliage stuck in hat bands, code words, or even untucked shirts.

The Foot

Each regiment consisted of musketeers and pikemen, in a theoretical ratio of two to one. They were composed of 1,300 men divided into ten companies. Those belonging to the field officers were larger than the others; thus the colonel's company had 200, the lieutenant colonel's 150 and the major's 140. Each of the seven captains would have roughly 100 men. The proportion of musket to pike would be roughly two to one in each company, and there would be a lieutenant, an ensign and several non-commissioned officers. In the field officers' regiments basic company duties would be undertaken by a captain-lieutenant. These sizes were theoretical ones; most regiments in the war were under size, even in the New Model Army. Most were probably less than half size and the ratio of muskets to pikes would vary immensely. In Royalist regiments there were often as many pikes – which were cheaper – as muskets.

Basic elements were the same for both types of foot soldier. They had a standard two-piece woollen suit of jacket and breeches, two pairs of woollen socks to keep the unshaped shoes or clogs on their feet and a coarse linen shirt with a large collar. Over this they should have all worn a jerkin of buffalo hide imported from the New World – a buff coat – which would protect them against glancing sword cuts. On their shoulders would be a selection of knapsacks, for food and spare socks etc. A cheap sword was slung over the right shoulder on a baldrick.

Pikemen also wore a set of armour. This consisted of at least a corselet – back and breast plates – and perhaps tassets (a pair of articulated thigh guards which hampered walking). On their heads a morion or 'pot' helmet

Pikeman

was worn. These could be either fancily fluted or plain depending upon their provenance. The pike itself was 18ft. (5.5m.) long and made of a hard wood such as ash. The final 4ft. (1.2m.) were protected from sword cuts by metal bracings surmounted by a point up to 2ft. (0.6.m.) long. Pikes were heavy and unwieldy and required strong men to use them successfully. Basically there were five positions: *charge,* at which the pike was horizontal to the ground at shoulder height; *advance,* at which the base was at waist height with the shaft at 45° to the vertical; *port,* at which it was carried in the palm of the right hand, resting against the shoulder, supported at times by the left hand; *trail,* at which it was either dragged along the ground whilst held at the pointed end in the

Musketeer

Trooper

right hand or, at night in the dark, held also at the butt in the left hand of the following soldier. The final position was that in which it was held with the butt against the instep of the right foot by the soldier's left hand at an angle of 30° to the ground to ward off an attack by horse.

The musketeer did not wear armour and often, but not always, wore a wide brimmed felt hat. His weapon was a matchlock – a musket up to 5ft (1.5m.) long, fired by lowering a piece of burning matchcord into a small pan of powder which was attached to the right-hand side of the barrel. The resulting flash passed through a small hole into the main charge of powder in the barrel, thus firing the lead bullet down the smooth bore. The good musketeer could fire perhaps as many as three times a minute. This was his job, until the enemy came into contact with the pike body of his regiment. Then, he was either to pile up behind the pike, to add weight to the 'push', or turn his musket round and use it as a club. If the regiment was attacked by horse, the musketeer could shelter under the pikes and fire at the attackers from this safe place. If caught in the open he was particularly vulnerable but at least was unencumbered by heavy armour or a pike. On many occasions, groups of musketeers were placed in front of the main army, or to the flanks as a forlorn hope, where they were to commence firing upon the enemy as the battle began.

The Horse

These regiments were, in theory, 600 strong divided into six troops. Due to the high raising and running costs many regiments, particularly in regional armies, were very small, often less than a hundred strong. Only in good regiments, such as Prince Rupert's or Cromwell's were there likely to be large numbers; in fact the latter seems to have been double size by 1645. The troopers carried a heavy sword and possibly two pistols, perhaps supplemented by a wheel or flintlock carbine. They wore a woollen suit supplemented by a helmet, back and breast plates and a buffcoat. On their feet they had heavy leather boots which if unrolled would reach their thighs, but they were often turned down into a bucket top.

Before the war contemporary military practice suggested that a horse attack would have been conducted at a leisurely pace with both sides stopping and firing at each other before coming into hand-to-hand combat. Rupert dispensed with this, preferring the shock of a headlong charge. The horses were only put into a gallop for the last 50 or so yards (46 metres). This ensured that there would be as straight a line as possible and therefore the maximum impact when the charge hit home.

Dragoons

These were dressed similarly to the horse but were really mounted foot. In general they fought on foot after riding quickly to a place of advantage, such as the flanks of an army, and then used their muskets. In hard times they had to give up their horses and fight as foot all the time. Many dragoon regiments were small and in regional armies they tagged along with the horse, possibly only one company strong.

Artillery

Gun sizes ranged from ⅓ lb. (150g.) shot to 64lb. (29 kg.). The larger guns were used in siege warfare whilst only the smaller ones firing balls of 20lb. (9kg.) and under were used in most battles. Only one of the gun team was trained in artillery lore. The others were expendable assistants. There was, in the Civil War, no use of mass batteries in the field, and many guns were dispersed about the field with the brigades, or tertias, of foot. Sometimes they never came into action at all!

POWICK BRIDGE

Powick Bridge.

THE COMMISSIONERS OF ARRAY and the officers working under the auspices of the Militia Ordinance, were largely redundant once they had failed to raise the Trained Bands. Individuals, often drawn from these two bodies, began to raise the regiments which went to form the two armies by virtue of personal commissions. Parliament gave each troop commander £280 expenses towards the cost of mounting a troop; Royalist commanders had to fend for themselves.

This haphazard finance was not seen as a problem: both sides expected the war to be a short one, which would not necessitate long term plans. The King gathered his army together as he left Nottingham, having raised the royal banner on 23 August. He placed himself at Shrewsbury to join up with recruits raised in the West and Wales. Sections of the Royalist horse under the command of the King's nephew, Prince Rupert of the Rhine, went southwards to occupy Worcester. Parliament's army, under the command of the Earl of Essex, had been based around Northampton and in late September it too began to march on Worcester.

A detachment of Essex's horse, ten troops under Colonel John Brown, was sent ahead towards Worcester as Essex moved into the central Midlands. On 23 September Prince Rupert and eleven troops of Royalist horse were in the fields between the Severn and Worcester, watching for the expected advance of Essex's army. Brown and the Parliamentarian horse arrived on the opposite bank of the river and made to cross Powick Bridge.

Rupert allowed them to do so, and Brown crossed in peace; he then drew up in the meadows, facing Rupert. Both sides had around a thousand men. Some of the Royalist forces were dragoons and these opened fire on the Parliamentarians. An immediate

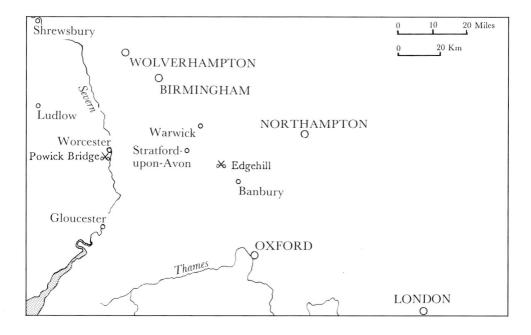

Essex's men occupied Worcester Cathedral in September 1642, stabling horses and lighting camp fires in the nave.

charge followed and some of the Parliamentarian horse, notably those under Captain Nathaniel Fiennes, managed a counter-attack. Fiennes's men charged into Sir Lewis Dives's troop who stood still and received the attack with pistol fire. Dives's men were defeated but saved from rout by the fact that the rest of the Parliamentarian horse had fled, leaving Fiennes isolated. The Earl of Essex's own lifeguard claimed that they misinterpreted an order to wheel about, intended to place them on better ground, as being an instruction to save their own skins. They cleared off with the rest.

This tragic farce cost 150 lives. Essex ordered a tougher training programme aimed at getting his horse to 'fall on with discretion' and, perhaps more appropriate in the circumstances, 'to retreat with care'. Rupert learned something too. Never was Dives's stand to be repeated: charges were to be undertaken and received with swords drawn and at the gallop. Rupert began to gain his reputation as a great cavalry commander, but the fame was out of all proportion to the action at Powick. The Prince drew off to join the King at Shewsbury via Ludlow, and Essex occupied Worcester on 24 September.

The field lies halfway between the town of Stratford-upon-Avon and Banbury, just off the B4086 between Kineton and Radway. The road along the ridge of Edgehill, between the A422 and the B4086, gives the traveller the best views of the field from the King's army's side of the battlefield. Much of the area is Ministry of Defence property, but the road from Radway to Kineton takes the driver along the line of Prince Rupert's charge and thus crosses the field.

The battlefield from Edgehill, looking towards Kineton

THE BATTLE OF EDGEHILL

IT WAS IMPERATIVE that the Earl of Essex should stop the King reaching London. To do this the Earl marched his still incomplete army from Worcester towards Warwick. By 22 October this army lay just to the south of the town, part of it in a village called Kineton. During the night quartermasters from both armies stumbled into each other at nearby Wormleighton. The Royalist army had marched from Shrewsbury during the previous ten days, via Bridgnorth and Wolverhampton and had got between the Earl of Essex and the capital. It is not surprising that Essex knew not where the King was. Neither side had much experience of scouting techniques and the Earl did not know of the route Charles intended to follow. As for the King, he had little in the way of a direct plan, just the vague objective of reaching London.

The Royalist forces drew up on Edgehill, a beautiful steep slope, then unwooded. Throughout the morning, regiments of horse and then foot gathered on the hillside from where the Earl of Essex could be seen marshalling his army in the valley below. Politically it would have been unwise for him to launch an attack on the annointed King, for it was not yet openly accepted that the King himself was responsible for the disastrous state of war. Militarily it would have been stupid to lead an attack up the steep hill with a partly trained army. So Essex waited roughly halfway between Kineton and the foot of Edgehill. His left flank rested on Radway ground. Here was Sir James Ramsey with around 1,200 horse interspersed with 300 musketeers. Flanking this wing were a further 300 musketeers behind a line of hedges. In the Parliamentarian centre were three brigades of foot: Charles Essex's on the left, Sir John Meldrum's to the right with Thomas Ballard's to the left rear. Behind Meldrum were two regiments of horse under Sir Philip Stapleton and Sir William Balfour. Two separate regiments of foot, Denzill Holles's and Sir William Fairfax's also stood in the centre, the former between Charles Essex's brigade and Ramsey's horse, the latter flanking Stapleton and

Meldrum. The right wing consisted chiefly of one regiment of horse, Lord Fielding's, which stood approximately where the Oaks Coppice now lies. This regiment was flanked to its right by dragoons. In all, Essex probably fielded around 2,000 horse, 12,000 foot, 700 dragoons and possibly in excess of thirty cannon.

Over on Edgehill the King's army was in position by mid-day with, unlike Essex, roughly equal amounts of horse on each flank. The right wing was under Prince Rupert and the left under Lord Wilmot; both men were leading around 1,500 men. According to the plan drawn by the King's engineer, Bernard de Gomme, each of these wings consisted of nine groups, seven to the front with two to the rear. In the centre the foot was drawn up into five brigades; a total of somewhat over 10,000 men. The King's army had a total of twenty cannon.

The marshalling of this army was marred by a dispute at high level. Rupert, the King's nephew, had been given command over the horse, but saw fit to interfere with the disposition of the foot in the centre. The Lord General, the Earl of Lindsey, had drawn them up in the Dutch manner which he had become familiar with whilst serving on the continent. The Earl of Forth, as Field Marshal, wanted to use the Swedish formation which he had learned abroad. Rupert agreed, the King gave in to them and let Forth have his way. Lindsey was right: the Dutch formation was a simpler affair suitable for a half-trained army; quite rightly he flung down his redundant baton. He fought and received a mortal wound at the head of his regiment.

Essex was not to be enticed up the hill and so the Royalists moved down the slope, through Radway, into the valley. At the foot of Edgehill they reordered their foot within ½ mile (¾ kilometre) of the enemy without any hindrance being offered. It was not until later that the Parliamentarian cannons opened

The monument to the battle, situated on the B4086.

BETWEEN HERE AND THE VILLAGE OF RADWAY THE BATTLE OF EDGEHILL THE FIRST OF THE CIVIL WAR WAS FOUGHT ON SUNDAY THE 23 OCTOBER 1642 MANY OF THOSE WHO LOST THEIR LIVES IN THE BATTLE ARE BURIED THREE QUARTERS OF A MILE TO THE SOUTH OF THIS STONE

fire on the section of the army where Charles stood. The Royalists replied, with little success, and began a general advance. On their left Usher's dragoons drove back the dragoons flanking Fielding's horse, and to their right Sir Arthur Aston drove off Ramsey's musketeers.

It was on this latter wing that the fighting first got under way. Rupert's horse thundered into their charge parallel to the road between Kineton and Knowle End. The inappropriately named Sir Faithful Fortesque and his troop instantly changed sides, ripping off their tawny orange sashes and turning on their erstwhile Parliamentarian colleagues. As soon as contact was made, Ramsey's wing virtually melted away. Only Holles's foot made any firm resistance to the Royalists, the majority of whom chased after the fleeing enemy. On the far side of the field, Lord Wilmot's horse drove Fielding off with even less difficulty. Here too the majority of the Royalists rushed off towards Kineton.

Action began in the centre just after the brief cavalry actions. Here it was a very different affair. Initially Parliament suffered a series of setbacks when Charles Essex's brigade crumbled as Ramsey's horse ran off. Nevertheless Ballard's brigade moved forward into the gap and the Royalists were held back. Sir William Balfour brought his regiment of horse up from the Parliamentarian rear along with Stapleton's horse and charged into the two brigades led by Sir Nicholas Byron and Richard Fielding. Stapleton achieved little but Balfour broke Fielding's brigade and charged the Royalist artillery.

Darkness, on this short October day, began to fall as Balfour, who had saved the day for Parliament, led his men back through the shattered Royalist centre and the Parliamentarian foot pressed forward, breaking Byron's brigade. At this point Sir Edmund Verney, who had only taken up arms out of a feeling of gratitude for the honours done to him by the King, was killed whilst fiercely defending the Royalist Standard entrusted to him. Lindsey was severely wounded and the whole Royalist centre was badly disordered. Sir Charles Lucas who had rallied a small number of horse attempted to lead an attack into the Parliamentarian flank, only to run into a group of frightened deserters. Luckily, the right centre of Royalist foot hung on, preventing any further collapse. In Kineton the foolish Royalist horse ran into several fresh Parliamentarian regiments, who pushed them back. Belatedly returning to the field, they were able to offer limited help to their foot as night fell. The fighting over, the casualties were highest in the foot fight: perhaps as many as 1,500 were killed on both sides, with Parliament's casualties a little higher than their enemy's.

Night added to the confusion of the day. The only clear thing was that the war was not over. Both sides attempted to claim victory with little justification. The Royalists had marred their chance when the horse ran off the field. Essex's foot matched the determination of their commander, who fought pike in hand and held back the onrush of the Royalist centre but could not overwhelm them. The Royalist army drew back to the foot of Edgehill to collect in scattered forces and Essex fell back onto Kineton to meet the regiments marching to join him.

On the following morning the Earl of Essex drew the army out for a second day's fighting, but nothing happened. The Royalist horse was jumbled, exhausted and anyway the horses had been fed little during the night. The King could not attack. Across the field, Essex realized his army was enfeebled and badly shaken. He withdrew to Warwick. The King had his passage to London; it was a victory he hardly deserved.

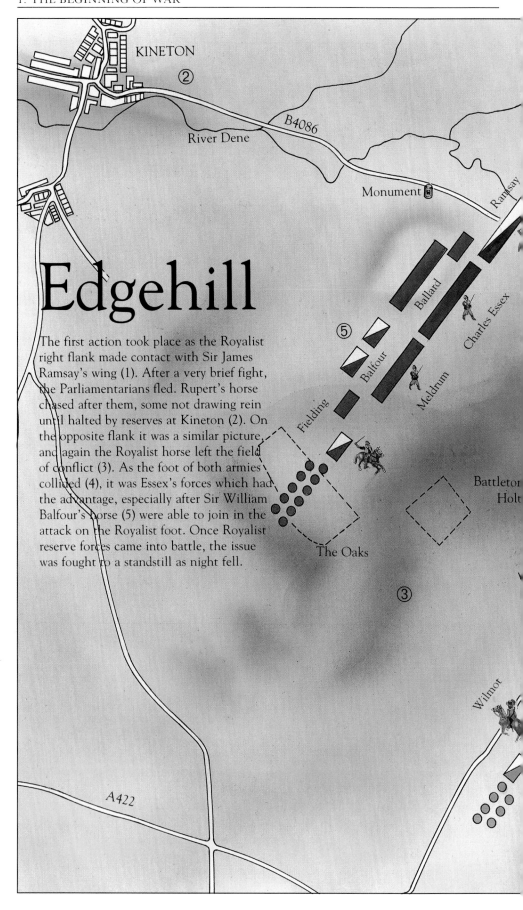

KINETON

②

B4086

River Dene

Monument

Ramsay

Ballard

⑤

Charles Essex

Balfour

Meldrum

Fielding

Edgehill

The first action took place as the Royalist right flank made contact with Sir James Ramsay's wing (1). After a very brief fight, the Parliamentarians fled. Rupert's horse chased after them, some not drawing rein until halted by reserves at Kineton (2). On the opposite flank it was a similar picture, and again the Royalist horse left the field of conflict (3). As the foot of both armies collided (4), it was Essex's forces which had the advantage, especially after Sir William Balfour's horse (5) were able to join in the attack on the Royalist foot. Once Royalist reserve forces came into battle, the issue was fought to a standstill as night fell.

Battleton Holt

The Oaks

③

Wilmot

A422

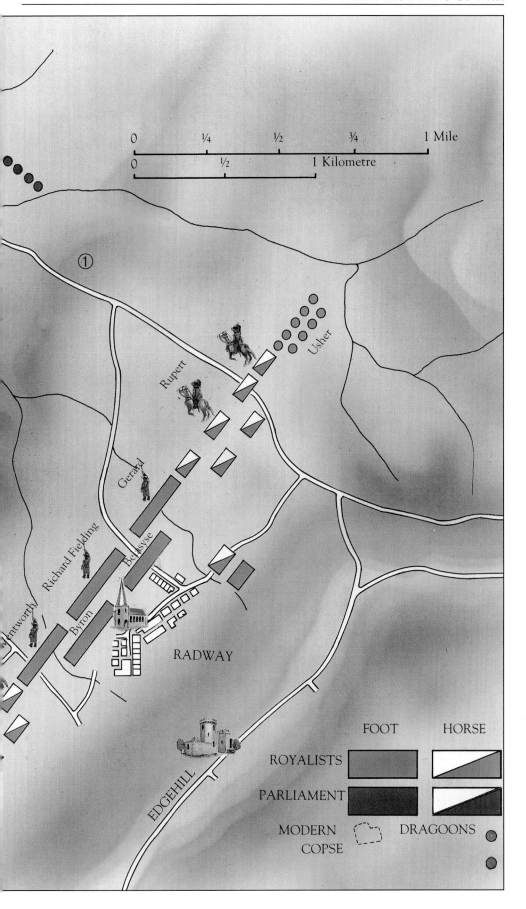

0 ¼ ½ ¾ 1 Mile

0 ½ 1 Kilometre

①

Usher

Rupert

Gerard

Wentworth

Richard Fielding

Byron

Bethsyse

RADWAY

EDGEHILL

	FOOT	HORSE
ROYALISTS		
PARLIAMENT		

MODERN COPSE

DRAGOONS

2. WINTER BATTLES

NOVEMBER 1642 – FEBRUARY 1643

> After Edgehill, the way to
> London was now open to the
> King. At the same time both
> sides were trying to establish
> themselves throughout the
> country; towns and castles
> were garrisoned and forces
> raised to man them.

York in the seventeenth century.

YORKSHIRE

IN YORKSHIRE, once the dilatory Earl of Cumberland had failed to check the vigorous activity of the Parliamentarian garrisons on the coast and at Hull, the Royalists had to call on outside help. Their opponents – the redoubtable Lord Fairfax and his son, Sir Thomas – were firmly established in the West Riding and were able to link up with the John Hothams, again father and son, in Hull. From the cloth-making towns of Leeds, Bradford and Halifax, the Fairfaxes were able to bottle Cumberland up in York. The Yorkshire Royalists, concerned about the inactivity of their leader and the financial harm caused by the Fairfaxes and the coastal garrisons, invited the Earl of Newcastle to their aid. He came down from the North where he was raising forces for the King and fortifying the town from where he derived his title. On 1 December he marched into Yorkshire.

It was necessary for the Parliamentarians to stop him. Hotham the younger attacked the Earl's forces at Piercebridge as he crossed the Tees, but was driven off. This victory persuaded all the Trained Bands in the North Riding to hand their weapons over to Newcastle. He then relieved York and pursued Lord Fairfax, who made a stand at Tadcaster, between York and the wool towns. Here Fairfax stood astride the River Wharfe. To the north-west his son was based at Wetherby, 6 miles (10 kilometres) away.

Newcastle decided to have Lord Newport attack Wetherby whilst he himself attacked Tadcaster. Hotham, who got wind of the plan, forged a letter to Newport, supposedly from Newcastle, telling him not to launch his attack. Thus only Newcastle went into action at the bridge in Tadcaster. Basically, the battle at Tadcaster was a long fire fight, interspersed with attempts by the Royalists to force the bridge. It could not be done. From eleven in the morning until dusk, Fairfax held them back; but he began to run low on ammunition and had to draw south to Selby. He thus left Newcastle a direct route to the cloth towns, but the Earl was unable to take

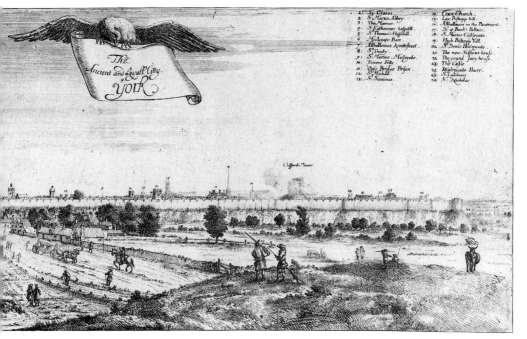

The
Ancient and Loyall Citty
of
York

1. St. Olaves
2. St. Maries Abbey
3. The Manner
4. St. Katherines hospitll
5. St. Thomas's Hospill
6. Micleyate Barr
7. Allhallowes Northstreet
8. St. Trinity
9. St. Martins Mileoyde
10. Tower Fells
11. Owse Bridge Prison
12. St. Michell
13. St. Sauiour

14. Cruxe Church
15. Low Bishopp hill
16. Allhallowes in the Pavement
17. D. of Buck: Pallaise
18. St. Marier Castlegate
19. High Bishopp hill
20. St. Denis Holygoode
21. The new Seffions house
22. The grand Jury house
23. The Castle
24. Malmgate Barr
25. St. Laurence
26. St. Nicholas

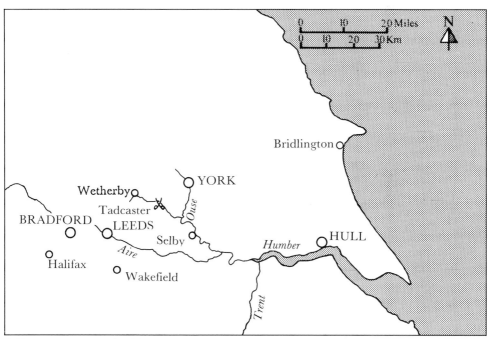

full advantage of this. Attempts to capture Bradford failed, even after the fall of Leeds and Wakefield. At the beginning of 1643 the Fairfaxes, whose retreat to Selby had put them closer to Hull and the source of ammunition supplies, went back on the offensive. Sir Thomas went back to Bradford and from there attacked the Earl's forces, driving them back on York. The Royalists' first attempt to take the county had failed.

Tadcaster stands on the A64 York to Leeds road and traffic still crosses the River Wharfe here, although the bridge is one of a later period. The area over which the battle was fought is now in the heart of the town but the salient features are long gone. It is best to visit Tadcaster at the same time as going to see Adwalton (Chapter Five) or Marston Moor (Chapter Ten).

Syon Park by Jan Griffier (late seventeenth century).

The battlefields at Brentford and the area of the confrontation at Turnham Green are now swamped by Greater London. The Great West Road follows the route that the King attempted to use, and some of the streets leading towards the Thames – Back Lane, Dock Road, Ferry Lane – may well follow the lines of those down which Parliament's soldiers were driven. Syon House still stands and its grounds are open to the public.

BRENTFORD

M4

B4R5

A4

A315

Kew Gardens

Syon House

Park Road

0 ¼ ½ Mile

0 ½ 1 Km

TOWARDS LONDON

WITH ESSEX out of the way, the King moved towards London. He was not fast enough. Rupert urged him on, yet older men like the Earl of Bristol held him back. He had not won at Edgehill and the capital was thus not supine. Instead of marching on London, he entered Oxford at the end of October and established himself there; only then did he begin the serious march on London, travelling along the Thames Valley via Reading, which he reached on 4 November.

Essex had begun his circuitous route to London much earlier and by 8 November reached the capital city,

affair and, as their army left, the men and women who remained behind worked on the city walls. As the soldiers marched under their colours, the logistical arrangements were largely the responsibility of the women, who followed the army with food.

On 12 November, Charles moved along the road from Colnbrook via Hounslow, on towards Brentford. The town was only guarded by two regiments: Lord Brooke's purplecoats and Denzil Holles's redcoats. Rupert charged into the town with the Royalist horse, backed by some foot. Although the fight was uneven in terms of numbers, the two Parliamentarian regiments fought from every possible vantage point in the small town. Many of these men were pushed backwards down the narrow lanes into the Thames as the Royalists pressed into Brentford. Despite the arrival of John Hampden's greencoats, the Royalists captured the town. However, elated by victory, they drank themselves to a standstill in the wrecked town.

On the morning of 13 November, a Sunday, as Brooke's, Holles's and Hampden's men still hovered to the east of the town, Essex sent supplies up the river to them. One of these ammunition boats was hit by artillery fire from the grounds of Syon House and it exploded. Others were sunk and yet more captured. Nevertheless, just 3 miles (5 kilometres) up the London road, 24,000 men under arms awaited the King's approach. Although many of these were raw recruits, it was unthinkable that the King with just 12,000 would attack them where they stood on Turnham Green. After a day spent facing his enemy, Charles had to turn back. His army was not as well supplied as Essex's and was in need of succour and rest. This was the closest that Charles came to capturing his city; the campaign was over but the war was not. With the alternative capital established at Oxford, it was time for a complete reassessment of the war.

ending any advantage that the King had gained after Edgehill. What finally decided the issue was not the presence of Essex or even the half-hearted attitude of the King: it was the action of the people of London themselves. They ended the Royalists' first and greatest design on the city. Whilst Essex was no longer between them and the King's forces, the Londoners had to fend for themselves, especially as Parliament was seriously considering suing for peace and the vanguard of the Royalist army got ever closer. Within London 6,000 recruits were raised and then added to the Earl's army, giving him greater numbers than the King possessed.

Whilst Parliament attempted to get him to talk, the King, confident of victory, pressed on. By 11 November he was approaching Brentford as Essex and Sir Phillip Skippon with the Trained Bands marched out towards him. As far as London was concerned the defence of the city was a communal

THE WEST COUNTRY

IN THE WEST COUNTRY the King's cause had since the summer of 1642 been in the hands of the Marquis of Hertford. After being driven out of Somerset, Hertford's horse, under Sir Ralph Hopton, had fled into Cornwall. The Marquis shipped across the Bristol Channel into Glamorganshire, from where he began to organize considerable support for Charles from the southern Welsh counties, with the exception of Pembrokeshire. Parlia-ment had established a line of garrisons between the King at Oxford and Wales, but in November Worcester and Hereford were abandoned, allowing Hertford into the West Midlands, whilst the Earl of Stamford took his Parliamentarian forces to Gloucester.

Hopton had tried and failed to raise Cornwall's Trained Bands; instead he had created an army of 1,500 volunteers with the help of Sir Bevil Grenville. With these he marched into Devon and attempted to dominate the county. Stamford, now in command of

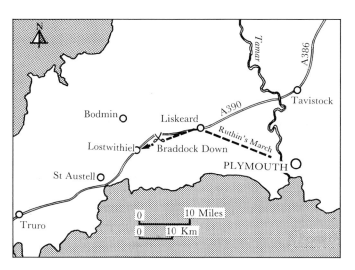

Braddock Down is perhaps best incorporated in a visit to Lostwithiel (Chapter Eleven). From Lostwithiel take the A390 eastwards. Turn off onto the minor road to Trewindle and Boconnoc. Go through Trewindle and after the junction of three roads you will be on the down. The battle was on your left.

MUSKETS

Civil War muskets were generally up to, and sometimes over 4ft. (1.2m.) long. Their length and weight often meant that a rest had to be used to make them steady for firing. They were smooth-bore, and fired a solid-lead bullet which was often made by the musketeer in his own mould and then trimmed to fit! As a result they were inaccurate at as little as 100 yds. (92m.).

The firing process was as follows. Coarse-grain powder was put down the barrel, followed by the ball and some wadding – chewed paper or some such – to hold the bullet in. This was rammed down tightly. The musketeer would carry the powder in ready made-up amounts in the small flasks attached to his bandolier. Fine-grain powder was transferred from his flask into the small pan attached to the right-hand side of the breech. When the trigger

Parliament's Western Army, was dispatched from Gloucester to prevent this. In January parts of this army entered Devon. Regiments under Lord Ruthin pressed Hopton back into Cornwall from their base at Plymouth on their own, as Stamford progressed only slowly into the county.

As Ruthin crossed high ground on the road from Liskeard, which he had just occupied, to Bodmin on 19 January, he detected a small force of Royalists to his east on Braddock Down. Hopton had actually hidden a large portion of his forces behind the brow of a hill, leaving only this small group as a decoy. As Ruthin crossed the down towards what, he thought, were retreating stragglers, a furious cannonade from six guns stopped him. The following charge by the hitherto concealed Royalists routed the startled enemy. Ruthin's men ran into Lostwithiel, but did not make a stand there. Over 1,200 prisoners were taken, along with four cannon and a thousand muskets. Hopton was able to establish a hold on Cornwall which, throughout the spring, he was to strengthen.

GARRISONS

DURING THESE WINTER MONTHS, towns and castles were garrisoned all over England. Several places tried desperately to avoid becoming embroiled in the war. Leicester prevaricated for as long as possible, but by early 1643 it had acquired a resident force under Lord Grey. Many places, of course, had little say in the matter. Worcester and Hereford had to accept the stationing of forces within their walls and even Stafford which had, along with the whole county, attempted to remain neutral, was taken over by Royalist forces. Naturally some garrisons were situated in castles like Dudley, Ashby de la Zouch, and Belvoir, in the Midlands; and Basing House, Brampton Bryan and Donnington Castle in the South and West. These were private homes, mostly garrisoned by their owners or their agents. Some, however, like Belvoir were garrisoned without their owner's approval. Belvoir was seized by Gervais Lucas, for the King. Lucas was a servant to the Parliamentarian owner.

was pulled, a smouldering match cord was lowered into the pan. The match cord was several feet long and was wrapped around the musketeer's arm. The fire in the pan set off an explosion in the barrel by sending sparks through a small hole. This discharged the bullet.

Garrisons varied in size. Oxford, for instance, was a major military base, being the headquarters of a field army. Around it were minor garrisons like Reading, which, until it was captured in the spring of 1643, acted as a base for some of the Oxford field army units. Smaller garrisons, like the Parliamentarian-held Nottingham Castle, were probably manned by only about 500 men. Nearby Belvoir was even smaller, having as few as 300 men in it. In addition to these chief garrisons, there were also a number of tiny outposts with only a handful of men. Along the Trent, in Derbyshire and Leicestershire, there was a string of small forts defending crossing-points on the river.

The establishment of a garrison required a great deal of work. In the case of towns like Chester, York, Newark, Gloucester and even London, a series of defensive works had to be made. In some cases these were built to supplement existing medieval walls, but in the case of Ashby de la Zouch they were necessary because there were no town walls at all. The construction of earthworks was undertaken by local people under the supervision of the garrison engineer. At Newark the construction of the earthworks was undertaken by the men of the nearby villages, like Upton. Workers from Upton were sent at the village's charge to build the breastworks, and after the war the same men had to dismantle most of them again! Within the garrisoned town it was necessary to try and achieve some form of self-sufficiency in case of attack. This could mean the creation of vast food stores, as at Oxford, or even the building of corn and gunpowder mills and brass foundries, as at Lichfield. Garrisoned towns like Stafford came under vigorous military law. Curfews were imposed and the town had to supply guards for the watch. The Parliamentarian committee for the county established there after spring 1643, also instructed local people to

A modern painting of the construction of Chester's fortifications during the Civil War.

dismantle the houses that stood outside the town walls. This was to prevent them being used as vantage points by attackers. If the townspeople did this voluntarily, then they could keep the building materials and reconstruct their houses on the common ground within the walls. If, on the other hand, they refused then, if the place was attacked, the soldiers would demolish the buildings and keep the materials.

Garrisons served a number of purposes. Gloucester secured the route to Wales from the South-west of England. Newark defended the road north and Chester provided the King with a port through which he could

receive support from Ireland. Many places were simply occupied in order to gain mastery over the surrounding area. Others simply provided lodging for part of a nearby army. Places like Uttoxeter, for example, were not garrisons in the full sense of the word. Instead they seem to have been lodgings for soldiers. Both sides appear to have used Uttoxeter for this purpose. Small garrisons provided convenient staging-posts for messengers travelling across the country and for collection-points for the war-time taxes imposed by both sides. From the beginning of 1643 the Royalists began the collection of 'Contribution' and the Parliamen-

tarians instituted the 'Assessment'. Both of these were property and income taxes designed to pay for the local forces. Collection was undertaken by the troops from the garrisons in the area. Royalist quartermasters of horse rode a circuit of villages, often on a weekly basis, to collect the tax from the village constables who had levied the taxes on their community.

Some of the most bitter tragedies of the war occurred when these garrisons came under attack. And it was in these cases that the civilian population was at its most vulnerable.

○ CHESTER

N

Nantwich
●

Hopton Heath is best visited from Stafford or Lichfield. Both of these towns were garrisoned and played an important part in the campaign. The castle at Stafford is undergoing considerable work at the moment and is worth a visit. The building known as High House, on Greengate Street, which now houses a Gas showroom, was once used as a prison for Royalists whilst the town was in Parliamentarian hands (see page 127). Lichfield is a beautiful town with an excellent cathedral. The close is still visible but much of it is now built up.

To reach Hopton Heath from Stafford take the A518 towards Weston and Uttoxeter. After passing the County Showground the road runs south-east of the battlefield. The minor road to Hopton (on the left, 3 miles (4¾ kilometres) from the centre of Stafford) takes you across the battlefield along the line of the Royalists' forces as they arrived on the field. From Lichfield, it is best to use the A51 to Rugeley and Weston. At Weston take the A518 to Stafford and the field is to the right after Weston Hall.

DER

Hopton Heath
⚔
Stafford ●   Rugeley
⊕

○

Lichfield
Tamwort
●

⊕ WOLVERHAMPTON

○ Dudley   ⊕ Coleshill

○ R(
● Pa
⊕ T(

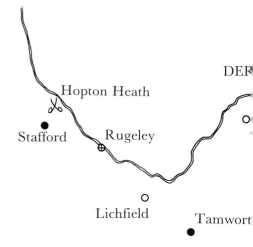

3. MIDLAND STRUGGLES

DECEMBER 1642 – APRIL 1643

Parliament moved swiftly in the Midlands and Charles saw the danger of losing this important area as major towns were occupied by his enemies. ○ WORCESTER

HEREFORD
○

0   10   20 Miles
0   10   20   30 Kilometres

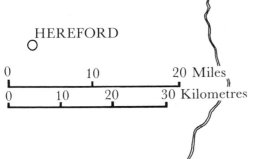

EARL OF RAWDON, &c &c &c

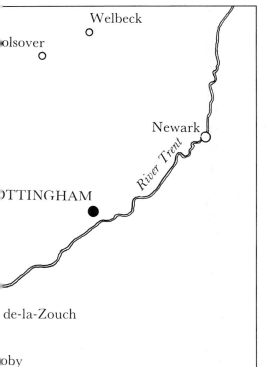

Welbeck
olsover

Newark

River Trent

OTTINGHAM

de-la-Zouch

oby

LEICESTER

Garrisons, Autumn 1643

ntary Garrisons, Autumn 1643

ot garrisoned

Ashby-de-la-Zouch Castle in 1730.

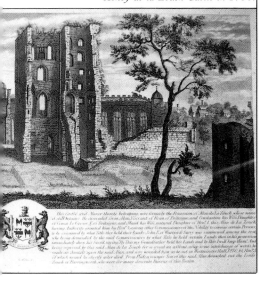

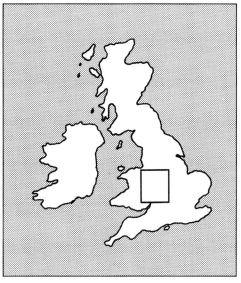

WHEN THE KING created the field army at Shrewsbury in September 1642, he took most of his active supporters out of the North Midland area. The most prominent of these was Henry Hastings. He was not the only one, however. From Nottinghamshire John Digby, the high sheriff, joined the King, and from Derbyshire two sons of the Earl of Chesterfield, Phillip and Ferdinando Stanhope, led troops to Shrewsbury, as did John Freschville. From Stafford-shire two sons of Sir Harvey Bagot joined the King, and from Hastings's own county of Leicestershire Sir John Beaumont and at least one of the Nevills of Holt went to Shrewsbury. The result of this was devastating, as Parliamentarians rapidly seized Derby and Nottingham.

Sir John Gell of Hopton in Derby-shire borrowed troops from Hull and occupied Derby. He also drove out the only remaining Royalists in the north of the county, Sir Francis Whortley's dragoons, and lent help to John Hutchinson in Nottinghamshire. Only the Earl of Chesterfield's little garrison at Bretby remained. Over in Nottinghamshire, Hutchinson took possession of the county town and the castle, largely on his own initiative after the Royalists had left. He was to be ensconced there for the duration. In Leicestershire little happened as the county's leading Parliamentarian was the Earl of Stamford, now busy in the South-west. Leicester, once a flashpoint in the war, now attempted to maintain some form of neutrality.

This was a stance for which some twenty-five counties strove. In the immediate area, Cheshire, Lincolnshire and Staffordshire all attempted to achieve armed neutrality. When Whortley had been driven out of Derbyshire by Gell he had gone into neighbouring Staffordshire and the county JPs went into special session, with the aim of creating a third force to repel all intruders.

The centre of England was too important, for its wealth as well as its communications routes, for the King to ignore. After the fiasco of Turnham Green, Charles faced up to the dual crisis in the North Midlands, the Parliamentarian successes and the rise of neutralism. His response was thorough. Henry Hastings was sent back home with his troop or regiment of horse, a commission to raise a regiment of dragoons and ammunition for a foot regiment. He was to create a garrison at Ashby de la Zouch and undertake co-ordinated action with the other returnees. At least one of the Stanhope brothers was sent to join his father at Bretby, which fell shortly afterwards. Sir John Digby was returned to Nottinghamshire where, with help from the Earl of Newcastle, he established a garrison at Newark. In Staffordshire Thomas Leveson, the Catholic black sheep of the county, garrisoned Dudley Castle and Wolverhampton, whilst the high sheriff, William Comberford, with Hastings's help garrisoned Stafford.

At the same time Parliament created its county committees. Based on the informal meetings of the deputy lieutenants and militia commissioners, these bodies' county gentry were to run the local government but had special responsibility for military/financial matters. These committees also had to work with their neighbouring counterparts. The Royalists utilized the almost defunct Commissions of Array to the same effect.

Hastings was too great a threat to Parliament's hold on the area, and concerted efforts were made to dislodge him. Newark was attacked, and by the middle of January Ashby itself was under siege. To the Royalists Hastings was too good an asset to lose and Prince Rupert was sent to his rescue. Upon the Prince's approach, the young Lord Grey (he was only twenty-two years old), now Parliament's Commander-in-Chief in the East Midlands, called off the siege. During February attempts were made to dislodge the garrison in Stafford. Sir John Gell and the Cheshire Parliamentarian, Sir William Brereton, joined with the inhabitants of the moorlands in north-east Staffordshire in several attempts to capture the town. By the end of the same month, Newark had also briefly come under siege. But the greatest challenge to the local Royalists was launched by Lord Brooke when he entered Staffordshire in late February and headed for Lichfield, now a garrison under the Earl of Chesterfield.

HOPTON HEATH

ON 2 MARCH 1643, as he inspected the siegeworks around the city of Lichfield, Lord Brooke was shot dead by a sniper in the cathedral tower. Much was made of the fact that it happened on St Chad's day as the cathedral was dedicated to this saint. Despite this auspicious accomplishment by the defenders, the town fell to Sir John Gell, who garrisoned it with Brooke's own purplecoats and other regiments which had come with the late lord. Gell then planned an attack on Stafford. To this end he aimed at linking up with Brereton.

At the same time, the Royalists were

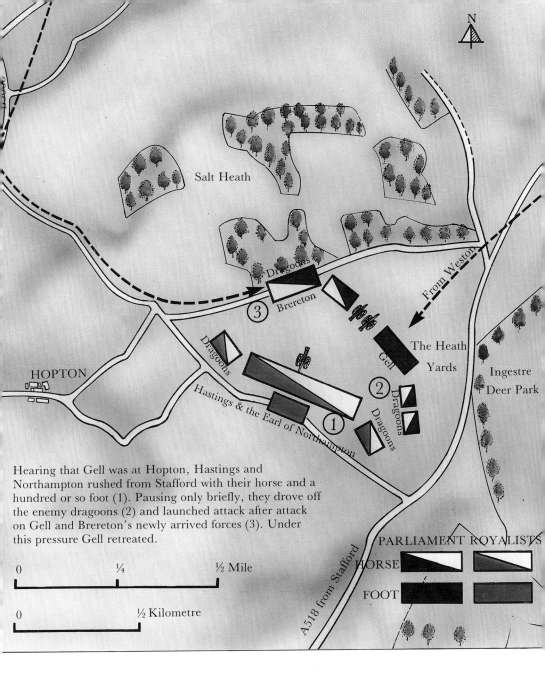

Salt Heath

Dragoons

③ Brereton

From Weston

HOPTON

Dragoons

The Heath Yards

Gell

Ingestre Deer Park

Hastings & the Earl of Northampton

② Dragoons

① Dragoons

Hearing that Gell was at Hopton, Hastings and Northampton rushed from Stafford with their horse and a hundred or so foot (1). Pausing only briefly, they drove off the enemy dragoons (2) and launched attack after attack on Gell and Brereton's newly arrived forces (3). Under this pressure Gell retreated.

| 0 | ¼ | ½ Mile |

| 0 | | ½ Kilometre |

A518 from Stafford

PARLIAMENT ROYALISTS

HORSE

FOOT

N

---

planning to redeem the situation. Hastings now had an army of some 2,000 men, but this was not enough to launch a major siege against Lichfield. To support him the Earl of Northampton marched into Staffordshire from Warwickshire, where he had undone all Brooke's good works. He joined Hastings near Tamworth and on 17 March they were at Coleshill.

Gell arranged to team up with Brereton on Hopton Heath, about 3 miles (5 kilometres) from Stafford. Accordingly, Gell left Lichfield and went on to Hopton via Rugeley (probably along the route of the A51 until crossing the Trent at Weston and then more along the route of the A518). Brereton made his approach again along the line of the A51 to Sandon, on the route of the Stafford road (now the B5066). Gell arrived on the heath on the morning of 19 March and drew his troops into a defensive position along the top of a ridge, running from Heathyards towards Salt Heath. In the front he placed his guns, and in the Heathyards Lodge close he positioned dragoons. The foot, chiefly his own regiment and Lord Brooke's, were on

Lichfield Cathedral Close.

after them. They lost no time: dragoons were sent out to tackle Gell's flanking units. During the half hour from three o'clock Brereton's dragoons on the right flank were driven back. On the opposite flank Gell's musketeers and dragoons were also chased off, abandoning supporting artillery as they did so. Then Northampton led a furious charge upon the Parliamentarian centre after firing a few shots from his massive cannon, Roaring Meg. Brereton's horse were defeated and fled the field taking their leader with them. Northampton turned on Gell's foot but was held at bay by the musketeers, covered as they were by the pikes. The Earl pulled back and launched another charge to the same effect.

Gell fought alongside his men, pike in hand, determined to keep their morale up. They fended off this second charge too, although each time they retired the Royalists took yet more of Gell's cannon with them. Northampton fell victim to Gell's well chosen ground. His horse stumbled in a rabbit hole and the Earl toppled fully armoured into the Parliamentarian ranks where he was killed. As Hastings and Sir Thomas Byron drew the Royalist horse up again for another attack, Brereton's foot arrived on the field. With their help Gell was again able to drive his attackers down the hill. This time, in the gathering darkness, they stayed.

Gell drew his men off under cover of the spring night. His band of terrified boys and men, many in their first fight, had done well – they had saved themselves from destruction. Had they broken and run, they would have been cut down. The Royalists were exhausted and disheartened by Northampton's death. The death of so many officers had left them dejected, if victorious. With the departure of Gell, Stafford was saved. Northampton's body was held to ransom by the dishonourable, if brave, Gell. The asking price was the return of the captured cannon. It was never paid.

the ridge protected by rabbit warrens which were difficult for approaching forces to negotiate. A few hundred ill-armed moorlanders were placed in the rear. Brereton arrived only at two o'clock and he joined the right-hand end of Gell's line, putting his dragoons in the Hayfield close. This would have the effect of creating a withering crossfire.

It was as well that they were prepared. Gell's march to the Heath and Brereton's attempt to join him had been so laboured that the Royalists had reached Stafford. These in turn relaxed too much and spread their billets far and wide on the night of 18 March. The next morning, a Sunday, Northampton and Hastings were in church when at eleven o'clock they heard that Gell was marshalling forces on Hopton Heath; it was only then that they realized their error. Although the horse were assembled fairly quickly, the foot were far behind.

With this horse Hastings and Northampton rushed out towards Hopton. They had about a thousand men: a hundred or so foot were trailing

Sir William Waller (1598 – 1668)

As RUPERT WAS engaged at Lichfield and the King was dealing with Essex's threat to his east, havoc was wreaked in the rear of the Royalist centre. Sir William Waller, MP for Andover and Chief Butler of England, was earning his reputation as 'the conquerer'. He was the son of a past lieutenant of Dover and had fought in Bohemia for the Elector Palatine. After the battle of the White Mountain he and his later rival and friend, Sir Ralph Hopton, were amongst the escort of the Elector's wife, the Winter Queen, Charles I's sister. Between them they carried the infant Prince Rupert. By the 1640s, as both men sat in the Commons, Waller saw the liberties of England best defended by Parliament, long after Hopton went over to the King.

In September 1642 Waller received Lord Goring's surrender of Portsmouth. He served at Edgehill and was swept away by Prince Rupert's charge. During the winter he captured a series of castles and towns in the South-east. By February, he took charge of the Western Associated Counties' forces defeating Lord Herbert at Newnham on 24 March, only to be checked himself a fortnight later by Prince Maurice at Ripple Field. As Maurice went to join the King before Reading, Waller began to take over the West Midlands.

During the summer, Waller was defeated by Hopton. He got his own back at Cheriton, the following year, but the King defeated him at Cropredy Bridge. At the second battle of Newbury, his plan to attack the Royalists in the rear failed due to ineffectual timing by the Earl of Manchester. After the passing of the Self-Denying Ordinance in 1645, Waller willingly resigned his military command, devoting himself to Presbyterian politics. He was a victim of the purge in 1648 and was imprisoned for four years. He worked for the Restoration and found some favour from Charles II.

GARRISONS: LICHFIELD AND HEREFORD

WHILST the battle of Hopton Heath had saved Stafford, Lichfield was still in the hands of Gell's garrison. Nevertheless it was not safe. Just over a week after the battle, Prince Rupert was sent to Hastings's aid; with him were 1,900 men. He and Hastings commenced the siege of Lichfield on 10 April 1643. The town had two distinct parts – the medieval town proper with its grid pattern streets, and the close around the cathedral separated from the town by the meres, the town's water supply. These two sections can still be seen.

It took twelve days to force a surrender. Miners from Hastings's Derbyshire coal mines sprang a mine under the town walls and the Royalists rushed in. After considerable fighting, the garrison surrendered to Hastings. He and Rupert installed Richard Bagot as governor. His elder brother Harvey was his lieutenant-colonel and both had served in Lord Paget's foot at Edgehill.

(Above) The Old House, Hereford, dating from 1621. It is now a museum in which Civil War artefacts are on display.

(Left) Lichfield Cathedral. The meres can be seen on the right.

A model of the city of Hereford as it was in 1645.

Lichfield became an important garrison in the county and the seat of the Commission of Array, which included the Bagots' father. Richard began to rebuild and add to the walls. Inside he had gunpowder factories, brass foundries and mills for producing food stocks for the town and the garrison, which lived there for the next three years.

Hereford, which the Marquis of Hertford had garrisoned earlier in the year, fell when the Parliamentarian commander, Sir William Waller, struck into the West Midlands in April. As the King recalled his nephew from Lichfield to help him against the Earl of Essex, who had besieged Reading, Waller took Tewkesbury. Reading fell to Essex before the King and Rupert could get there and on 25 April Waller captured Hereford. The third garrison there in four months was established; this too was short lived. Before many months a new Royalist garrison was installed, which remained until 1645. In the spring of 1643, however, the central Royalist territories were in deep trouble.

MIDLAND PARLIAMENTARIAN COMMANDERS

Lord Grey of Groby (1620 – 1657)

At the head of the Midland Parliamentarians was the young Thomas, Lord Grey of Groby, heir to the Earl of Stamford. He was referred to as 'a grinning dwarf' when, in 1648, he helped Colonel Pride exclude Presbyterian members from the House of Commons, or as 'a man of no eminent parts' by the Royalist minister and later historian, the Earl of Clarendon. He was not particularly successful in his role. He failed to take Ashby in January 1643 and held up the attempts to capture Newark in the following May. Within the next few months parts of his command were hived off and given to other commanders. By 1644 Grey was more-or-less a cypher.

Sir John Gell (1593 – 1671)

The presence of the Parliamentarian garrisons in the region was due largely to Sir John Gell of Hopton, Derbyshire. He was a lead-mine lessee and had served as High Sheriff in 1635. He achieved some notoriety when he suggested that his county could actually afford to pay more Ship Money. He had also served as a JP and a deputy lieutenant. During the war, he led the dominant section on the county committee and was suspected of rigging the election of his brother to Parliament in 1645. By the end of the war he was largely at odds with the Government – to such an extent that he tried to hold a siege of Tutbury at the same time as Sir William Brereton's siege yet independent of it. He had disliked Brereton ever since Hopton Heath.

John Hutchinson (1616 – 1664)

The career of the other leading Parliamentarian commander, John Hutchinson, of Owthorpe in Nottinghamshire is well known to us, thanks to the labours of Lucy his wife who wrote a record of his life. She keenly felt the injustices done to him, both before and after the Restoration. Her work is filled with wonderful thumbnail sketches of the men with whom he worked and what she thought of them. John's father, Sir Thomas, had served as a JP and an MP. Given the normal course of events John would have followed in his footsteps. As it was, he garrisoned Nottingham Castle in the autumn of 1642 and held it thereafter, facing several sieges, with the help of his wife and brother. At least one attempt was made to get him to give the castle to the King by his mother's relatives, the Byron family also of Nottinghamshire. John was a regicide and served as JP in his county during the 1650s and also sat in the Commons. He was imprisoned at the Restoration and left to die within the crumbling walls of Sandown Castle.

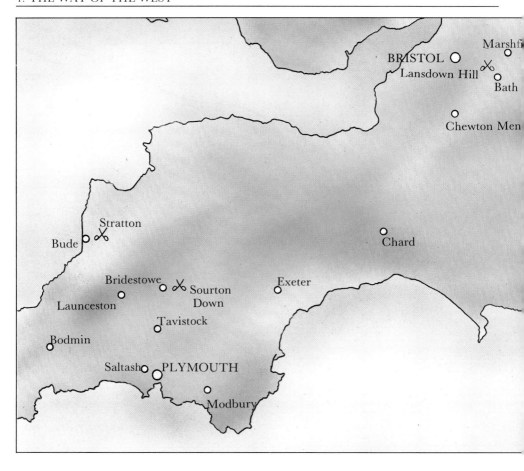

4. THE
WAY
OF THE
WEST

Whilst the Midlands had been dominated for Parliament by Sir William Waller, Royalist forces under Sir Ralph Hopton and Sir Bevil Grenville achieved successes in the South-west – even the devastation of Waller's army at Roundway Down.

FEBRUARY – JUNE 1643

Stratton is a few miles inland from Bude, on the A39. The battle took place on the hill to the west of the village. By using the Poughill road off the A39, the traveller can reach the summit of the hill where the action took place. Some of the earthworks, which the Earl of Stamford built, are still visible.

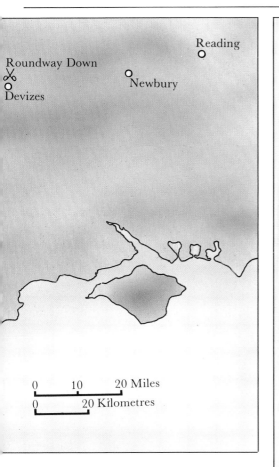

Anthony Payne (c. 1612 – 1691). Known as 'The Cornish Giant', he was 7ft. 4 ins. (2.2m.) tall and was born and died in what is now the Tree Inn, once a manor house, in Stratton. As servant to Sir Bevil Grenville, he fought at Stratton and brought his master's body home from the battle of Lansdown.

STRATTON

HOPTON'S VICTORY at Braddock Down (page 33) had settled very little. True, he had then marched into Devon, stormed Saltash, and prepared to besiege Plymouth, but by the end of February 1643 he was again pushed back to Tavistock. The Earl of Stamford had arrived and defeated Hopton's van at Modbury on 21 February. Nevertheless the Royalists somehow got the Earl to accept a forty-day truce, with later extensions, which eventually expired in April. Thus, on 22 April, Stamford sent Sir James Chudleigh and 2,100 men from Exeter to lure Hopton out of Cornwall.

Hopton was lured towards Chudleigh's trap at Sourton Down, where he was defeated and driven back on Bridestowe. Half of Hopton's army fled in panic and Hopton and Grenville only escaped because of heavy rain.

Even so, Hopton's correspondence was found, containing details of a projected advance into Somerset. Stamford, believing that he had Hopton at his mercy, set about finishing him off. He had 6,800 men as he advanced into Cornwall; Hopton had less than half this number.

With 800 horse sent to prevent Hopton raising men in Bodmin, Stamford waited with the rest of his army on a hill near Stratton, now called Stamford Hill, which he had reached via the Poughill Road out of Stratton. The hill, about 1 mile (1½ kilometres) inland from Bude, should have been secure enough. The east side was too

The monument to the battle of Stratton on Stamford Hill.

(Opposite) Horseman's armour as worn by Haselrigg's 'Lobsters' (see page 50).

The original plaque commemorating the battle of Stratton, now displayed outside the Tree Inn, Stratton.

steep to climb easily and at the top Stamford constructed a series of earthworks to guard the western approach.

At Launceston, Hopton and Sir Bevil Grenville could only muster 2,400 foot and 500 horse. Nevertheless, on 16 May, they went on the offensive. Despite the odds they planned a three-pronged attack on the hill. Hopton himself led a column of 600 up the south side, Grenville took two columns up the easier western slope whilst Sir John Berkeley took a fourth column up the north side. Until around three o'clock Stamford was able to hold the Royalists back and they began to run out of ammunition. Yet it was too dangerous for Hopton to call a retreat: if they had begun to draw off Stamford could have destroyed them. In effect then, there was no alternative but to continue the attack. Luckily Grenville's pikemen managed to gain a foothold on the plateau at the top of the hill. Suddenly Stamford's horse panicked, taking the Earl with them as they ran down the hill. Some said that he led them.

Chudleigh was made of sterner stuff and began to force Grenville back off the hill. By now, to the north, Berkeley was also on the top of the hill and even Hopton was beginning to make headway. Chudleigh's counter-attack went awry; as his forces pressed forward, he became cut off from his men. Leaderless, the Parliamentarians began to waver and fall back. The other two Royalist columns also pushed further onto the plateau, turning captured cannon onto the enemy. Declining any foolish bravado many fled down the precipitous eastern slope and 1,700 were taken prisoner. Chudleigh, thoroughly demoralized, changed sides. The Royalists owed their victory not only to the determination of the commanders but to the tenacity of the Cornish foot. Even so, the gross incompetence of Stamford had made it all possible. On the debit side, 300 Parliamentarians had been killed.

The Cask open

The Gorget

The Fore part of the Armed Lancier

The right Pouldron & Vambrace

The Left Pouldron & Vambrace

The Placcate

The Breast

The Back

The guard de reine

The Spanner

The Pistol

Pistol with the appurtenances

A HORSEMAN'S ARMS, ARMOUR & ACCOUTREMENTS

PARLIAMENT'S EARLY WESTERN COMMANDERS

The Earl of Stamford (1599 – 1673)

Prominent in the South and West in the early stages of the war, were the Earl of Stamford and his fellow Leicestershireman, Sir Arthur Haselrigg. Both had been long-standing opponents of the King's government in their own county during the 1630s, much of which had been put into effect by the Hastings family, led by the Earl of Huntingdon. Stamford was the head of the same Grey family which had sacrificed Queen Jane on the altar of her father's ambition and which had vied for power with the Hastings for over a century. In 1642 this struggle was seemingly won, as Stamford was made Lord Lieutenant, in Huntingdon's stead, by the Militia Ordinance. It was to counteract Stamford's and his son's, Lord Grey's, raising the Trained Bands that Henry Hastings was given the first Commission of Array. Stamford went on to recruit a regiment of bluecoats with which he garrisoned Hereford during the Edgehill campaign. In 1643 when given the task of destroying Hopton, he was clearly out of his depth and the defeat at Stratton effectively ended his military career. He then took up his seat in the Lords and at one point assaulted a man who accused his son's Leicestershire forces of incompetence, with his cane. He was not in favour of the Revolution and told his son, who was the first signatory of the King's death warrant after the court's Lord President, that no King meant no Lord Grey.

Sir Arthur Haselrigg (1625 – 1661)

Sir Arthur Haselrigg, of Noseley in Leicestershire, whilst not a regicide, had stood out firmly against the King in the 1630s. In 1638 he had arrested a constable for collecting Ship Money distraint, and had no less than five of the Earl of Huntingdon's deputy lieutenants called before a Parliamentary committee for alleged misdemeanours. Four of these men, Henry Hastings, his uncle (also Henry Hastings), Sir John Bale and Richard Halford, were all later to become Commissioners of Array, whilst the fifth, Sir Thomas Hartop, served on Parliament's county committee in Leicestershire.

Haselrigg sat in the Long Parliament and later formed his own small regiment of Cuirassiers, armoured cap-à-pie and nicknamed the 'Lobsters'. Similarly armed himself, he successfully fought off several assailants at the battle of Roundway Down. This caused the King to make one of his few jokes. When told of the incident, Charles commented that had Haselrigg, whom he had attempted to seize in the Commons in 1642, been victualled as well as fortified he might have endured a siege of seven years. Later in the war Haselrigg adhered to Cromwell and in the second Civil War fought with him in the North.

He was a Republican by conviction and opposed the army's interference in politics. He left Cromwell's side after the dissolution of Parliament in 1653. So implacable an enemy was he of the Restoration that he was arrested and later died in the Tower in 1661.

LANSDOWN AND ROUNDWAY DOWN

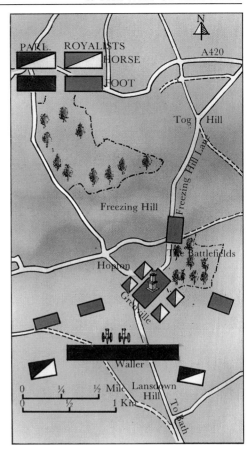

IT WAS NOW POSSIBLE for Hopton to work in conjunction with the Marquis of Hertford in the planned operation in Somerset and Wiltshire. Prince Maurice had also returned to Oxford to receive orders to follow Sir William Waller's army as it now entered the South-west. Waller was not really keen. Believing that Hertford would stay in Wiltshire and that Hopton would be kept immobile besieging Exeter, he would rather have concentrated on defeating the King. Charles, he was certain, was in an untenable position after the capture of Reading. Oxford would be abandoned, Charles would fall back on Worcester and Waller wanted to be there to finish him off. He was wrong. Hopton and Hertford joined forces at Chard and intended to clear Somerset before attacking Exeter. In response, Waller marched to Bath on 8 June 1643 to face them.

On 10 June there was a brief engagement at Chewton Mendip but it was not until 3 July that the Royalists' main forces encountered Waller on Landsown Hill, blocking the road to Bath. On 5 July they attacked. Lansdown Hill is about 5 miles (8 kilometres) from Bath on what is a minor road, leading from A420 towards Bath from Tog Hill. Hopton wished to use this route to Bath from Marshfield, where his army lay from 3 July. But Waller's position was a strong one. On the north-western end of the hill Waller had constructed fortifications controlling the road. Behind these he planted his cannon and ranged his horse and foot on the flanks to cover any approach. Hopton's initial attack with horse and dragoons was repulsed and the army pulled back to Tog Hill. Hoping to keep him moving, Waller sent his own horse and dragoons under Sir Arthur Haselrigg in pursuit. But Haselrigg was defeated and this time Hopton's foot moved after the

Lansdown can best be seen by using the route across Freezing Hill, which Hopton travelled to reach Waller. A minor road leading to Bath probably follows the exact route. This can be joined from the A420, just west of where it crosses the A46. Travel towards Bath. A steep descent down Freezing Hill brings you to Hopton's position in the valley. Join another minor but very busy road on a tight corner and this will bring you to the plateau of Lansdown Hill. On the left, behind trees, is the monument to Sir Bevil Grenville. A few hundred yards in from the edge of the hill is the place where the hill narrows. This is where Waller re-formed after pulling back.

The monument to Sir Bevil Grenville on Lansdown Hill.

The view of the battlefield from the road looking north-east towards Grenville's monument and the position where his regiment made its stand.

retreating Parliamentarians, on towards the hill.

The attack was a costly one: several officers and a large number of soldiers were killed assaulting the well prepared positions. Grenville's regiment made it up the hill and stood there despite Grenville receiving a mortal wound. They made an excellent target for Waller's guns but were also an anchor for the Royalist forces who followed. Hopton's horse were devastated by the cannon fire and put out of action; the foot had to make all the running. Eventually, as Grenville's men drove off his horse and increasing numbers of musketeers pressed in on his flanks, Waller ordered a retreat. He only moved about 400 yards (370 metres) to a series of stone walls which ran across a neck on the hill. It was a shrewd move. Hopton's men were exhausted and in no condition for another fight. During the night Waller pulled off towards Bath and the Royalists withdrew to Marshfield. It was really a victory for Waller, despite his inability to hold on to the edge of Lansdown Hill. Hopton's army was exhausted, and Grenville was dead: moreover, Hopton had lost a thousand horse. Yet Waller's army was not seriously damaged and he was still able to keep the Royalists out of Bath.

The next day, the discomfort of the

Sir Ralph Hopton (1598 – 1652)

SIR Ralph, later Lord Hopton of Stratton, had been involved in the same retreat from Prague as his friend Waller. He accompanied the Winter Queen as she carried the as yet unborn Prince Maurice. It was ironic that both men were to die in the same year.

During the 1620s Hopton sat as MP for Wells and Somerset. In 1640 he sat again for Wells. In the early days of Parliament's attempts to limit the King's power, Hopton supported the attack on the Earl of Strafford. He later went on to present Charles with the Grand Remonstrance, the list of complaints against the King's government and the remedies so far enacted by Parliament. Nevertheless, rebellion was not his aim and Hopton switched sides and even defended the King's attempt to seize five members of the Commons and Lord Mandeville (later the Earl of Manchester) only a month after the presentation of the Grand Remonstrance.

In October 1642 he raised troops in his native Cornwall and voluntarily stood trial at the Lostwithiel sitting of the Quarter Sessions, where he was cleared of disturbing the peace. After his victories over Stamford and Waller he was ennobled. But the following year he was defeated at Cheriton by Waller and his army was absorbed into the main Royalist army. Later in the war he became one of the advisers to Prince Charles when the Prince was given command of the West. As Lieutenant-General of the new Western Army he was eventually defeated by Sir Thomas Fairfax and the New Model Army. He, like Rupert and Maurice, found a career at sea in 1650 but was left out of Charles II's counsels when he opposed the new King's acceptance of a Scottish alliance. He retired from public life after this and in 1652 died 'of an ague'.

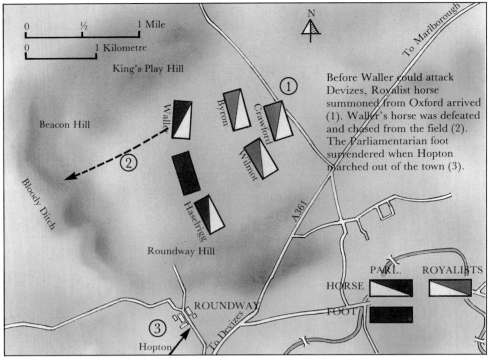

Before Waller could attack Devizes, Royalist horse summoned from Oxford arrived (1). Waller's horse was defeated and chased from the field (2). The Parliamentarian foot surrendered when Hopton marched out of the town (3).

Roundway Down.

Roundway Down is best explored on foot. It can be reached from the A361 Devizes-Swindon road, taking the turning for Roundway on the left, 1 mile (1½ kilometres) out of Devizes. Go into Roundway and turn right to Roundway Hill. This is perhaps the best vantage point and stands to the righthand rear of Waller's position. Looking north-eastwards, the line of Maurice's attack can be seen. Bloody Ditch is still a steep bank, lying back along the road to the south-west.

Royalists was enhanced by a bizarre accident. An ammunition wagon exploded and Hopton was very badly burned. With him out of action it was too dangerous to stay at Marshfield: the army was running low on ammunition and Waller was too close by for Hopton to recuperate in safety. They retreated to Devizes, and Waller followed. On 10 July, Waller drew his army up on Roundway Down to the north of the town, to try to tempt Hopton out into open battle. The Royalist commander had been temporarily blinded and paralysed by the blast. Moreover, ammunition was still short and a battle was out of the question. Waller was now

convinced of the advantage he had gained at Lansdown and set to besiege Devizes. By 11 July the town was encircled, but not before Prince Maurice and Hertford were able to get the horse out and set off to Oxford.

When they arrived there, they were told that a rescue party was already on its way under Lord Wilmot. The day before, however, an ammunition convoy under the Earl of Crawford had been captured by Waller on 9 July as it went towards Devizes. Without resting, Maurice and Hertford turned back; by now the horse had travelled over 50 miles (80 kilometres) in two days. Even so they caught up with Wilmot at Marlborough on 12 July. The following day was the one Waller had set for his storm of the town. Before he could launch the attack, Wilmot, Hertford and Maurice arrived on Roundway Down. Waller still had the advantage: in numbers he had 2,000 horse and 2,500 foot; ranged against him were only 1,800 horse and he was between them and 3,000 foot in Devizes. Waller turned from the town and drew up his army between Roundway Hill and Beacon Hill with his horse on the flanks. He had already intercepted the message sent by Wilmot to Hopton telling him to attack Waller's rear upon hearing signal gunshots. As a result, when these shots were heard in the town, Hopton's men were reluctant to come out.

There was a danger for Wilmot that if he waited too long, he would be taken at a disadvantage. To overcome this he attacked first. On his left was Sir John Byron's brigade, on his right his own brigade and in the rear the Earl of Crawford. Charging so quickly that they caught Waller's horse unprepared, the Royalists drove Haselrigg's own regiment, the 'Lobsters', into panic-stricken retreat and they took with them what remained of Stamford's old army, to which they belonged. Soon all of Waller's horse had run off leaving the foot standing unscathed. The Royalist horse pursued the retreating enemy to the edge of 'bloody ditch', a 300 foot (90 metre) drop at the edge of the down.

Hopton's foot now came out of the town and began to attack Waller's foot as Wilmot's men also began to return. There followed a brief pointless fight in which, sadly, a great number of Waller's foot were killed before the rest surrendered. In effect Roundway Down destroyed Waller's army. It was the second western army devastated in two months. Waller, who had escaped, fled to Gloucester and then on to London. Hopton occupied Bath. Prince Rupert joined him and his brother Maurice and an attack on Bristol was launched.

Prince Maurice (1621 – 1652)

The younger brother of Prince Rupert, Maurice is often passed over. This Prince was not as flamboyant as his brother nor as gifted, but he was of crucial importance in the western war and later in the West Midlands. Prince Maurice learned the 'art' of war with his brother in Europe, under William of Orange. In the early days of the Civil War, he raised a regiment of horse and fought at Powick Bridge and, in January 1643, at the taking of Chichester. By March he commanded the Gloucestershire forces and defeated Waller at Ripple Field in April. He then became Hertford's Lieutenant-General of Horse during the campaigns which culminated in the siege of Bristol. He fought in the King's army at Lostwithiel and at the second battle of Newbury. In 1645 he took charge of the Marcher counties along the Welsh border where he performed well. After Rupert's surrender of Bristol to the New Model Army he stuck by his brother and went into exile with him. In the later Civil Wars the two served with the small Royalist Navy.

THE SIEGE OF BRISTOL

BRISTOL was the second seaport in the country and Parliament had held it since the beginning of the war despite lukewarm support from anyone besides the town's few puritan stalwarts. From the King's point of view its capture would be valuable, not only as a morale-booster and fitting end to a successful western campaign but because of its undoubted value as a port. Apart from Chester and some small Welsh ports the Royalists had very few harbours of their own, especially ones with good links with Europe and Ireland from where they were expecting military help. Bristol was indeed a glittering prize. It was no less essential to Parliament as it provided a means by which to supply armies in the west of England.

As soon as Rupert joined his brother and the other western Royalists, they moved on Bristol and summoned the garrison's governor, Nathaniel Fiennes, son of Lord Saye and Sele, on 24 July. Bristol was well fortified but the line of circumvallation was over 3 miles (4¾ kilometres) long and Fiennes's garrison was too small to man the whole length in strength. With this in mind the Royalists decided to storm the town, in spite of the risk this would entail – they could barely afford to risk their Western Army. As it was, the attack on 26 July got off to a bad start when the Cornish foot stormed Temple Gate too early. This forced all the other attacks to begin before full preparations were made. As a result, only one of the four separate assaults succeeded. The breach was made in the wall between Windmill Hill and Brandon Hill and Royalist forces entered the town. The fighting continued over much of the day, but eventually Fiennes decided to surrender.

Although it was an important victory, Royalist casualties were very high. For Fiennes it was nearly fatal; he was court-martialled for his surrender of the town despite assertions by Prince Rupert, among others, that it would have been impossible for him to have held out after the town had been entered.

By careless error, Hertford, the commander of the Royalist forces at the siege, was not mentioned in the surrender document. It was a diplomatic slip by Rupert. The Marquis was quite incensed and to spite Rupert, who had led and planned the attack, he appointed Hopton as governor of the town in his stead. Thus the rankled Rupert returned to Oxford. Maurice and Hopton went on to besiege Exeter and Plymouth.

The medal struck to commemorate the successful siege of Bristol. The obverse depicts the fortified city.

Prince Rupert 1619 – 1682

RUPERT was the third son of Elizabeth, sister of Charles I, who had married Frederick V Elector Palatine, sometime King of Bohemia. He fought for the Protestant cause in Europe, and when he crossed to England in 1642 he was quickly given command of the King's Horse.

Rupert's first success was at Powick Bridge (see Chapter One). From lessons he learned here, he formulated the headlong but ordered charge which, by dispensing with the preliminary volley of pistol-fire, enabled an attacking force to hit an enemy unit with both speed and weight. This formula was successful at Edgehill and even at Naseby. However, it proved difficult to control the cavalry once a charge had been successful. Nonetheless, on a strategic level, Rupert was a more than able commander. His rapid advance on Newark in March 1644 (Chapter Eight) caught Sir John Meldrum napping, and the march to York in June and July 1644 confounded the allied Scots and Parliamentarians (Chapter Ten). Moreover, he was an effective organizer of the Royalist war effort and had great success in the West Midlands in early 1644.

Rupert was one of the more perceptive Royalists in the high command. He knew that the New Model Army should not have been underestimated in 1645 at Naseby. Likewise he recognized soon afterwards that the war was lost. His surrender of Bristol later that year should be seen in the light of his realization that it was futile to kill unnecessarily in the name of a defeated cause. Charles considered this tantamount to treachery, but Rupert had not deserted the cause. In 1648 he served in the small Royalist Navy and continued in this capacity throughout much of the 1650s. After the Restoration he was Admiral of the White Squadron and later Admiral of the Fleet. He was also a keen scientist and a member of the Royal Society.

5. NEWCASTLE'S COMMAND

FEBRUARY – OCTOBER 1643

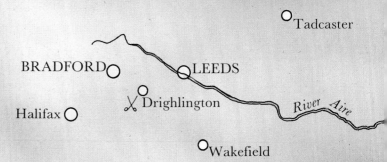

○YOR
●Tadcaster
BRADFORD○   ○LEEDS
Halifax○   ○Drighlington
         ○Wakefield
River Aire

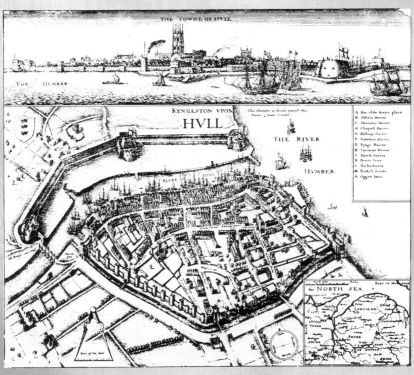

Plan of Hull in 1640 by Wenceslaus Hollar.

NOTTIN
○

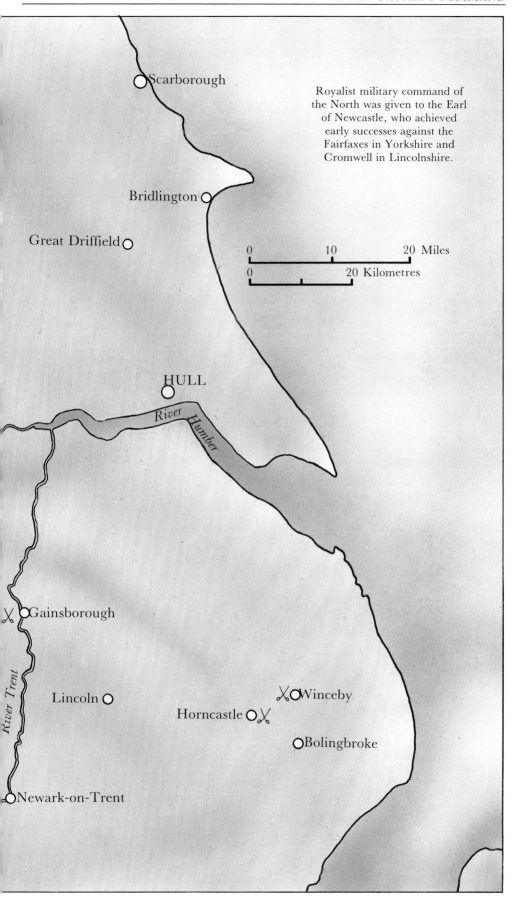

Scarborough

Royalist military command of
the North was given to the Earl
of Newcastle, who achieved
early successes against the
Fairfaxes in Yorkshire and
Cromwell in Lincolnshire.

Bridlington

Great Driffield

0   10   20 Miles
0   20 Kilometres

HULL

River Humber

Gainsborough

River Trent

Lincoln

Winceby

Horncastle

Bolingbroke

Newark-on-Trent

A Victorian engraving of Queen Henrietta Maria's arrival at Bridlington.

THE EARL OF NEWCASTLE was the King's lieutenant in the counties stretching from the Scottish borders to East Anglia. By the beginning of 1643 the Earl had secured the East Midland section with garrisons at Newark and Belvoir in the area commanded by Henry Hastings. Thereby he had gained an approach road into the southern section of his territory. In the far North, Northumberland and Durham were also firmly held down and the same was true of the North-west; but Yorkshire was a great problem. The offensive launched by Sir Thomas Fairfax in January 1643 had dislodged the Royalist garrisons at Leeds and Wakefield, and the Earl was too busy with the arrival of the Queen during February to deal with this situation.

A year earlier Queen Henrietta Maria had left England with a portion of the crown jewels to pawn for arms abroad. In the last week of February 1643 she arrived off the east coast and landed at Hildathorpe or Bridlington Quay in the Bay of Bridlington. She was bombarded on arrival by several Parliamentarian ships and had to take refuge in the down by the Gypsy Race brook. The Dutch ships which had accompanied the Queen from Holland then threatened to open fire on her assailants and the firing ceased. The Queen travelled inland to Bridlington, the small town grouped around the remains of a once great Augustinian priory. From there she went on to Boynton Hall and so on to meet the Earl of Newcastle. In York she began to gather an army around her and toyed with taking the field as a She-Generalissima.

In March Newcastle went on the offensive. He prevented the Fairfaxes destroying the bridge at Tadcaster, which would have secured them in the West Riding, and on 30 March Lord Goring, who had come over from Holland with the Queen, caught Sir Thomas Fairfax near Leeds. 5 miles (8 kilometres) out from the town Fairfax was hustling his tired foot across Bramham Moor. It was a hot day for

William Cavendish, Marquis of Newcastle (1593 – 1676)

NEWCASTLE was an old-fashioned man even in his youth. Described as a dilettante, he fancied himself as a poet but his verse was poor. He lived the role of rural magnate but at the same time wanted national status. He was on good terms with the powers behind Charles's throne – Archbishop Laud, the Earl of Strafford and the Queen. With their influence he became the tutor to the Prince of Wales, a dignified but not a political role: as such it just suited Newcastle. When the war broke out it was his ownership of large parts of the North-east and North Midlands which resulted in his being given military command over the whole North. He appointed experts to lead under him yet appeared in the field as Commander-in-Chief, perhaps just a little in the role of poet at war. In the war he was often described as being lethargic, but his offensive campaigns against the Fairfax's in late 1642 and the summer of 1643 do not bear this out. He showed fine strategic sense at Adwalton Moor although it was obvious that he sadly lacked Lord Goring, who by this time had been sent to the Tower. However, the decision to besiege Hull, albeit forced on him by the nervous Yorkshire Royalists, was a gross error. At that point he had been at his strongest and a march into the South should have been undertaken. There was also a series of political blunders at Oxford.

In 1644 the fruits of these blunders appeared. Parliament had brought the Scots into the war and Newcastle was the only line of defence against their invading army. He undertook strenuous efforts to defeat Lord Leven's forces, only to see the Yorkshire army in his rear collapse. The defeat at Marston Moor in July 1644 ended his role in the war. His flight to Holland was completely in character. The blame for defeat may well have fallen upon his shoulders, rather than on the King's nephew, Prince Rupert. The fact that he had advised against doing battle would, in a court which mocked him and called him lazy, have gone unnoticed.

early spring and at Seacroft, now a suburb of Leeds beside the A63-A64 linkroad, the soldiers halted for a drink. Here Goring caught up with them. Easily evading the three troops of horse which Fairfax had, the Royalists charged straight at the foot. These were short of pikes and could not hold off the furious assault. As a result they were broken. Those men not taken prisoner ran off to Leeds across the moor. It was not a great victory. Goring had not tackled the larger Parliamentarian army under Lord Fairfax which was able to reach Leeds safely. The reoccupation of Wakefield which followed Bramham Moor soon ended as Fairfax stormed the town capturing 1,400 men and Lord Goring. The common soldiers taken at Wakefield were soon exchanged for the men Sir Thomas had lost at Bramham Moor.

The Fairfaxes still needed help. Scarborough's governor, Sir Hugh Cholmeley, had changed sides when the Queen arrived and the Hothams, Sir John and his son John, who had held Hull since before the war began, looked like wavering in their loyalty. It was hoped that the Parliamentarians in the East Midlands would be able to offer support. During May these forces were gathered at Nottingham, planning to capture Newark in order that the Queen could be prevented from coming south with her army. However, they were riven by dissent. Lord Grey was unwilling to leave Leicestershire to the mercy of Henry Hastings, and the younger Hotham was likewise unwilling to press any attack which would damage his attempt to change sides on favourable terms. As a result the allied Parliamentarians at Nottingham, John Hutchinson, Sir John Gell, Lord Grey, John Hotham and the now Colonel Oliver Cromwell did nothing, except blithely tell the Fairfaxes that they had full confidence in their ability to defeat Newcastle. On the arrival of the Queen's army at Newark, Grey and the others scattered.

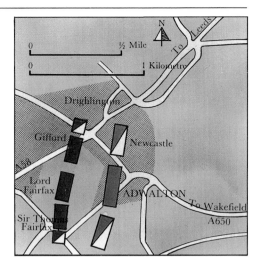

Adwalton Moor can be reached via the A58 from Leeds or the A650 from Bradford. The field is bounded by Drighlington to the north and Adwalton to the south-east and east. Whilst industrial land surrounds it, there is still a green between the two villages, and this marks part of the battlefield. To the south, the minor roads via Oakwell and Cleckheaton are along the lines of those down which Sir Thomas Fairfax made his retreat. To the north, the A650 is the line of retreat for Lord Fairfax and Gifford. Both armies would have stretched from the area of the A650/A58 crossroads to the position of the old Adwalton/ Drighlington Station.

ADWALTON

THE QUEEN'S DEPARTURE from York on 14 June 1643 left Newcastle with no excuse for inactivity. The Earl went on the offensive and the Fairfaxes, fearing an attack on Bradford, led their 3,000 trained men and a large number of raw recruits towards Wakefield along the route of the present A650. When the Parliamentarians arrived at Adwalton they discovered Newcastle waiting for them. It was already a strategic and tactical success for the Earl. By 30 June he had concentrated no less than 10,000 men at Adwalton and he had also secured the open fields south of the village.

The battlefield is now encompassed

Ferdinando, second Baron Fairfax of Cameron.

on three sides by the villages of Drighlington to the north and Adwalton to the south and east. In 1643 Drighlington was on the Parliamentarian's left flank which was led by General Gifford. Lord Fairfax was in the centre sheltered by the hedges of enclosed fields. On the right was Sir Thomas. His flank, consisting of a thousand foot and five troops of horse, was drawn up amongst a series of coal pits. These provided excellent cover for the foot but put the horse in a difficult position, at a distinct disadvantage to Newcastle's horse on the open ground opposite them.

The Fairfaxes went on the attack in an attempt to offset the disadvantages of numbers and ground. Even on the right Sir Thomas's horse met with some success as Newcastle's horse crashed off the open ground into the coal-pit area. Sections of the Royalist horse who overlapped Sir Thomas's left and charged the foot in the centre were assailed by well covered musket fire. The low number of pikes which had been such a problem at Seacroft did not matter here, and Newcastle's horse

reeled back allowing Fairfax's foot to progress from hedge to hedge. It is probable that the advancing Parliamentarian army was able to reach the line of the Royalist guns in this confusion.

However a major problem now beset Lord Fairfax's army. At a 90° angle to the front of the army lay a ridge. This was the line of the road which they had been following on their march to Wakefield. Although an admirable route, it presented a problem now as Sir Thomas's flank was separated from the bulk of his father's army by it and was actually out of Lord Fairfax's line of sight. Thus, as the Royalist Colonel Skirton counter-attacked against the Parliamentarian centre, and with his greater numbers of pikemen was able to halt their advance and begin to force them back, Sir Thomas was left out on a limb. Newcastle, leading his horse in person also drove back the Parliamentarian left under Gifford. Lord Fairfax began a retreat towards Bradford with the left and centre of his army, but the Royalist forces were between them and Sir Thomas, and had blocked off all the routes to the town. By the time the younger Fairfax realized his dilemma, it was too late to attempt to follow his father. Instead he began to retreat down the lanes south of the ridge in the direction of Halifax, along the line of the present A58. After an 8 mile (13 kilometre) march, unmolested by Newcastle's army, Fairfax reached Halifax and began a march to Bradford straightaway. The Royalist army was somewhat discomforted by its none-too-impressive performance at Adwalton Moor, and its advance on Bradford was slow and half-hearted. Nevertheless Newcastle was soon able to secure the capture of the town. The Fairfaxes with the remains of their army fled to Hull. All of Yorkshire, with the exception of the great port, lay at the feet of the Earl of Newcastle.

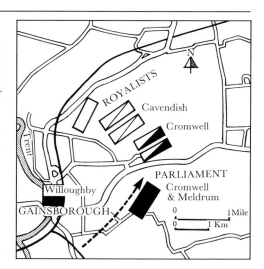

It is likely that the battle of Gainsborough took place to the north and east of the town and the field is now bisected by the railway line to Grimsby. Cromwell's attack was, probably, along the line of the minor roads to the east of the A159 near the old Lea Road Station. From around here, he and Meldrum climbed Summerhill. The main fighting would have been in the Highfield Grange Area, from where the Royalists were chased to Morton.

EVEN SO, the southern part of Newcastle's command now gave cause for concern. In the North Midlands, Colonel-General Hastings was making progress in his attempts to hold down the indigenous Parliamentarians. But in Lincolnshire there was trouble. In April 1643 the Eastern Association, the Parliamentarian counties of East Anglia, had sent Colonel Cromwell into the county. From there he had become part of the abortive attempt to capture Newark in May. By July the Parliamentarian commander in Lincolnshire, Lord Willoughby of Parham, with Cromwell's help, had captured Gainsborough, thereby closing in on Newark. In response Sir Charles Cavendish, son of the Earl of Devonshire and cousin to the Earl of Newcastle, returned to the area after escorting the Queen to Oxford. Once there he set about besieging Gainsborough. Cromwell and Sir John Meldrum, now commanding part of the horse which had been under Lord Grey, went to its rescue. The town was important: it was a crossing-point on the Trent and a part of the route from Yorkshire to the South. Even now it lies on the crossroads of the A631 which crosses the Trent there and the A561, important roads from the North and into Lincolnshire. When Lord Willoughby captured the town he had not only captured the leading Lincolnshire Royalist, The Earl of Kingston, but he had deprived Newark of its direct communications with the Earl of Newcastle.

Cromwell and Meldrum joined forces at North Scarle, 9 miles (14 kilometres) or so north of Newark, and marched on Gainsborough. When there they drew up north of the river Lea and were faced by Cavendish who pulled away from the town. The ensuing fight probably took place to the north-east of Gainsborough. The

Parliamentarians pushed forward up the steep hill to where they were attacked by Cavendish leading his horse. The first Royalist charge was defeated but Cavendish brought up a second line and drove the Lincolnshire horse back. Having pressed these too far, Cavendish left himself open to attack by Cromwell in his rear. The Royalists were scattered and began a retreat on Morton. Cavendish was killed in the pursuit. Cromwell and Meldrum then entered Gainsborough for a meeting with Lord Willoughby. Whilst they were in the town, reports came in of a small Royalist force approaching from the direction of East Stockwith on the east bank of the River Trent.

It was not a small force however; the reports were wrong about that. It was in fact the Earl of Newcastle himself with his whole army. Cromwell's forces were easily caught and defeated outside the town and Gainsborough was soon surrendered. Newcastle went on to capture Lincoln without a blow being struck. Cromwell retreated to Peterborough and the Lincolnshire Parliamentarians were bottled up in Boston. Newcastle appointed Sir William Widdrington as the Lieutenant General in the county and took his army back to deal with Hull. The Earl was nervous of leaving the Fairfaxes behind him, or at least the nervousness of the Royalist Yorkshiremen with him was sufficient to make him retire to the north again. The siege which he opened upon his return was to waste away the great Northern Army. Had he continued south he could have led 15,000 men to join the King in the Thames valley.

PARLIAMENTARIANS RESURGENT

THE DISASTER in Lincolnshire spurred the Parliamentarians on. The whole of the Eastern Association was re-organized and the Earl of

Lincoln Castle, which fell to the Earl of Newcastle following the battle of Gainsborough.

Manchester was given command of the army raised in the region. Cromwell was made Lieutenant-General and set off to help Sir Thomas Fairfax evacuate his Yorkshire horse from Hull over the Humber. Once over, these twenty-seven troops were joined to Manchester's forces besieging Bolingbroke Castle. The siege was really only a ruse to draw a Royalist force from Newark into open battle. Widdrington and the Newark governor, Sir John Henderson, took the bait. On 10 October 1643 elements of Royalist horse defeated Manchester's horse at Horncastle on the Lincoln to Skegness road (A158). The day after they pushed on towards Bolingbroke.

Manchester's army marched via Old Bolingbroke towards Horncastle on the Winceby Road. In the vicinity of Winceby they encountered twenty-one colours of dragoons and seventy-four

Sir Thomas, Third Baron Fairfax of Cameron (1612 – 1671)

FERDINANDO, second Baron Fairfax of Cameron, and his son, Sir Thomas, were not only the two most important Yorkshire Parliamentarians but the latter was one of the most important men in the whole war. In the early years of the war they faced the problem of having to work with generally unsatisfactory material. With the exception of Sir William Saville, their fellows were not as determined Parliamentarians.

But the Fairfax's were of different stuff. Even in defeat Sir Thomas was remarkable. His march to Bradford via Halifax after the battle at Adwalton was a magnificent piece of man-management. The father, Ferdinando, was not so gifted but was just as dogged. His defence of Hull in 1643 was determined and successful; it was perhaps his finest hour.

Whilst Thomas was ultimately perhaps a lesser general than Cromwell, he was undoubtedly brave. At Marston Moor, where his flank was destroyed by Lord Goring, he declined to run. Instead he rode round the rear of the Royalist centre and met up with Cromwell, bringing him round to defeat Goring's horse. When the New Model Army was created he was appointed Commander-in-Chief and secured Cromwell's appointment as his second. At Naseby, Fairfax led the last attack himself and personally took a colour. His generalship at the head of the New Model was to be admired and his eclipse by Cromwell was not due to any military deficiency. Fairfax was not a revolutionary; indeed he was not much of a politician at all. He opposed the execution of the King, although he left it to his wife to voice opposition as he was hamstrung by being head of an army which brought about the trial. A year later he retired from the army after opposing the proposed war with Scotland. As the third Lord Fairfax (his father died in 1648) he lived on his estate at Bilborough. Although he later played a significant part in the early stages of the Restoration, he passed the rest of his days in rural retreat. In this way he lived out his life like his old adversary, Newcastle.

colours of horse. In theory each of these colours represented a troop of sixty men, but twenty to forty was a more likely figure. Cromwell, leading Manchester's horse had only half that amount of colours, but in fact his troops were much nearer to full strength and therefore he probably had similar total numbers. At noon the battle began. The Parliamentarian horse with Vermuyden leading, Cromwell second and Fairfax bringing up the rear, followed up a dragoon engagement with a charge. Willoughby's front line was defeated and plunged back into his second. Hampered by this and by being on poor ground to the north of Winceby, this line could not counter Cromwell's attack. A rout soon developed and a large number of Royalists were killed in a lane to the west of Winceby now known as Slash Lane (this is now incorporated into the modern A1115). The battle was over before Manchester's foot could enter the fight and they had to content themselves with rounding up the Royalist stragglers. Many of the dead were found in marshlands which no longer exist. This area, which is now know as Snipe Dale, is still uncultivated land to the east of the battlefield.

Newcastle ended his disastrous siege and again brought his army south to redress the situation after Winceby. Henderson was replaced by a local man, Richard Byron. Hastings's army was enlarged with a series of Derbyshire regiments installed in several garrisons created to hold Gell in check. Newcastle, in recognition of his earlier successes, was given a marquisate and Hastings was made Lord Loughborough. Lincolnshire was now a divided county, but the North Midlands was firmly held by Hastings. If Newcastle was ever able to march south he could draw on a large number of reserves from the area. He had need to. The siege of Hull had reduced the numbers of the Northern Army significantly.

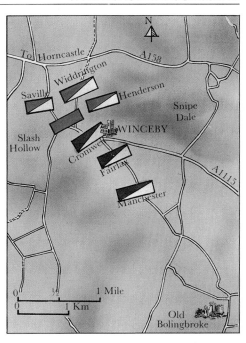

Winceby is best reached by taking the A1115 southwards, roughly east of Horncastle along the A158. The fighting took place to the north of this road, above the junction with the Hammeringham road. Manchester's forces appeared from the direction of Asgardby and Old Bolingbroke, and attacked the Royalists as they came from the direction of Horncastle. Slash Lane, along which the Royalists routed, is now seemingly incorporated into the A1115. One of their dead, Sir Ingram Hopton, is entombed in Horncastle Church.

Bolingbroke Castle. After the battle of Winceby, Lord Willoughby took over the siege of the Royalist garrison begun by the Earl of Manchester. The castle surrendered to him on 14 November 1643.

The monument to John Hampden at Chalgrove.

6. THE FIRST BATTLE OF NEWBURY

SEPTEMBER 1643

CHALGROVE FIELD

DURING THE MIDDLE OF THE YEAR events of importance were usually taking place on the periphery of the Royalist centre. Hopton was clearing the South-west, Hastings and Newcastle were working away at the opposition in the North. Once Essex had taken Reading, he was largely ineffective. This was shown up very clearly when Rupert made a dash at one of Essex's pay convoys in June 1643.

Sir John Urry changed sides (not for the last time) and fled to Oxford, bringing information about a pay train carrying £21,000 to Essex at Thame. Prince Rupert set out with 1,000 horse, 500 foot and over 300 dragoons. At Chinor, he attacked the tiny garrison. However, this gave warning of his approach and the convoy scuttled to safety. Having failed in the mission, Rupert turned back to Oxford. After all he was in an area dominated by Essex's army and his mission had depended upon his not being discovered. Once he had been found several Parliamentarian units began to follow him. At Chiselhampton they caught up with him. Rupert turned from his crossing of the bridge on the Thame and drew up his forces in Chalgrove Field, which is west of the road from there to Warpsgrove.

The enemy dragoons approached his line and commenced firing. Rupert charged through them straight at the main column behind. It was only a brief fight before the Parliamentarian horse fled. In the skirmish John Hampden, the man who had stood out against the continued imposition of Ship Money, was mortally wounded. He led regiments of greencoats (his foot had been involved at Edgehill and Brentford). The King offered to send his personal physician but Hampden was beyond help. He managed to ride to his home at Thame, where he died six days later. Meanwhile, on the afternoon of the fight on 18 June, Rupert returned to Oxford. This was to be only the first of his attacks on Parliamentarian outposts in the Chilterns using the information he had got from Urry. A monument was later erected to Hampden's memory near the crossroads on the road from Chalgrove to Warpsgrove.

E

The first battle of Newbury was a remarkable achievement by the Earl of Essex and Parliament's London Trained Bands. Having marched to Gloucester to relieve Charles's siege of the city, they encountered the King's army at Newbury on the return journey.

JRY

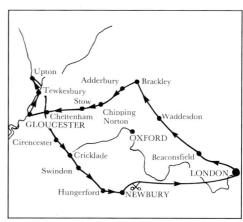

Essex's march from London to Gloucester and back.

ESSEX'S MARCH

JUST AS the Earl of Newcastle became mesmerized by Hull so, it can be argued, was the King by Gloucester. The town was the last major Parliamentarian bastion in the Severn Valley and thus in the King's rear. If Charles could remove it then access to Wales would be much easier. Yet it has to be argued that the time spent besieging the town could have been better spent. If Essex's army had been attacked – after all it was the only army left in the centre of England after Waller's defeat at Lansdown – victory could have been his. As it was, the prospect of dominating the West Midlands was very tempting to the King.

Thus on 10 August 1643, Charles summoned the governor of Gloucester, Edward Massey, to surrender. Massey had been placed there by the Earl of Stamford earlier that year. He was a Scot by birth and a soldier by profession. He had been the Lieutenant-Colonel of Stamford's own Leicestershire regiment of bluecoats. In his refusal to surrender,

Massey expressed his hope that there would be relief coming from Waller's or Essex's forces. To this the King replied: 'Waller is extinct and Essex cannot come.' Preliminary attacks began almost immediately as the King's forces began to take over the suburbs and to build earthworks. A storm was likely to be expensive in terms of Royalist lives and the King settled for a siege. Massey was known to be short of ammunition and besides he had a garrison of only 1,500. Nevertheless, he had significant support from the townspeople and this was important. With the spirited resistance shown by the people, a relief attempt became politically desirable in London. A proposed attempt was projected under Waller's command but Essex, ever mindful of any diminution of his status, decided to do the job himself.

So, as Massey fought off the Royalist attempts to mine the town walls and their use of 'Roman' siege engines, Essex led his army out of London. He marched up the Thames Valley with 15,000 men, including five regiments of London Trained Band foot and its regiment of horse. It proved an easy march. Prince Rupert and Lord Wilmot made only small raids on the column. As the Earl arrived at Prestbury on 5 September, Massey tried to prevent his men from firing back at the Royalists – he had only one barrel of gunpowder left!

'The Setting Out of the Trained Bands from London to Raise the Siege of Gloucester' by the Victorian artist C. W. Cope.

THE SIEGE OF GLOUCESTER

THE SIEGE OF GLOUCESTER as later recorded by Massey's chaplain, John Corbet, was an affair conducted by God and Godly people working in unison:

The sadness of the times did not cloud the countenances of the people. They beheld their fortunes with a clear brow, and were deliberate and cheerful in the endeavours of safety. No great complainings were heard in our streets; no discontent seized upon the soldiers, at other times prone to mutiny; men of suspected fidelity did not fail in action; every valuable person was active in his own place. The usual outcries of women were not then heard, the weakness of whose sex was not overcome by the terrible engines of war. And our becalmed spirits did implore divine assistance without confusion. The Governor personally performed, ready at every turning of affairs and gracing the business with speech and gesture.

Edward Massey, Governor of Gloucester

contemplating surrendering to the Royalists, in the hope of favour. If so this letter may have been preparing the ground by presenting a series of excuses beforehand. He nevertheless remained loyal to the cause throughout the first Civil War. It was only after the aims of that cause changed that he changed sides.

THE BATTLE

CHARLES did not risk fighting Essex with Gloucester at his back, and he pulled his forces to the south-east. After relieving the town with much needed supplies and ammunition, Essex had to contemplate the hazardous journey back. For the first time he demonstrated real tactical skill by taking the army up the west bank of the Severn and then across it and the Avon at Tewkesbury. The King assumed, just as Essex had hoped, that the Earl was returning to London by the same route as he had come – that is to the north of Oxford. To block his route, the King moved his army north-east from Painswick to Cheltenham, then on past Sudbury Castle to Pershore and Evesham. Meanwhile, Essex left Tewkesbury and marched south to Cricklade and Swindon, thereby leaving the King to the north of him and

Yet at the same time, Massey himself was telling Parliament a different story, partly to entice their help:

But now, what with the general discontent of both, of the city soldiers and our own, we stand at present as betrayed unless speedily you can prevent it. Alderman Pury and some few of the citizens, I dare say, are still cordial to us, but I fear ten to one incline the other way.

Massey may well have been playing a double game. It is possible that he was

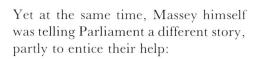

Much of the area where the battle was fought has now been built over, but you emerge very quickly from the housing estates of Wash Common into the open countryside around Round Hill.

To reach Wash Common, take the A343 to Andover from Newbury. At crossroads about 1 mile (1½ kilometres) from the town centre, you will see the Falkland Monument on your right; you are at this point in the centre of the Royalist lines. Take the road to the right in front of the monument and in about ½ mile (¾ kilometre) you come to open country and the beginning of the Parliamentarian lines.

The view north-west from Round Hill towards the Parliamentarian positions.

putting valuable miles between the two armies.

This advantage was lost all too soon. On 16 September 1643 when Essex reached Cricklade, the King was still at Evesham. But within one day as Essex made it to Swindon, the King marched to Abrescot north of Farringdon. On 18 September Rupert with the Royalist horse encountered the advance guards of Essex's army at Newbury and pushed them back on Hungerford. By the following day the King's army stood between the Parliamentarians and London.

On 20 September the Royalist forces were drawn up from the Newbury to Kintbury road in the north, to Wash Common to the south and east of Newbury itself. Much of the main army stood in the open lands now covered by housing estates. This clear ground was where Rupert had placed most of the horse under Sir John Byron to the right and Rupert himself to the left. Essex's army had its left flank resting near the Endbourne to Kintbury road, where his baggage train stood, down to Wash Common and Endbourne Heath. The Earl had positioned horse on both flanks; in the centre was the regular army foot with the London Trained Bands to the rear.

It was up to Essex to attack: he was short of food and, after all, he was attempting to reach London. He had little choice but to push on through Wash Common and then go to the south of Newbury and round onto the London road. Forcing his way to the common was easy as he had plenty of foot which would be necessary for the hard slog this would involve. Crossing the common was a different matter, given Rupert's superiority in horse. The King had only to play a defensive role to minimize damage to his own army whilst holding Essex back from the route to London. However from the very outset the Royalist plan was badly executed. Just to the north of the common was Round Hill, a promontory

The Earl of Essex (1591 – 1648)

Robert Devereaux, third Earl of Essex, was the son of Elizabeth I's piqued favourite and had gained considerable experience of war at sea and by sea. In the war between Scotland and England he was second in command of the King's army, yet he always favoured the calling of Parliament. In March 1642 he was named as Lord Lieutenant in several counties in the Militia Ordinance. Still Charles tried to gain his support, inviting him to join the Court at York. On 12 July he became the commander of Parliament's army and undertook the task with gusto. He welded together an army of some 14,000 only to dissipate this strength by creating several garrisons in the South Midlands. Even so, despite being the first to quit the field at Edgehill, he was still the first to reach London from where he drove the King back.

The Newbury campaign was his greatest triumph: Essex reached Gloucester without having to fight a battle and then fended off the attempt to intercept him as he marched home again. It was important that he achieved this success, for there was already a great deal of criticism levelled at him, and hitherto 1643 had not been much of a success. Nevertheless, despite the revelation of his strategic capabilities, Parliament began to diminish his status. Essex kept on fighting for the cause in the following year, but was outgeneralled by the King at Lostwithiel and a partly diplomatic illness prevented him from playing any role at the second battle of Newbury. By the time that the nobility lost their military commands at the end of 1644, Essex had already lost his authority. The cause he fought for triumphed just before he died: it is unlikely that he would have appreciated the victory.

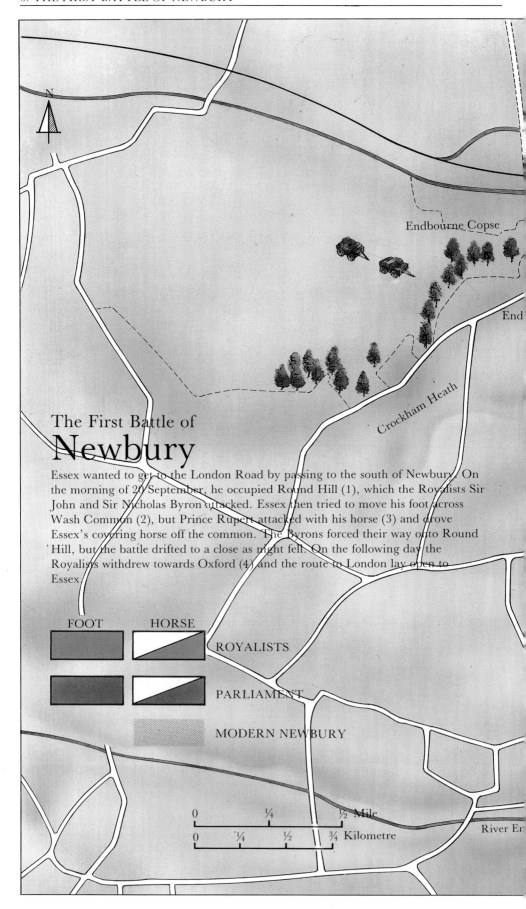

Endbourne Copse

End

Crockham Heath

The First Battle of
Newbury

Essex wanted to get to the London Road by passing to the south of Newbury. On the morning of 20 September, he occupied Round Hill (1), which the Royalists Sir John and Sir Nicholas Byron attacked. Essex then tried to move his foot across Wash Common (2), but Prince Rupert attacked with his horse (3) and drove Essex's covering horse off the common. The Byrons forced their way onto Round Hill, but the battle drifted to a close as night fell. On the following day the Royalists withdrew towards Oxford (4) and the route to London lay open to Essex.

FOOT   HORSE

ROYALISTS

PARLIAMENT

MODERN NEWBURY

| 0 | ¼ | ½ Mile |
| 0 | ¼ | ½ | ¾ Kilometre |

River En

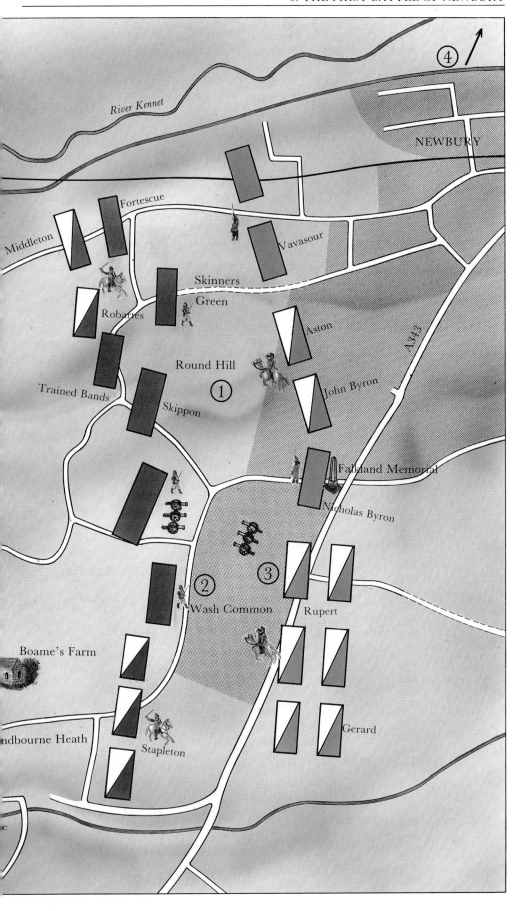

River Kennet

NEWBURY

Fortescue

Middleton

Vavasour

Skinners

Green

Robartes

Aston

Round Hill

John Byron

①

Trained Bands

Skippon

A343

Falkland Memorial

Nicholas Byron

②

Wash Common

③

Rupert

Boame's Farm

Gerard

ndbourne Heath

Stapleton

The Falkland Monument on the A343.

which dominated the whole battlefield. Before the King and his generals were aware of the importance of the hill, Essex's army had captured it.

Therefore the first task of the Royalist army was to redress this by storming the hill. At seven o'clock in the morning, Sir Nicholas Byron led several regiments of foot in an attack on the hill; he was supported by Sir John Byron's, his nephew's, horse. Their task was a difficult one. Essex had placed two light cannons on the hill and the Trained Bands which had advanced onto it were firmly ensconced behind the hedgerows. Casualties were high in the Royalist horse and it took a long time to establish any foothold on the north-east corner. Nevertheless, eventually this was achieved and the Trained Bands began to give some ground. It was in this fierce fighting that Lord Falkland was killed. Once the Byrons gained their grip on the hill, it was the turn of the Trained Bands to suffer heavily, but for up to three hours they held their ground against heavy pressure. Sir Phillip Skippon drew the Trained Bands back slowly, contesting every foot of ground. At one point the Royalist horse attempted to fool them by adopting the Parliamentarian field

sign of a green sprig in their hat bands, but this failed. By midday, Sir John's horse were too exhausted and retired from the hill, leaving Sir Nicholas to hold on alone.

On Wash Common, Rupert was tempted on by the open ground. He need only have waited until the Parliamentarian foot emerged from the enclosures but instead charged at the covering horse of Sir Phillip Stapleton, only to be driven back twice. Eventually the sheer weight of numbers enabled Rupert to push Stapleton off the common back into the lanes between the enclosed fields. Here the Earl of Essex rallied them and prepared again to push onto the common. It was clear that it was Skippon who was controlling the Parliamentarian army, as the Earl was again to be found pike in hand down by the common. Skippon brought the artillery up from behind the hill and began a successful bombardment of the Royalist centre, which took the pressure off the battered Trained Band regiments on Round Hill. They were then able to keep their hold on the southern side of the hill. According to one participant, Sergeant Henry Foster, the Red and Blue regiments 'stood like so many stakes against the shot of the cannon, quitting themselves like men of undaunted spirits'.

To the north of the field little happened. As the Royalists held Newbury, there was no real point in the Parliamentarians trying to push round their lines at this place. What fighting there was, that between Lord Robartes's Parliamentarians and Vavasour's foot, was as hard as any on the field. At one point Robartes looked in danger and Skippon had to send some reinforcements to him.

Sporadic fighting went on all day and may have continued until ten o'clock at night. Nevertheless, it was the Royalists who lost the battle. Essex had not only gained the advantage of the ground but he had held onto it. Although he had not made any progress on his march to

London, his army had not suffered much harm. The same could not be said for the Royalist forces, who had been mauled in several areas with so little result. Moreover, it was the King who was running low on ammunition. On the morning of 21 September, Essex awoke to find that the King had marched off to Oxford. The London road lay open.

Essex and the army were able to progress via Greenham Common and Aldermarston. Only one serious attempt was made to impede his progress. But the attack, launched near Aldermarston, was driven off. The Parliamentarians were refreshed and fed at Reading and Essex entered London on 28 September to a justly deserved hero's welcome.

The Newbury campaign looked remarkable to contemporaries. For Parliament it was an excellent propaganda coup. In addition Gloucester and the road to Wales were still in their hands. But it is possible that the full significance was unnoticed at first. The King's obsession with Gloucester was matched by the Earl of Newcastle's with Hull and the south-western Royalists' preoccupation with Plymouth. Each siege had distracted attention from the central need to defeat Essex and march on London before any other army could be raised in its defence. If the major Royalist forces had combined in the Thames Valley this could have been achieved. Instead, the Northern Army wasted away at Hull and the King was defeated before Gloucester and at Newbury. This was the last time that any major Royalist initiative against London could have met with success. Political mistakes made at Oxford compounded this. Scottish representatives had been sent packing and the Scots were about to send an army into the North of England. This would end the possibility of the Earl of Newcastle marching south to the King. The initiative was fast leaving the King's party.

Lucius Cary, Second Viscount Falkland (1610 – 1643)

LUCIUS CARY, second Viscount Falkland, was educated at Cambridge and Trinity College, Dublin. He succeeded to the title and the estate at Great Tew, north of Oxford, in 1633. He had sat in the two Parliaments of 1640 and opposed the extremes of the personal rule and agreed with the execution of the Earl of Strafford. He only left Parliament's side in August 1642 and from then on adhered to the King.

He was a man of high intellect and capable of showing great tolerance in debate. As one who believed in logic and discussion, the war was anathema to his very soul. By the time of the siege of Gloucester, the tragedy of the kingdom kept him awake at nights. It is probable that his death at Newbury was suicide. He received communion that morning and dressed in clean linen. As a volunteer in Sir John Byron's horse, he spurred his mount through a small gap in one of the hedges on Round Hill only to be killed instantly in a hail of musket fire.

Goodrich Castle, near Monmouth – a Royalist stronghold.

7. NANTWICH
JANUARY 1644

Parliament saw Nantwich as an important post from which to check the movement of Royalist troops brought into England from Ireland through the port of Chester. They were determined to hold it.

Haverfordwest

Pembroke

Tenby

IT IS FAIR TO SAY that, with the exception of Pembroke and Tenby, Wales was largely Royalist territory, or it was indeed content, while circumstances demanded, to remain in Royalist hands. It was from the Principality that Charles I was able to recruit large numbers of foot for his army. Lord Hertford had failed to secure further the south of Wales in the late months of 1642 and the early days of 1643, but the north was firmly held and guarded by the garrison at Chester. That is why Gloucester and its route into the south of the country was so important to both Charles and Parliament in late 1643.

The Royalists had not had a quiet time in Wales, however. In spring 1643 Waller had advanced into the south and taken Chepstow and Monmouth after capturing Hereford. In the north Sir William Brereton had tried to overrun Cheshire preparatory to a march into North Wales, or at least cut the area off from Oxford. In the following summer Parliament had felt confident enough to appoint a Major General, Sir Thomas Middleton, to North Wales, but he and Brereton concentrated on capturing Eccleshall in Staffordshire and Wem in Shropshire to secure their rear before

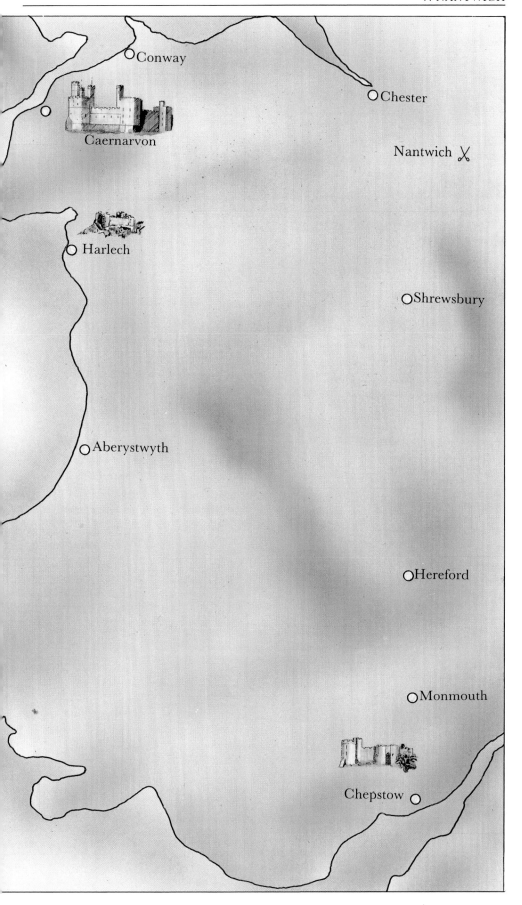

Conway

Chester

Caernarvon

Nantwich ✂

Harlech

Shrewsbury

Aberystwyth

Hereford

Monmouth

Chepstow

entering the Principality. Lord Capel, the Royalist commander in the region, was unable to cope despite having a large army of his own and support from Henry Hastings. He attacked Nantwich in October, only to be repulsed. He likewise failed to take Wem. When he retreated to Shrewsbury, Brereton and Middleton went into North Wales. Although it only took them a few weeks to secure the northeast they were driven out when Sir Michael Earnley landed in Flintshire with 1,500 English soldiers from the army in Ireland.

In view of his failures, Capel was replaced by Sir John Byron who was sent from Oxford at the end of 1643. Attacks were launched on minor garrisons in the south of Cheshire and Brereton's army was wrecked at the battle of Middlewich. As Brereton fled to Manchester, the remains of his forces took refuge in Nantwich.

THE BATTLE OF NANTWICH

Byron was created Field Marshal of Wales and the Marches which left scope for him to work with, rather than replace, Capel. Nevertheless the latter's failures were too great to allow him to continue long in the post. Therefore Byron succeeded to the task of securing Cheshire, recapturing 'lost' areas of North Wales and protecting it from further Parliamentarian incursions. After Middlewich, Byron had bottled up the remains of Brereton's army in Nantwich. The town had long been a thorn in the side of Chester's Royalist garrison and Capel had long tried to extract it. By early January Byron took up the task.

Parliament was determined to hold on to Nantwich. If the Royalists began to bring large numbers of English, and perhaps Irish, soliders over from Ireland, then Chester would be one of the main ports used. If Nantwich remained in Parliament's hands, then

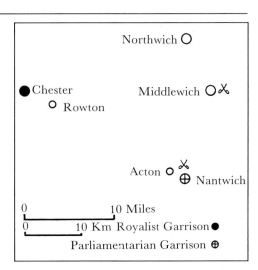

the movement inland of these Royalist levies could be halted or at least interrupted. Most of the troops landed at Chester were Englishmen from the army fighting the Catholic rebels. Nevertheless they were labelled as being Irish and subjected to a variety of diatribes in the Parliamentarian press: one called them 'vipers returned to eat out of the bowels of their own mother'. At the same time Charles was trying to bring an end to the war in Ireland so he could enlist large numbers of Catholics to his cause, but by the beginning of 1644 only English regiments had crossed the Irish Sea.

If Parliament held on in Cheshire, the eventual aim was to capture Chester, and Brereton had been trying to conduct a siege of the port in 1643. When he and Middleton had entered Flintshire and Denbighshire after taking Wem, such a siege became a strong possibility. But at the beginning of 1644 all such plans lay in tatters.

Brereton's position was desperate. There were no reserves in Lancashire and, besides, Byron had an army of 4,000 horse and 1,000 foot composed of Earnley's men, Capel's regiments, local levies and those troops he had brought with him from Oxford. The nearest field army Parliament had was in Lincolnshire under Sir Thomas

Chester city walls: King Charles Tower.

Fairfax. The county had been overrun by the Eastern Association and Fairfax had captured embattled Gainsborough in late December. Within days he was ordered to march to Cheshire. He tried to gain time for his forces were badly paid, clothed and fed. Parliament was not sympathetic and by 29 December 1643 Fairfax was on his way. He skirted around the Nottinghamshire, Derbyshire and Staffordshire Royalist garrisons and tried to solicit help from local Parliamentarians, to supplement his 1,800 horse and 500 dragoons. He bought cloth for 1,500 new uniforms out of his own pocket and gathered soldiers from the army which had been defeated at Adwalton Moor. Some of these men were only armed with cudgels, but he did manage to gather around 3,000 foot by the time he reached Manchester. From there he and Brereton began a march on Nantwich.

It was a long and tiring march in deep snow and it was three days before he got near the town. On 24 January Fairfax's army camped at Tilstone on the road from Chester to Nantwich (now the A51). The following morning he was attacked at Barbridge by some of Byron's forces. It was a skirmish lasting but half an hour and Fairfax was able to press on to Hurleston. At Nantwich Byron's army was smaller than it had been in December, casualties had mounted up in the short campaign at the end of the year, and the cold conditions of the siege at Nantwich had also taken their toll – he probably had only 2,400 foot and less than 1,000 horse left.

Byron's army was spread around the town right up until the night of 24 January, although Byron had known of Fairfax's approach. It is possible that the units which engaged the Parliamentarians at Barbridge were intended as only part of a more serious attempt to stop Fairfax there. However, if Barbridge was the intended site of the battle, Byron's plans were wrecked by a

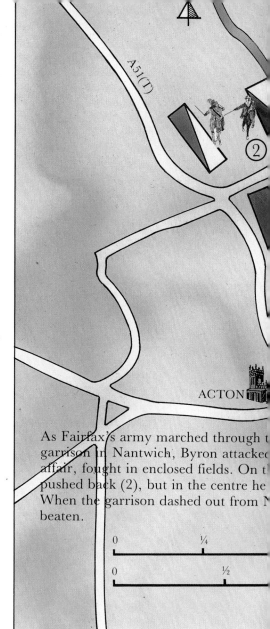

As Fairfax's army marched through t garrison in Nantwich, Byron attacked affair, fought in enclosed fields. On t pushed back (2), but in the centre he When the garrison dashed out from N beaten.

sudden thaw. Rushing water swept down the River Weaver and destroyed the bridge over which Byron planned to move the rest of his horse. As it was, the foot had arrived at Acton via the road which became the A534 en route for Barbridge, but a large number of horse were still on the wrong side of the river and faced with a march south to Shrewbridge before they could cross over. From Shrewbridge (on the A530) Byron's horse then had to go roughly north, across country, to Acton.

As for Fairfax, he continued along the line of the A51 to Hurleston where he held a council of war. Here it was

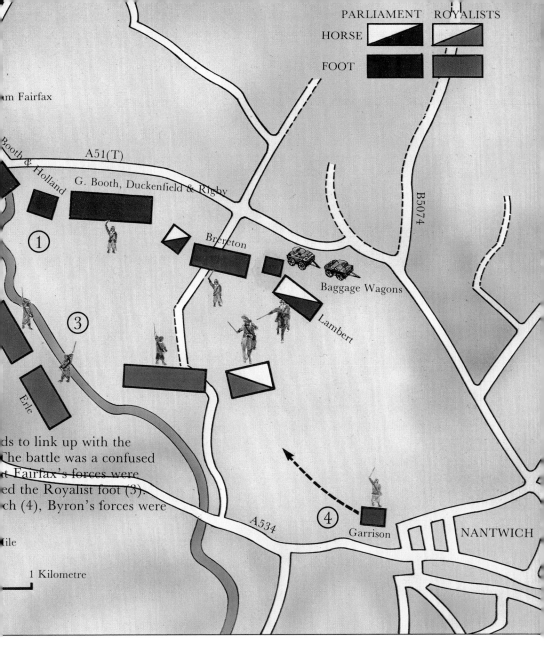

PARLIAMENT   ROYALISTS

HORSE

FOOT

m Fairfax

Booth & Holland

A51(T)

G. Booth, Duckenfield & Rigby

①

③

Brereton

Baggage Wagons

Lambert

Erle

B5074

ds to link up with the

he battle was a confused

t Fairfax's forces were

ed the Royalist foot (3).

ch (4), Byron's forces were

ile

④ Garrison

A534

NANTWICH

1 Kilometre

decided that after the foot column had slogged it uphill to catch the horse, the army should try to get to Nantwich and join the garrison before engaging Byron. Because of this delay, Byron's horse was able to link up with the rest of the army at Acton before the battle began. In the light of the council of war's decision, Fairfax continued to go straight on towards Nantwich, passing north of Byron's army at Acton, travelling through the intervening fields rather than on the road, which the Royalists now occupied.

Fairfax's target was Welsh Row, a settlement to the north-west of

The battlefield is almost surrounded by 'A' roads. The A51 runs to the north and the A534, which almost marks the Royalist lines, to the south. The chief action was fought in the ring formed by the roads. A minor road, which bisects this ring, is a suitable viewpoint from which to examine what was then an area of enclosed fields. The last action of the day centred upon Acton Church which stands beside the A534.

Nantwich, clearly in view of the town. Byron moved from the roads onto the attack, attempting to catch Fairfax in the flank. The two wings of the Royalist army made contact with the van and rear of the Parliamentarian army at about half-past three o'clock in the afternoon. The battle which followed was not a set-piece affair. The enforced separation of sections of the armies by the hedges of the enclosed fields ensured that the foot battle in the centre was fought in three distinct parts. Byron's horse found it difficult to get across the fields and moved only a little way from the road. Fairfax's horse, too, found movement difficult in the snow-covered fields and could initially offer only limited support to the foot.

The Royalist left wing, composed partly of Byron's horse and his brother's, Colonel Robert Byron's horse, caused problems for Colonel Booth and Holland, until caught in the series of narrow lanes by Sir William Fairfax's horse, whereupon they were driven back. Sir Thomas Fairfax's rear, now in effect his right flank, was pushed back by Major-General Gibson's attack. In the centre, though, the Royalists found themselves in trouble. As it had taken longer for this part of Byron's army to reach the enemy, the regiments in Fairfax's centre were ready for them. Colonels Warren and Earle's 'Irish' regiments were assailed by a determined push of pike and Warren's regiment broke under the pressure. Earle's regiment held on until a party of 800 musketeers dashed out of Nantwich, pushed aside a small force intended to prevent such an eventuality, and hit Earle's regiment in the right flank.

The Royalist centre now crumbled and the two separate Royalist flanks, under Gibson and the Byrons, were assailed on their own flanks by the centre units of Fairfax's army as they turned outwards. Gibson's regiment collapsed and fled to Acton church where it and the remains of the Royalist centre surrendered along with a large number of Byron's officer corps. The Byron brothers drew their own horse and foot off in good order and made a circuitous journey to Chester.

It was a crushing defeat. Fairfax had captured over 1,500 men including every Royalist colonel except Robert Byron. Brereton was now able to reconstruct the Parliamentarian presence in Cheshire. Moreover the first contingent of troops from Ireland had been destroyed and Byron's command was in tatters. He was no longer able to contemplate a march into Lancashire to try and establish a Royalist hold over the county. The initiative was firmly slipping from the Royalists.

Acton Church.

Sir William Brereton (1604 – 1661)

Brereton was born at Hansworth in Cheshire. He attended Brasenose College, Oxford, in the early 1620s and went on to Grays Inn in 1623. William became a baronet in 1627 and in the following year sat as MP for Cheshire. During the 1630s he further established himself in Cheshire society and sat again for the county in the Short Parliament in 1640 and was also elected to the Long Parliament. At the beginning of 1643 he was sent from London with a detachment of horse to try and combat the Royalists in Cheshire. On the way Lord Grey got him to help out at the siege at Ashby. By the time he arrived in Cheshire, Royalists had already seized Chester.

Brereton recruited forces in his own county and in Lancashire and sought to attack the Royalist presence in Wales. He confounded Lord Capel and in the end, with Fairfax's help, defeated Byron's attempts to control the county of Cheshire. The presence of Prince Rupert in 1644 kept him very much on the defensive, but Marston Moor ended any serious threat to his power-base in Lancashire and facilitated an ever more effective blockade on Chester. Nevertheless, it was not until the February of 1646 that he was able to capture the town and port.

Following this success he went on through the western section of what had been Lord Loughborough's territory and captured Tutbury, Lichfield and Dudley. In March 1646 he had also defeated the last Royalist army at Stow-on-the-Wold. Although as an MP he was technically barred from military command by the Self-Denying Ordinance, Brereton had proved himself to be perhaps the greatest of Parliament's commanders. He played little part in the subsequent events of the 1640s but, when the Rump Parliament was restored in 1659, he took his seat. He died in 1661.

8. THE SIEGES OF
NEWARK

Defences at the Third Siege

Balderton Gate

Defences 1642–3

Barnby Gate

Carter Gate

Governor's House

M

Appleton Gate

Castle

North Gate

Newark Castle.

Newark is situated on the A1, the modern version of the old Great North Road, and on the A46, the old Fosse Way, down which Leicester lies 35 miles (56 kilometres) to the south-west and Lincoln 16 miles (26 kilometres) to the north-east. It is 23 miles (37 kilometres) from Nottingham on the A612. By train the town can be reached by regular services.

Within the town several Civil War sites are preserved. The castle, centre point of the military occupation, stands in ruins by the River Trent. It was here that the King and Prince Rupert had their stormy scene after the latter's surrender of Bristol. The house where the first Governor, Sir John Henderson, lodged still stands in the market-place and is known as the Governor's House. Buildings in Kirkgate, which also still exist, are supposedly those wherein the Queen, Henrietta Maria, stayed whilst in the town. One of the aldermen of the town, Hercules Clay, dreamed during the second siege that his house was destroyed by cannon fire. After having the dream a third time, he moved out – whereupon it was wrecked by gunfire. Naturally the house is no longer there, but its site is marked by the National Westminster Bank in the market-place.

Most of the defence works are long gone, but some interesting earthworks still survive, the best of these being the Queen's Sconce. This is just off the A46 to the south-west of the town. Within the town itself, the Newark Museum in Appleton Gate has a display of Civil War items and maps of the fortifications.

A few miles out of Newark on the A612 is Southwell where, at the still extant Saracen's Head, King Charles surrendered on 5 May 1646 to the Scots army besieging Newark.

1. 27 – 28 February 1643   Royalist defenders repulse Parliament's forces.
2. 29 February – 21 March 1644   The town is relieved by Prince Rupert.
3. 26 November 1645 – 8 May 1646   The town surrenders on orders from the King.

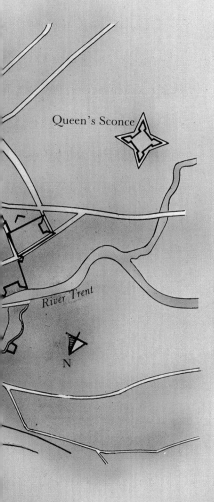

Newark was a town of strategic importance in the war. Here the Great North Road crosses the River Trent and also meets Fosse Way, the Roman road that connected the Royalist headquarters at Oxford to the vital centres in the North-east. The town also gave the Royalists a counterbalance to the Parliamentarians' possession of Nottingham, posing a constant threat to the garrison in that town and a hindrance to the extension of Parliamentarian control over Lincolnshire.

The Governor's House, Newark.

THE FIRST SIEGE

NEWARK had been seized for the Royalists towards the end of 1642 by Sir John Digby, the Nottinghamshire High Sheriff, and Sir John Henderson – a Scottish professional soldier. Henderson had been sent into the county by the Earl of Newcastle, to add military acumen to the Royalist cause in Nottinghamshire and became the first Governor of Newark.

The importance of the town was not lost on Parliament and an attempt to capture it was first made in February 1643. Taking advantage of the absence of the local Royalist commander, Henry Hastings, Major-General Thomas Ballard began a siege on 27 February with his own forces from Lincolnshire and those of the various garrisons in Nottinghamshire, Leicestershire and Derbyshire. Ballard failed to make any headway against the defenders and the siege ended the next day.

THE SECOND SIEGE

AT THE BEGINNING of 1644 the North Midland Royalists should have been at the height of their power. By the end of the previous year, with the help of the now Marquis of Newcastle, forces under Henry Hastings, by this time raised to the nobility as Lord Loughborough, had established control over the region and had kept the Parliamentarians in Derby, Nottingham, Leicester and Stafford at bay. The Royalists had been able to collect taxation – contribution – from under the very walls of these towns themselves. Local Parliamentarians were in such dire financial straits that they had to be subsidized from the more secure Parliamentarian counties such as Kent. With their network of eight major and sixteen minor garrisons, the Royalists could not only tap the resources of the region but also make movement and communication very difficult for their adversaries. However, this success was blighted by the entry of the Scots into the war on the side of Parliament. As the Marquis of Newcastle desperately tried to hold up their advance along the east coast, units of the North Midlands Army were dispatched to him. Sections of all the major garrisons in the region were sent north under the command of Sir Charles Lucas, and for some reason the burden fell particularly heavily upon Newark. The new governor, Sir Richard Byron, who had replaced Henderson after several minor disasters in Lincolnshire the previous year, realized the danger posed by the resurgence of Parliamentarian power in Lincolnshire and requested urgent aid. It was not forthcoming and the town came under a second siege at the end of February. On this occasion it was led by a man of very different mettle to Ballard, the tough and gifted Scot, Sir John Meldrum.

Meldrum had, since the previous summer, been the commander of part of the North Midland Parliamentarian horse and with him he had Lord Willoughby of Parham's Lincolnshire forces and a collection of forces from the regions' garrisons. In total he was able to surround Newark with between 6,000 and 7,000 men, 2,000 of which were cavalry. Such a conglomeration was, however, fraught with problems, as the various commanders who had carved out little power-bases for themselves began to bicker over superiority. Nevertheless, the imposition of a close siege was a serious problem for the Royalists in the region.

Under his command, Lord Loughborough had an army of between 4,000 and 5,000 men. Of these, he was capable of putting 3,000 into the field, whilst maintaining soldiers in the garrisons. This number was woefully inadequate for mounting an attack capable of dislodging Meldrum's army. Loughborough needed outside help, just as he always had when confronted by a major problem. Whilst he began to inveigle Prince Rupert into providing the necessary help, Loughborough instructed his colonels to begin harassing attacks on Meldrum's regiments.

Meldrum had stormed the island formed to the north-west of Newark by the Trent's division into two channels. The island was used by the garrison to pasture their livestock, and Meldrum's possession of it not only deprived them of grazing land but also completed their isolation. On the island on 6 March when Meldrum's forces attacked, were the Royalist horse under Major-General George Porter and Colonel Gervaise Holles's regiment of foot. As the attack began, Porter and the Royalist horse rapidly fled the island, leaving Holles's regiment to be overwhelmed by over 2,000 men. Porter then led his force north towards Tuxford.

At about the same time, Colonel John Freschville, one of Loughborough's Derbyshire colonels,

proposed linking up with Porter and assembling the majority of the North Midland Army at Mansfield, from where they would launch an attack on Meldrum. However, Loughborough had managed to interest the Prince in the plan for a joint campaign and Freschville's idea was shelved. On 9 March Rupert instructed Hastings and Porter to send him 700 horses to mount musketeers for a rapid march, and sections of the North Midland Army dismantled hedges and fences between Ashby and Newark in preparation for the cross-country march. On 15 March, as Rupert reached Bridgnorth, Loughborough dispatched a small force to Leicester to probe the defences of the Parliamentarian garrison.

At the same time Meldrum got wind of the plan to link Loughborough's forces at Ashby with those of Porter, and he sent Sir Edward Hartop, Commander of the Leicestershire and Derbyshire horse, to prevent it by capturing the bridge over the River Soar at Cotes in Leicestershire. The Royalists had begun to fortify themselves on the western side of the bridge in expectation of an attempt to deny them communications with Porter. On 18 March, after initially capturing the bridge, Hartop withdrew his forces from the battle. It appears that he was alarmed by the increasing numbers of soldiers that Loughborough was pouring into the area. Yet, even though the Prince himself had arrived at Ashby on the same day, it seems that both Hartop and Meldrum were unaware of his march eastwards.

On 19 March Rupert and Loughborough crossed the Soar at Cotes and marched as far as Rempstone. The following day they reached Bingham – a few hours march from Newark – where they linked up with Porter. Between them, the three commanders led a force of around 6,400, 3,000 of which were provided by Loughborough. It was only at this juncture that Meldrum became aware of the

Sir John Meldrum

MELDRUM UNAWARE OF DANGER!

The Governor of Nottingham [Sir John Hutchinson] kept out spies upon the enemy's motions and sent word to the Leaguer, but the gentlemen there were so over-confident they would not believe any force could come to raise their siege. At length, the governor of Nottingham being there himself, word was brought Prince Rupert was at Ashby, wherefore he, fearing some attempt upon his garrison to divert the forces at the siege, returned home with his brother to look to their charge. It was late upon Wednesday night when the governor came home, and was certainly informed that Prince Rupert was, that afternoon, marched by to raise the siege, with about six thousand men. Immediately the governor sent two men, excellently well mounted upon his own horses, to carry the alarm to Sir John Meldrum, who by two of the clock on Thursday morning delivered him their letters . . .

From *Colonel Hutchinson, The Record of his Life by Lucy Hutchinson His Widow.*

presence of the Prince in the region: but he still did not know that the Prince was only two hours march away. When he and his commanders suddenly learnt this fact, some urged him to withdraw to Lincoln. Rupert was, however, aware that this option lay open to Meldrum and at midnight on 20 March began a march around the south of Newark; by two o'clock in the morning on 21 March he had positioned himself on Meldrum's line of retreat. The Scotsman decided to fight it out and concentrated his army to the north of Newark, between the town and the ruined hospice, known as the Spittal, where he had constructed fortifications. Behind him lay a bridge of boats to the island via which he intended to escape if necessary.

From the top of Beacon Hill, Rupert's horse charged the 1,500 Parliamentarian horse led by Thornhaugh and Colonel Edward Rossiter in the valley below. At one point Rossiter forced part of the Royalist horse back onto their second line led by Loughborough. But a subsequent charge pushed the Parliamentarian horse back to the Spittal. Whilst some regiments began an orderly withdrawal, others ran off in panic as Meldrum hustled his remaining cavalry over the bridge onto the island and strove to fend off Rupert's attacks designed to capture this link.

As a full assault on the Spittal would have proved costly in manpower, Rupert settled down to whittle away at the Parliamentarian resolve. Attention turned to the northern exit point from the island: the bridge at Muskham. When units from Newark crossed onto the island and began heading towards the bridge, the Derbyshire horse guarding it fled, leaving a small garrison in a fort by the crossing. The other regiments of Parliamentarian horse, which Meldrum had evacuated onto the island realizing that they too might be cut off if the bridge fell, also

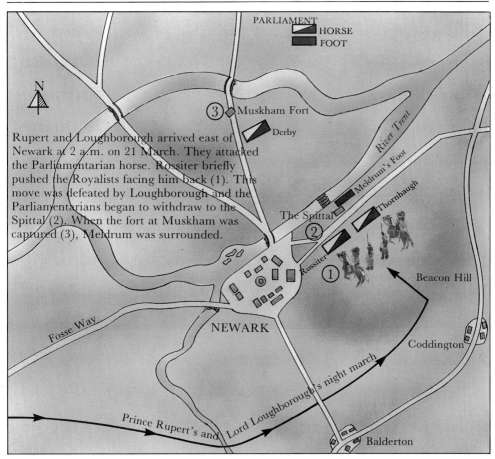

Inside the map:

PARLIAMENT
HORSE
FOOT

N

③ ◈ Muskham Fort

Derby

River Trent

Meldrum's Foot

Thornhaugh

Rupert and Loughborough arrived east of
Newark at 2 a.m. on 21 March. They attacked
the Parliamentarian horse. Rossiter briefly
pushed the Royalists facing him back (1). This
move was defeated by Loughborough and the
Parliamentarians began to withdraw to the
Spittal (2). When the fort at Muskham was
captured (3), Meldrum was surrounded.

The Spittal

②

Rossiter

①

Beacon Hill

Fosse Way

NEWARK

Coddington

Prince Rupert's and Lord Loughborough's night march

Balderton

Rupert's attack on Newark to raise the second siege.

abandoned the island. The subsequent capture of the small fort rendered Meldrum's isolation complete.

It was now impossible for the Parliamentarian army to escape and at around nine o'clock that night Meldrum sued for terms. By seven o'clock on the morning of 22 March, these had been agreed and Meldrum's army marched away with a safe conduct. By the conditions of the surrender, Loughborough and Rupert had bagged over 3,000 muskets, 2 mortars and 11 cannons – a useful booty of arms for both men.

The effect on the region was electrifying. Lincoln was abandoned by its Parliamentarian garrison and Derby and Nottingham braced themselves for a siege. No doubt Loughborough hoped that Rupert would stay and help him

attack at least one of the Parliamentarian strongholds. The Prince, however, was determined to continue his work in the West and after resting his troops marched out of the region.

Parliament was not willing to allow this state of affairs to continue: the Earl of Manchester gathered his Eastern Association forces and entered Lincolnshire whilst the Earl of Denbigh began to destabilize the southern part of Lord Loughborough's command. To the north Lord Fairfax and his son Sir Thomas continued their offensive against the Yorkshire Royalists. Demands were soon made upon Loughborough's resources from all these sectors: the success at Newark had, for him, only provided a breathing-space.

THE THIRD SIEGE

I<small>N</small> J<small>ULY</small> 1644 Rupert's new army engaged Cromwell and Fairfax at Marston Moor and units from Newark were defeated along with it. Despite attempts by Lord Loughborough and Sir Richard Byron to raise a force to rescue the Prince, the collapse of the Royalist North curtailed the activities of Newark. A defeat at Denton near Belvoir in October 1644 destroyed confidence in Byron's leadership and he was soon replaced by an associate of Prince Rupert, Sir Richard Willis. The battle of Naseby wrecked any chance of a reorganization of the North Midland war effort. Yet the garrison at Newark did remain active: forces from it recaptured Welbeck and Bolsover during the summer months.

Once the King's diminutive wandering army had left the area, the Scots took up siege positions to the north of the town on 26 November 1645 and the south was covered by Pointz's forces, and Rossiter, after their failure to storm Belvoir Castle. Bellasyse and the garrison were aggressive from the start and in January almost captured Pointz himself. The harsh winter months saw the Scots construct siegeworks around the town and attempt to dam the River Devon to stop the town corn mills working and to facilitate an easier approach to the south of Newark. The siegeworks were manned by a total of 16,000 men by the end of March but Bellasyse refused to consider surrender until April.

However, the arrival of the beardless King as a fugitive, and his subsequent surrender to the Scots at Southwell, forced Bellasyse's hand. Charles was forced by his captors to order the garrison to surrender. Neither the town nor the governor wished to give in yet, and plans were made for a fighting escape from the town. But Charles ordered the surrender and Bellasyse, with tears in his eyes, signed the terms. The war was over in all but name.

Plan of the third siege of Newark by Richard Clampe and silver coins struck during the third siege.

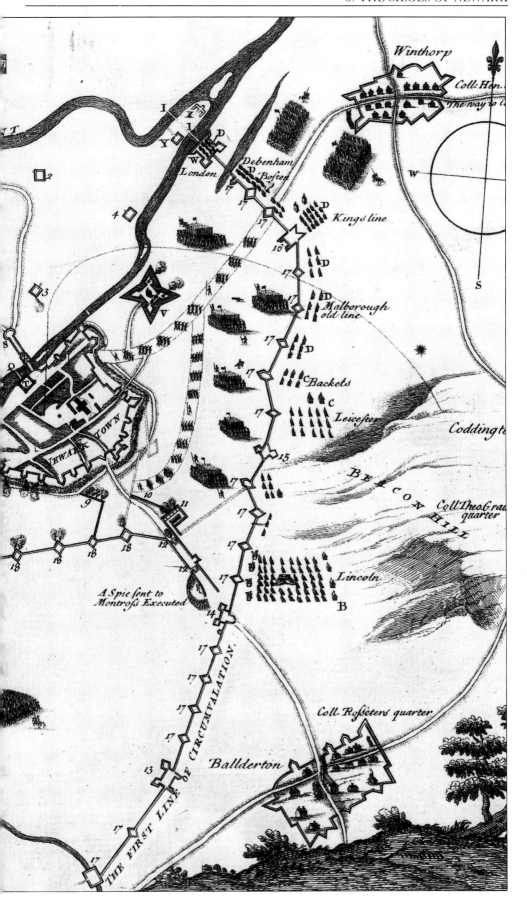

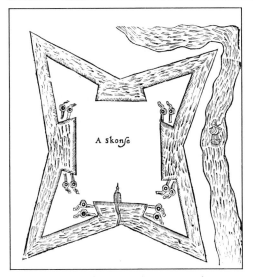

Plan of a quadrangle sconce, often constructed to defend besieged towns.

A mortar, called 'Roaring Meg', used by Parliamentary forces in the siege of Goodrich Castle (see page 78).

SIEGE WARFARE

DESPITE THE FACT that the medieval castles of England were technically outdated by the time of the Civil War, the lack of expertise in siegecraft gave them a new lease of life in the early days of the conflict. Long-outmoded methods of attack were used on the castles which declared for the King or Parliament: petards were again exploded against gates, a sow (covered battering-ram) was utilized at the sieges of Corfe Castle and Canon Frome, and mines were dug at Lichfield and York. Whilst much of this was conducted in an amateur way, both sides employed European engineers who provided professional skills. On the one hand there was the steady approach to the castle walls made possible by the construction of successive lines of circumvallation. Trenches and breastworks, often with elaborate series of forts, were dug around the castle or town and saps dug out towards it. As the garrison was steadily driven from outposts, such as the sconces around Newark, the besiegers incorporated them into their lines, drawing closer to their prey. On the other hand large guns firing shot up to 63lb. (29 kg.) could also be used to bring down walls and towers, effecting breaches through which the attacking forces could enter the defences.

Following the example of Gustavus Adolphus (the Swedish King and military leader in the Thirty Years' War), several commanders on both sides preferred the short siege, and stormed the towns after an artillery barrage, as happened at Leicester. Patient sieges such as that at Oxford and Newark took time and were costly. However, in the long run they were probably less expensive in lives, unless a plague broke out amongst the defenders or the attackers.

Sieges were damaging to the populus of towns. To some, the necessity for the defenders to destroy suburbs to prevent a covered approach by the enemy, cost

The Queen's Sconce at Newark.

them a home. Most people would suffer privations as food became scarce, as at York in 1644. Sieges were therefore unpopular. It was more unusual to find people in the town in favour of the garrison holding out, as at Newark, than it was to find them putting pressure on the military to give up the struggle, as at Colchester in 1648.

THE COST

The following extract is taken from page 24 of the constables' accounts from Upton in Nottinghamshire and deals with the period of the second siege. It shows that the villages around Newark were faced with additional burdens during the siege. As well as paying the normal levies of contribution to the garrison at Newark, they had to hand over provisions to the forces brought by Prince Rupert and Lord Loughborough.

given to 2 soldiers which would have had horses 6d

spent at Kerkes when the Quartermaster and ten soldiers came from Roulston for pease and oats being of the Lord Loughborough his regiment 1s 2d

Colonell Harpur his men would have had horses there owne being tyred to have ridden to Thurgarton I going to the Captayne & could have noe Releefe was constrayned to give them haulfe a Crowne to drinke to spare our horses. 2s 6d

given to Twoe of Colonell Eyre of hossoper [Hassop, Derbyshire] his men which had lost their company. 1s

payed to foure Carters which went with the carts when Prince Rupert was at Newarke. 1s

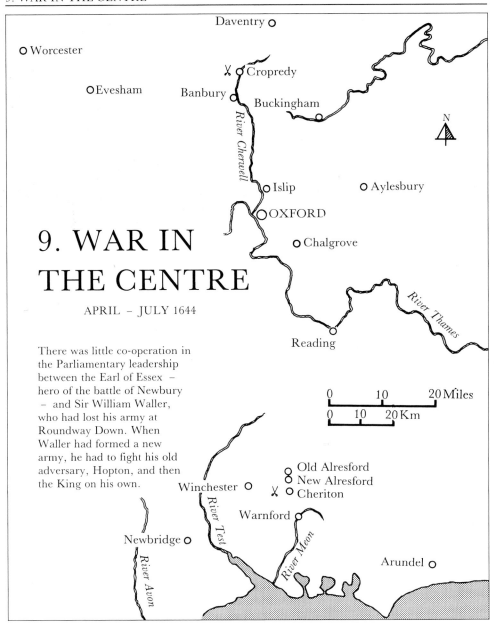

9. WAR IN THE CENTRE

APRIL – JULY 1644

There was little co-operation in the Parliamentary leadership between the Earl of Essex – hero of the battle of Newbury – and Sir William Waller, who had lost his army at Roundway Down. When Waller had formed a new army, he had to fight his old adversary, Hopton, and then the King on his own.

OXFORD IN THE WAR

OXFORD became Charles I's capital after the battle of Edgehill. It turned from a city of intellectual activity into one geared to the pursuit of humanity's basest impulse – the need to destroy. The townsfolk and the Trained Bands were disarmed in November 1642 when the King began to create the military capital. He took up residence in Christ Church and the Privy Council used Oriel. New College became the arsenal and Magdalen Grove the artillery depot. Uniforms were made at the Music and Astronomy schools whilst Law and Logic became granaries. Even so, a few scholars hung on, trying to work as best they could, until being asked to leave in 1644 to make room for more soldiers.

Oxford had to be fortified – and these defences can be seen in the painting overleaf. They consisted chiefly of breastworks and water. Dams and sluices were constructed so as to flood large areas outside the town. The building of these defences had been slow work and in the summer of 1643 all residents of the halls and colleges between the ages of sixteen and sixty had been ordered to do one day's work a week building them.

Financially, the honour of being the capital cost the town dear. Once the mint had arrived in January 1643 Charles began using the college plate to make coinage. He asked for a loan of £200 in the same month and a further £2,000 in June. Food gathered from the local area was stored in the colleges for distribution to the court and garrison. As the war turned against the King the collections became increasingly draconian: by 1644 all surplus foodstocks in the Oxford region had to be handed over. When the city surrendered in June 1646 there was an estimated six months supply of food and other supplies in the town.

Throughout the war there were large numbers of resident aristocracy and gentry. From the end of 1643 onwards these numbers increased when the King summoned a Parliament to the town, which brought an influx of new permanent and temporary residents. As well as courtiers and politicians there were numerous agents representing the various garrisons. Sir Arthur Gorges was one of these men. He represented the interests of Lieutenant-General

The 'Oxford Crown Piece', minted in the city during the war.

Henry Hastings during much of the first Civil War. On behalf of his commander he had to negotiate arms purchases with the Oxford council of war. As defeat loomed ever nearer the town filled up with refugees; men and women with their families fleeing from Parliament's increasing control were supplemented by garrison commanders and loyal soldiers drifting in from their surrendered outposts.

Christ Church, the King's residence in Oxford.

The Siege of Oxford (1645) by Jan de Wyck.

CHERITON

SINCE THE DEFEAT of his army at Roundway (or Runaway) Down, Waller had been engaged chiefly in the creation of a new one. Hopton, meanwhile, had advanced south of the Thames into Hampshire. The Earl of Essex had done his best to limit Waller's power and left Waller to defeat Hopton alone. Whilst in the process of building up his new army, Waller had to avoid doing battle with Hopton and he achieved this with some skill. Nevertheless he captured Arundel Castle and destroyed the garrison at Alton. Hopton, marching roughly in the direction of London, was more or less brought to a standstill by these successes and the 1643 campaign petered out, with Hopton based at Winchester and Waller with about 8,000 men waiting for spring to attack him. In March, Waller went onto the attack.

The Parliamentarian army pushed on through the River Meon valley whilst Hopton moved to Wamford on the Meon to await him. Waller bypassed him and pressed on to Tichborne Down which he reached on 27 March. Hopton turned after him and got into Alresford

The trooper's main weapon was the basket-hilted, double-edged sword, illustrated here. Charges were undertaken, and received, at sword point. In any ensuing skirmish troopers would use the flintlock pistols which they also carried.

first after marching parallel to Waller for much of the way. Hopton's foot moved out towards the down and on 18 March the two armies faced each other. Waller still may have wished to avoid a pitched battle but he was unable to withdraw in the face of Hopton without being mauled. Despite the news that the relief of Newark had exposed the South Midlands to attack and therefore Waller's army might well be needed intact, the Parliamentarian general decided to accept battle.

During the night 1,000 musketeers, under Lieutenant-Colonel Leighton, pushed forward into Cheriton Wood which lay on Hopton's left flank and rear. Waller also concentrated artillery opposite the centre of Hopton's army with horse under Haselrigg and Balfour behind them. On Waller's left, foot moved forward onto the Lamborough Lane to the cover of the hedges bordering it.

In the early morning mist Hopton had the musketeers in Cheriton Woods driven out. Hopton was in favour of following this with an attack on the rest of Waller's left flank, but the Earl of Forth, Hopton's senior commander, was not convinced of the viability of this move. Instead the Royalist army began to consolidate its hold on the east down. Their line extended from Cheriton Wood to Broad Lane on their right. The horse was concentrated in their centre around Bramdean Lane by which they would have access to the common below the down. Hopton commanded the forces to the left of the lane, Forth those to the right. Forth's flank was too far forward for the centre to offer them much support as Sir Henry Bard led an attack in the direction of Hinton Ampner.

This was immediately obvious to Waller who launched Haselrigg's horse into Bard's exposed flank. The fight was brief and Bard's men routed. On the opposite flank Waller sent his own foot into an attack on the down and during the next three hours they advanced slowly up the hill, fighting for every step. Haselrigg and Balfour were able to use their horse to aid the right flank's attack and Forth tried at least to distract them from this process by launching an attack on the Parliamentarian centre. The problem here was that to get onto the common where Balfour and Haselrigg were, the Royalist horse had to use the narrow lane around which they were grouped in order to bypass the hedges of the enclosed fields on the down. As each troop debouched onto the common they were simply picked off one by one and chased back onto the down by Waller's horse. Waller himself rode at the head of his horse during this action, but he was unable to press his advantage further because Hopton had lined the hedges with musketeeers. The fire from these kept Waller's horse from getting onto the down.

On the left wing of Waller's army his foot were able to push their opponents back up the down following Bard's defeat. Some time after three o'clock Waller's army began to force Hopton and Forth back through the enclosed fields of the down. Before being trapped in this pincer movement the Royalists withdrew to the top of the hill, gaining time with a series of counter-attacks. This was so successful in disordering Waller's ranks that before any assault on the hill top could be considered the whole army had to be redressed. This gave Hopton and Forth enough time to withdraw from the field in good order. In the face of the exhausted Parliamentarians, the Royalist army made off to Basing House and then on to Reading. Within the next few weeks Hopton's army was absorbed into the King's own Oxford field army.

Waller, who had been the victor of Cheriton, had ended any chance of a Royalist advance south of the Thames Valley that spring. He had also established the reputation of his new army. His horse had proved themselves a match for the Royalists and the London

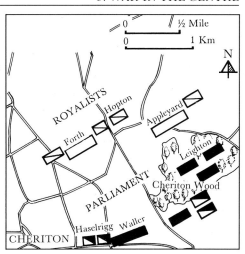

Cheriton can be reached via the A272 from Winchester, turning left onto the B3046 at Hinton Marsh. In the village of Cheriton, a road leading east brings you right into the centre of the field of action at about the point where Waller's horse stood during the battle: Cheriton Wood is directly ahead.

Trained Bands had again proved their courage and zeal, and with their help, Parliamentarians established themselves in the South again.

CROPREDY BRIDGE

THE KING absorbed Hopton's army because he wanted a strong force in the heart of England. To his north the Marquis of Newcastle was distracted by the Scottish invasion and the expected troops from Ireland had not materialized in any great number. Moreover, those which had arrived had been defeated at Nantwich.

In reality it was Parliament which held the initiative now that Waller had ended the threat in Hampshire. The large independent army of the Eastern Association was ordered to join the Earl of Essex and his army at Aylesbury, preparatory to launching a campaign directed at Oxford. But Manchester did not want to leave the East after Rupert had cleared Lincolnshire following the relief of Newark. Essex did not really want to join up with Manchester as he was angry at the independence Manchester had been given. In the event the junction never took place. Instead, Waller was forced into uniting his army with the Earl's and together they put pressure on Oxford, forcing the King to withdraw the outposts at Reading and Abingdon, during April and May 1644.

In the face of this pressure the King took personal charge of his army, moved out of Oxford and put pressure on Waller's line of communications with London by moving on Abingdon. It was essential that he should somehow distract the Parliamentarian generals as their presence had made some of the Oxford Royalists contemplate surrender. After threatening Waller's rear the King drew north to Worcester. The distraction worked; Essex had been at Islip and Waller at Newbridge on the River Thames, but following the move to Worcester Waller set off after him. Furthermore, the King's action destroyed what precious little harmony there was between Waller and Essex and the Earl did not follow on after Waller; instead he turned towards the South-west to deal with Prince Maurice, who was besieging Lyme.

Waller was lured on towards Shrewsbury where he suspected the King was headed, only to find that Charles, displaying uncommon strategic skill, had actually turned back to Evesham. At Witney the Oxford garrison met up with the King and then they marched on to Buckingham. Waller had come briefly to rest over in Gloucester before being apprised of the King's actual whereabouts. He turned east to seek the King out. At Banbury the King halted to meet him. Upon arriving Waller drew up on Crouch Hill, but it was too strong a site to draw the King into attacking him. So on 28 June the Royalist army moved north

along the line of the A361 towards Daventry. As the King marched along the eastern bank of the Cherwell, Waller, only 1 mile (1½ kilometres) away, followed on the west side. As he watched the King's progress, Waller realized that his enemy was becoming temptingly strung out. Lord Wilmot with the rear guard was almost 1½ miles (2½ kilometres) behind the King at the head of the column.

Waller seized his chance at Cropredy. Across the bridge which now carries the A361 from Cropredy to Williamscot, Waller sent Lieutenant-General John Middleton with Haselrigg's Lobsters, Colonel Vandruske's horse and nine companies of foot with eleven guns. His intention was to cut Wilmot off from the rest of the King's army. To do this Middleton headed quickly towards Wardington and Hay's Bridge which the rest of the King's forces had crossed. To complete the encirclement, Waller himself led a thousand horse over the Cherwell at Slats Mill. (The traveller will now find a convenient footbridge.) It was an excellent attempt at what would later be known as the strategy of the central position. Once he had defeated the rearguard, Waller would turn on the other sections of the King's army which would have been held fast by a small force at Hay's Bridge.

Unfortunately it all went horribly wrong. As Waller crossed the ford he was attacked by the brigade of the Earl of Northampton (the son of the Earl killed at Hopton Heath), which was the last of Wilmot's two brigades. As a result Waller's force was halted in its attempt to reach Williamscot. Wilmot's other brigade under the Earl of Cleveland attacked Middleton as his forces became strung out between Cropredy Bridge and Hay's Bridge. Middleton was pushed back on Cropredy by Cleveland who had now received support from the King who had turned the vanguard of the army and was now recrossing Hay's Bridge.

Middleton pushed forward again

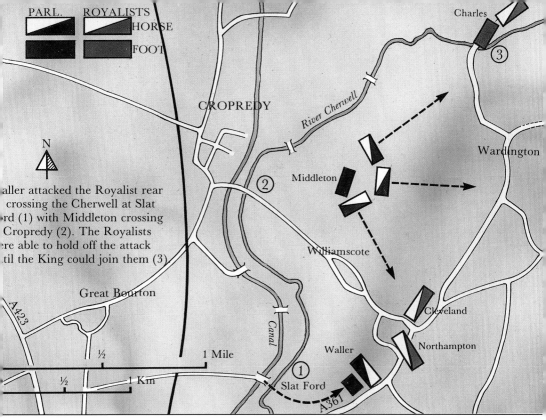

PARL.   ROYALISTS

HORSE

FOOT

...aller attacked the Royalist rear
...crossing the Cherwell at Slat
...rd (1) with Middleton crossing
Cropredy (2). The Royalists
...re able to hold off the attack
...til the King could join them (3).

only to be driven back more forcefully.
This time Cleveland pressed him over
the bridge, and the dragoons with
which Middleton tried to cover the
approaches to Cropredy were of no
avail. Cleveland captured all eleven
guns and the commander of Waller's
artillery. Cleveland then pulled back to
join the rest of the army and redress his
lines. Whereas Middleton had lost a
hundred men as prisoners and many
more killed, Cleveland lost only
fourteen men and two colonels.

Waller had also been driven right
over the Cherwell. The battle was now
over, for the King did not pursue
Waller across the river after Waller
received reinforcements. Nevertheless
the loss of all his guns seems to have
affected Waller's self-confidence and in
any case the defeat shattered the
cohesion in his army and it disintegrated as the King moved back on
Evesham. Within a week 2,000 men
had deserted from Waller's army and
he had to come to a standstill at
Northampton while trying to get money
for pay out of Parliament. Essex was
urgently recalled from the West. It was
too late: the King was now after him.

*Cropredy Bridge. This Victorian structure bears a
plaque commemorating the battle.*

Cropredy Bridge can be visited from
Oxford or Coventry by using the A423.
5 miles (8 kilometres) north of Banbury
there is a turning to Cropredy. The
present bridge is a Victorian one,
incorporating a small monument to the
battle. Slatt Mill is now along the canal
to the south and there is a convenient
footbridge replacing the ford over which
Waller led his attack. Although
Cropredy is largely built up, it has
remained to the west of the river. By
following the road over the bridge the
traveller reaches Cleveland's position
and then, going along the road, reaches
Northampton's, opposite Slatt Mill.
Hay's Bridge is on the A361.

Charles I (1600 – 1649)

CHARLES was second son to the King of Scotland. Three years after his birth his father became King of England and his brother, Prince of Wales. Charles, a weakly child, was very much in the shadow of his brother Henry, who was greatly praised for being a renaissance prince and much mourned when he died in 1612. Charles was a connoisseur of the arts – a collector of paintings and a lover of books. As a politician he was incapable of the depth of vision necessary to adjust to the changing political landscape in England. Moreover he was deceitful, untrustworthy and lazy. He was not regular in his attendance at Privy Council and he rarely examined state papers in any detail.

Alongside this, his view of kingship was different from that of the politicians with whom he had to work and his natural stubbornness meant that conflict was likely right from the start of his reign. His relationship with the early Parliaments was never harmonious and in 1629 he embarked on a period of government without one. To finance government he had to use a series of quasi-legal methods, often resurrecting what were probably obsolete exactions. These ranged from the thorough exploitation of the estates of orphans in care of the Court of Wards to the collection of Ship Money, normally an extraordinary coastal-county tax, from the whole country on a regular basis. This was a far more efficient tapping of the nation's wealth than the usual subsidies and was opposed increasingly as the Thirties went on. Charles's patronage of the Arminian reformation of church, through Archbishop Laud, was also unpopular in England; but its attempted enforcement in Scotland led to war. Only when forced by dire financial needs did Charles call a Parliament. And only when it refused to grant him money unless he allowed it to reform the 'evils' of the last eleven years, did he compromise with demands for political chance. Even then, he always looked for the chance to reverse his position and attempted to build up support in the Commons by appearing conciliatory. Nevertheless despair at his weakened status drove Charles to attempt a *coup d'état* aimed at depriving the opposition of its leadership. The ensuing bungled attempt to arrest the five members of the Commons and Lord Mandeville almost completely wrecked the moderate attempts to gain him wider support, and made it impossible for him to remain in London.

Once he left the capital the gulf between him and Parliament widened. By the middle of the year England stood on the brink of war – with no side able to compromise. Four years later the war was over and little had changed. The King was defeated but undauntedly confident that he was essential to the settling of the Kingdom. Few people could conceive of government without the King and stalemate ensued as he refused to come to terms with Parliament. In effect, he was again waiting for an upswing in his fortunes and by 1648 he had committed the country to a new war. His defeat and death were brought about not by revolutionaries intent upon the overthrow of the monarchy, but by tired and angry men seeking social stability. The execution of an intractable obstacle was the only way they could achieve it.

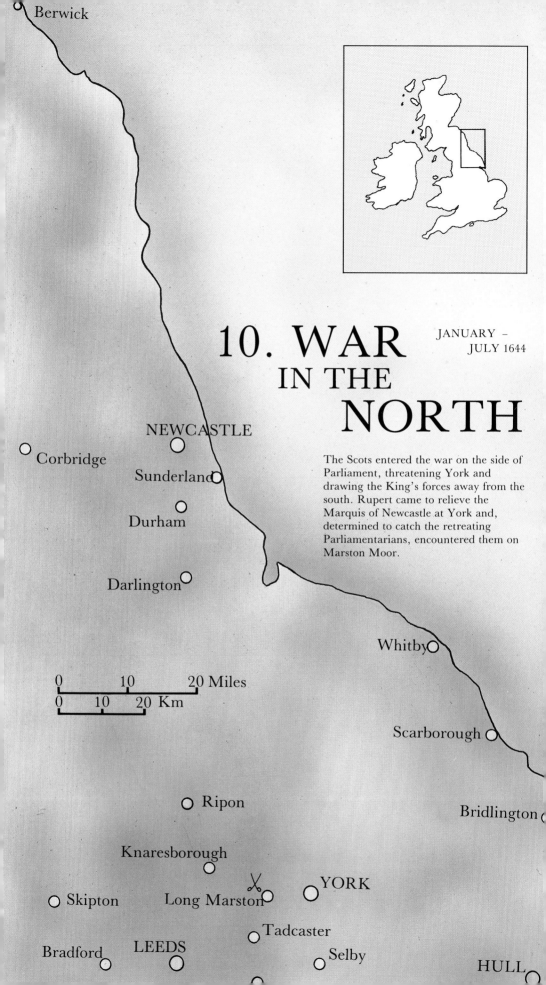

Berwick

10. WAR
IN THE
NORTH

The Scots entered the war on the side of
Parliament, threatening York and
drawing the King's forces away from the
south. Rupert came to relieve the
Marquis of Newcastle at York and,
determined to catch the retreating
Parliamentarians, encountered them on
Marston Moor.

Corbridge

NEWCASTLE

Sunderland

Durham

Darlington

Whitby

```
0        10        20 Miles
0   10    20 Km
```

Scarborough

Ripon

Bridlington

Knaresborough

Skipton   Long Marston   YORK

Tadcaster

Bradford   LEEDS

Selby

HULL

THE SCOTS ENTER THE NORTH

PROBABLY because of the disastrous political attitude in Oxford which the Scottish representatives had encountered in the spring of 1643, as much as through John Pym's diplomatic skill, the Scots entered the war against the King. They, like their allies, fought on the professed grounds of rescuing the King from his evil ministers, but they were also concerned to protect their Church. Charles had tried to destroy the Presbyterian system in the 1630s thereby prompting the two wars between the nations. Pym on the other hand promised to 'reform the English Church' if the Scots helped Parliament, thereby holding out the hope that Presbyterianism might be introduced in England. In return for monthly pay, to be squeezed from the already pressed county communities under Parliamentarian control, the Scots sent an army into the North.

Alexander Leslie, Earl of Leven.

This had the desired effect of drawing the Marquis of Newcastle north out of the Midlands and thus away from any intended march into the South where he was greatly feared by Parliament. As early as November the Marquis had sent Sir Thomas Glenham to fortify Newcastle-upon-Tyne and the county of Northumberland in case the Scots did invade. In January Newcastle himself hurried north, raising fresh troops *en route*. The Scottish army was watched closely as they crossed the Tweed on 18 January. By 22 January Newcastle arrived at the port from which he drew his title, as Glenham pulled south in the face of the Scots. The town was too strong for the Scots to take quickly and the Scots leader, the Earl of Leven, began to skirt around it. Royalist horse ranged out and defeated Leven's horse at Corbridge. Already the continuous bad weather, the failure to attack Newcastle and the defeat at Corbridge were sapping the morale of the invading army.

Nevertheless, by March Sunderland had fallen, as Leven took advantage of driving snow to evade the Marquis of Newcastle. The Marquis was desperate to bring Leven to battle, but the wily general was just as determined to reach Yorkshire unscathed. On 7 – 8 March Newcastle almost succeeded at Bowden Hills. But Leven found security on the hill tops, inaccessible in the snow. The unsuccessful Royalists pulled back to Durham City and Leven hovered in the vicinity. Newcastle held all the advantages. As his army was increasing in size and was in better shape than Leven's, if it came to battle it had the better chance of winning. It was 12 April before Leven left Sunderland and Newcastle moved towards him. As the Scots occupied the Quarrenden Hills the two armies faced each other. There was no battle. Newcastle was brought information which ended his chance of defeating the Scots. The Royalists in Yorkshire had been defeated.

THE FAIRFAXES IN YORKSHIRE

At the end of January 1644, with Glenham in the North and his replacement's, Sir William Saville's, sudden death, John Belasyse took command of the Royalist forces in Yorkshire. Superficially, all was secure. Sir Francis Mackworth was holding down the West Riding and Lord Fairfax was still bottled up in Hull. But the security was false. Sir Thomas Fairfax, the most potent threat, was still in Cheshire, and then Lancashire, mopping up garrisons, and his return was daily expected. Furthermore, the Marquis of Newcastle had drawn most of his horse into the North leaving only five or six regiments of foot and only a handful of horse with Belasyse.

The Parliamentarians soon sought to exploit this situation. Sir William Constable led raids into the wolds as far north as Pickering. He captured Bridlington and Whitby and defeated Royalists at Driffield. In March John Lambert, sent back from Lancashire by Sir Thomas Fairfax, led an excursion into the West Riding and captured Bradford, before going northwards to defeat the Royalist horse at Hunslet near Leeds. With pressure building up Belasyse took to the field and set up his headquarters at Selby so as to sever Lambert's communications with Hull. Belasyse then tried to get outside help from Lord Loughborough (Henry Hastings) amongst others. Loughborough sent Major-General George Porter and Colonel Gervaise Lucas to him. With these reinforcements Belasyse attacked Bradford on 25 March. The attack failed, Porter playing a large part in this failure and skulking off home. Loughborough ordered him to go back as Belasyse desperately needed his horse. But Porter went over Loughborough's head and gained Prince Rupert's approval for his remaining in Nottinghamshire.

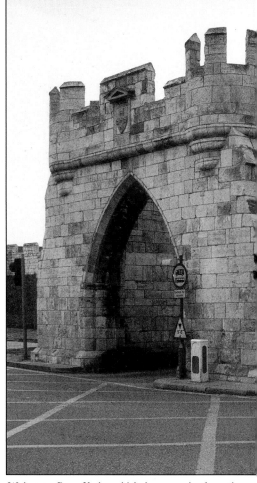

Walmgate Bar, York, which bears marks from the fighting of 1644.

Fairfax now crossed the Pennines and joined his father at Ferrybridge bringing 2,000 horse to add to Lord Fairfax's 1,000 horse and 1,000 foot. They were then joined by Sir John Meldrum and sections of the army he had led at the ill-fated siege of Newark. This army attacked Belasyse at Selby. The three Parliamentarians pressed into the town trapping the Royalists in the streets. Belasyse was wounded several times before he was captured. The Royalist foot was decimated; such as escaped the town were left leaderless due to the high mortality rate amongst the officers. In effect, half of the Yorkshire army was destroyed. York was exposed to attack and this was the dreadful news which was communicated to Newcastle at Quarrenden Hills.

YORK UNDER SIEGE

THE NEWS of Selby was shattering. Newcastle promptly withdrew and began a race to York. Two days later, on 14 April 1644 he arrived having dispatched his horse southwards on the way. Skirting the Fairfaxes by travelling via Knaresborough, these men travelled into Nottinghamshire to join up with Lord Loughborough.

The Scots chased after Newcastle but went past York and joined the Fairfaxes at Wetherby. The combined army now came to around 20,000; of these, 4,000 were horse. The allied commanders decided to besiege York. The Fairfaxes were positioned to the east, from Fulford to the south round through Heslington to the Fishpool (the part of the city defended by an expanse of water and marsh). The Scots were, for the time being, stretched around the

rest of the city. Because of the size of the town the forces around it were stretched thinly and the siege was not a very tight one. For much of the time there were skirmishes between the two sides with the Royalist forces generally coming off best.

In early June the Earl of Manchester arrived with 4,000 foot and 4,000 horse from the Eastern Association army. From then on the siege became a close one. At one point a mine was exploded under the Marygate Tower by Major-General Crawford. However, the subsequent entry into the Manor House defences was isolated and easily defeated. The explosion scattered and destroyed the records of the Abbey of St Marys which were being transcribed at the Fairfax's expense!

York was still considered the second city in the country, despite being smaller now than Norwich and the

Two musketeers from the English Civil War Society at the monument to the battle of Marston Moor.

(Opposite) Cromwell's Plump, looking towards the field of battle.

This battlefield is a good one for the traveller. Good views of the field can be obtained from the monument on the Long Marston to Tockwith road. No major road crosses the field or goes by it, but access is easy. The A59 from York brings you to Monkton Moor from where there is a road to Long Marston village. This road was once the Atterwith Lane which features in the battle. Coming from Leeds use the A64, turning onto the Rufforth Road at Buckles Inn. Long Marston can be reached on the B1224, the Wetherby road. The road from Long Marston to Tockwith takes the walker or driver between the position of the two armies.

economically more important Bristol, and to lose it would damage the crown's prestige. The King intimated as much to Prince Rupert. The Prince began to utilize the resources and manpower of the West Midlands as well as a good proportion of those from the neigbouring areas under Lord Loughborough. With the resulting forces which consisted of the Prince's own army and about a thousand men from Loughborough's, Rupert marched north through Cheshire and then Lancashire. He captured Stockport on 25 May, and stormed Bolton on 28 May. Two days later he was joined by the Northern Horse under Goring. By 10 June Liverpool was in Royalist hands, the King's forces were supreme in Lancashire and Rupert had an army of 14,000.

By 24 June the Prince was at Clitheroe; two days later he was at Skipton in Yorkshire. On 26 June he was at Denton, the home of the Fairfaxes. He had successfully fooled his enemies. The allies at York had assumed that the Prince would come down the west bank of the Ouse; this would have caught them split in two by the river. So, first, they united to the south of the city, then they moved southwards to avoid being attacked by Rupert from the west and having the Marquis of Newcastle with the Northern foot and the York garrison at their rear. They selected rising ground near Long Marston as a safe position from which to observe the Prince's approach. But Rupert did not take this route. Instead he stayed to the east of the river and entered York by the now unguarded northern approach. As Rupert entered the city on 1 July the disheartened Parliamentarians withdrew towards Tadcaster.

MARSTON MOOR

RUPERT was not content to let the enemy get away. If he had done so,

The Battle of Marston Moor by Abraham Cooper.

it is possible that the acrimonious relationship between the allied commanders might well have split their army into its component parts. Instead Rupert used the bridge of boats which the Parliamentarians had built at Poppleton to cross to the west bank of the Ouse on the night of 1 July. At dawn on 2 July the Marquis of Newcastle left the city in his coach. Released from the walls in which he had been long immured, the Marquis expected to be followed by his army under Lord Eythin. But Eythin was slow to leave the city, claiming that his men were plundering the siegeworks outside. Also Eythin was opposed to the attempt to catch the Parliamentarian army, and he may have delayed marching out of York to foil the Prince's plan. In the event it was after four o'clock in the afternoon when the Northern Army foot arrived at the battlefield, too late to be put onto the plan of the field drawn by Rupert's engineer Bernard de Gomme. In the end only 3,000 of Newcastle's foot made it onto the field.

On the morning of 2 July Lord Leven had begun to retreat with the army towards Tadcaster. But Rupert appeared on the moor between the Long Marston to Tockwith road and the road which is now the A59. Whilst the vanguard of the Parliamentarian army was only 1 mile (1½ kilometres) from Tadcaster, the Eastern Association Army foot was only 3 miles (4¾ kilometres) from Long Marston, and some of the horse were still on the edge of the moor. The Parliamentarian leaders, Leven, Manchester and Fairfax, turned the vanguard around and began to return to Long Marston; their seconds, David Leslie, Oliver Cromwell and Sir Thomas Fairfax, began to dispute ground with the approaching Royalists near Bilton Bream. In this preliminary scrap the Royalists came off worse. The Parliamentarian horse took up strong positions on the ridge covered by the cultived fields of Long Marston and Tockwith, leaving Prince Rupert to marshal his army on the moorland.

The edge of the moor began about 300 yards (275 metres) from the road linking Long Marston and Tockwith, starting on Atterwith Lane and then running in a rough semi-circle to join the road near its junction with the Fosse dyke. The line of the moor was marked by a series of hedges and ditches. Rupert placed musketeers behind this natural barrier as he moved onto the moor. Two tracks crossed the moor: to the east, Atterwith (or Hatterwith) Lane leading to the Boroughbridge Road (A59) – there was moorland from 300 yards (275 metres) on from where it joined the Tockwith Road and from 600 yards (550 metres) on its west side. The other lane, Moor Lane, left the Tockwith road 300 yards (275 metres) west of Atterwith Lane. After ½ a mile (¾ kilometre) this road branched into three lanes at Four Lanes Meet, two roads joining the Boroughbridge road and the other crossing the moor to link up with Atterwith Lane and then on to Hessay.

On this moor Rupert marshalled his army as it arrived bit by bit. The right flank of horse was under Sir John, now Lord Byron, seconded by Lord Molyneux. In the centre the foot was spread thinly because of the late arrival of the Northern Army. The left flank was again composed of horse under Lord Goring consisting of the Northern horse and some of Lord Lough-borough's horse. Across the road on the hill, Parliament mustered a much larger army (around 28,000 compared with around 18,000). Opposite Lord Byron was Oliver Cromwell and the Eastern Association horse backed by Scottish horse under David Leslie. In their centre the foot was marshalled in

the order in which the regiments returned from the Tadcaster road. From the right to the left, the front line consisted of Eastern Association foot, Yorkshire foot and Scots. The second line had more Scots and Eastern Association regiments, whilst the rear line contained Yorkshiremen and Scots. The right flank was under Sir Thomas Fairfax and was composed of Yorkshire and Scottish horse in three lines.

Byron's flank was the weakest link. He was heavily outnumbered and, unlike Goring who was firmly anchored on Atterwith and Moor Lanes, his flank was exposed. There were compensations. To his front there was a ditch lined with musketeers. Between this and the horse were a series of rabbit warrens. This meant that Byron was in fact protected by ground which would seriously disorder any attacking force attempting to cross it. In short, Byron was instructed not to move forward. Cromwell sent a couple of guns forward to deal with the musketeers in the ditch who posed a serious threat to his intended attack. The guns opened fire about seven o'clock in the early evening. Ever since five o'clock Leven had been aware that the Royalist foot was in disorder as the Northern Army foot appeared on the field and had to be fitted into the line. It was also observed that the majority of Royalist soldiers had stood down. Moreover, supply carts began to arrive on the field bringing food and water to the men who had last eaten at dawn. By seven o'clock as Cromwell's guns opened fire, the optimum moment seemed to have arrived.

Not surprisingly Byron's horse soon grew restless under the gunfire. Their morale was already low, having been chased off Bilton Bream and then having to stand in light rain all day. They and their commander were also thoroughly bored. Byron's impetuosity got the better of him and he led his men forward to attack. As they crossed the

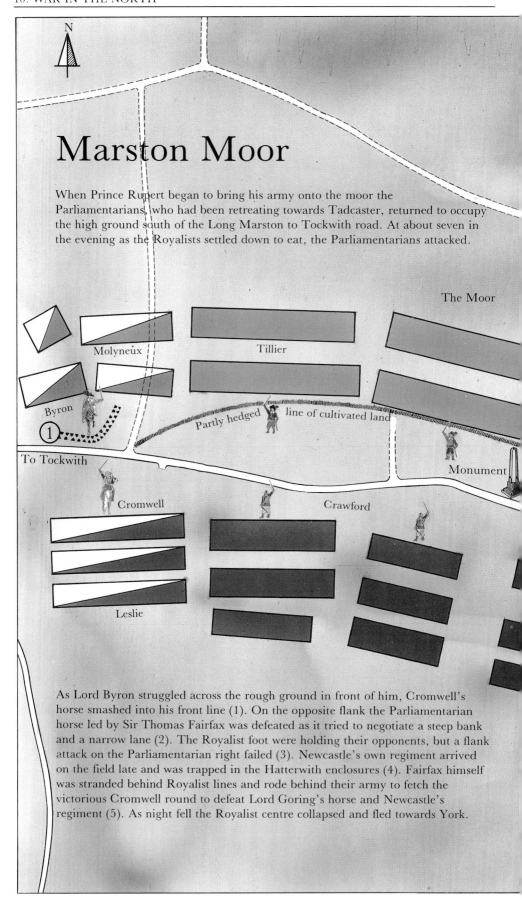

Marston Moor

When Prince Rupert began to bring his army onto the moor the
Parliamentarians, who had been retreating towards Tadcaster, returned to occupy
the high ground south of the Long Marston to Tockwith road. At about seven in
the evening as the Royalists settled down to eat, the Parliamentarians attacked.

The Moor

Molyneux

Tillier

Byron

Partly hedged   line of cultivated land

To Tockwith

Monument

Cromwell

Crawford

Leslie

As Lord Byron struggled across the rough ground in front of him, Cromwell's
horse smashed into his front line (1). On the opposite flank the Parliamentarian
horse led by Sir Thomas Fairfax was defeated as it tried to negotiate a steep bank
and a narrow lane (2). The Royalist foot were holding their opponents, but a flank
attack on the Parliamentarian right failed (3). Newcastle's own regiment arrived
on the field late and was trapped in the Hatterwith enclosures (4). Fairfax himself
was stranded behind Royalist lines and rode behind their army to fetch the
victorious Cromwell round to defeat Lord Goring's horse and Newcastle's
regiment (5). As night fell the Royalist centre collapsed and fled towards York.

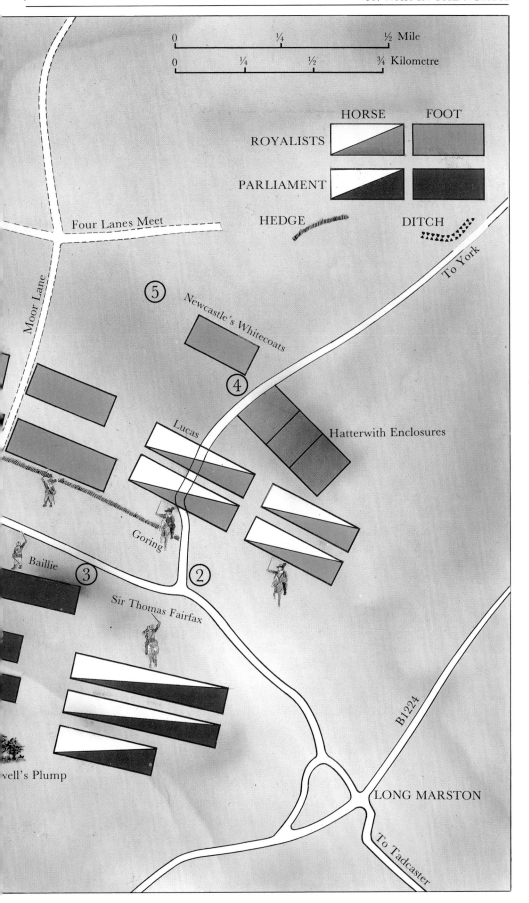

0 · ¼ · ½ Mile
0 · ¼ · ½ · ¾ Kilometre

HORSE · FOOT
ROYALISTS
PARLIAMENT
HEDGE · DITCH

Four Lanes Meet

Moor Lane

To York

⑤

Newcastle's Whitecoats

④

Lucas

Hatterwith Enclosures

Goring

③ Baillie

② Sir Thomas Fairfax

B1224

...well's Plump

LONG MARSTON

To Tadcaster

broken ground in front of them they naturally became disordered. Cromwell, relieved at the sudden advantage he had gained, counter-attacked. Byron's front line was defeated after only a short fight and Cromwell plunged on to the second Royalist line under Molyneux. These troops stopped Cromwell's advance but they were heavily outnumbered and although Rupert charged to their aid, they were eventually overcome.

On the opposite flank, Goring was protected by a steep bank sloping from the cultivated lands to the moor and crowned with a hedge. To get at him Fairfax had to pass his horse down Atterwith Lane in the face of musket fire. As he did so, his front lines were torn apart by the gunfire and turned back, colliding with the regiments behind them. These came on and reached the moor. At this point Goring, with perfect timing, launched his attack. He defeated Fairfax's horse and only received a check when he hit the Scots horse under the Earl of Eglington in the rear. Even here he was successful after a brief flight. As Goring reached the ridge, Sir Charles Lucas turned on the flank of the Parliamentarian foot.

Fairfax and possibly some of his officers found themselves stranded behind the Royalist lines. They pushed round behind the enemy lines and joined up with Cromwell's men. These were then led around the rear of the Royalist army and brought to stand where Goring had stood earlier. To the east of Atterwith Lane there was a series of enclosures and in them was Newcastle's regiment of foot which had only arrived as the battle began. They attempted to halt Cromwell's advance and managed to fend off several attacks.

In the centre of the field the foot of both sides had hit each other after the battle on the flanks had begun. Therefore Cromwell, after he had defeated Byron and Molyneux, could lend assistance to the foot to his right. On the opposite flank, Lucas attempted

the same thing. With assistance from Blakiston's horse and the Marquis of Newcastle himself, the Royalist foot drove off several attacking regiments. Blakiston pursued them to the ridge where their flight was joined by Leven and Lord Fairfax. But Lucas's forces failed to drive in the flank and after three charges he was captured; the weight of allied numbers had begun to tell.

Cromwell, meanwhile, charged Goring's tired horse. Goring put up a hard fight, all the more surprising because of the exhausted state of his horse and the fact that he was now fighting on the same terms as Fairfax had been earlier. Nevertheless, the outcome was a foregone conclusion. As night fell the remains of Goring's horse fled to York. As the Royalist foot also made off as fast as they could extricate themselves, resistance continued in one part of the field. In the Atterwith enclosures Newcastle's regiments held out for about an hour. Eventually dragoons forced their way into the field and the battle was over. Only about thirty men from Newcastle's whitecoats survived, many saved against their own will. At one stroke, Prince Rupert's relief-effort and the Marquis's once great army came to grief. The Royalist north collapsed, leaving only a few strong garrisons at Helmesley, Bolton, Skipton, Knaresborough, Pontefract and Scarborough. Newcastle himself left the country suspecting that he had become the laughing-stock of the court. Of the Royalist army, the foot had disintegrated but the horse made it over the Pennines with Rupert. The allied army split up as Eythin had thought it would once York fell. Manchester turned south, whilst the Scots and the Fairfaxes stayed on to mop up Yorkshire resistance. It was devastating for the Royalist cause. Although success in the South was seemingly to override the defeat, nothing could disguise the loss of resources for very long.

THE SCOTS ARMY

THE ARMY which Leven led over the Tweed in January 1644 was not of the same calibre as that which had defeated the King in 1640, despite having the same admired commander. Even Leven seems to have been past his best and no longer the man who a mere six years earlier had been accepted 'as if he had been the great Solyman'. Sir James Turner, a professional serving with the Scots in 1644, saw the army as being generally healthy ('lustie') but led by in-experienced men and being largely untrained. Turner had little doubt that if Newcastle had brought Leven to battle he would have defeated him.

The Scottish army differed in certain respects from the English forces: for example, a proportion of the horse were armed with lances. As the army were mainly lowlanders, they did not actually wear kilts, but there were still differences in the foot. Scottish foot made more use of their swords than the English soldiers who often ruined theirs by utilizing them as axes to chop wood. Scottish regiments also used the national flag as a basis for their colours. This was not done in the English armies except for the regiments of members of the Royal family.

At Marston Moor the Scots had six regiments of horse and fifteen foot regiments. This was a reduction in the number which they had brought across the border. Several regiments were left around Newcastle to pin down Royalists left in the North. During the battle they were to be a crucial part of the success which Cromwell was able to achieve on the left flank.

11. LOSTWITHIEL

AUGUST – SEPTEMBER 1644

Having left Waller to deal with the King's forces in the Oxford area, the Earl of Essex set off for the South-west. But Waller's army had disintegrated at Cropredy, and the King turned in pursuit of Essex.

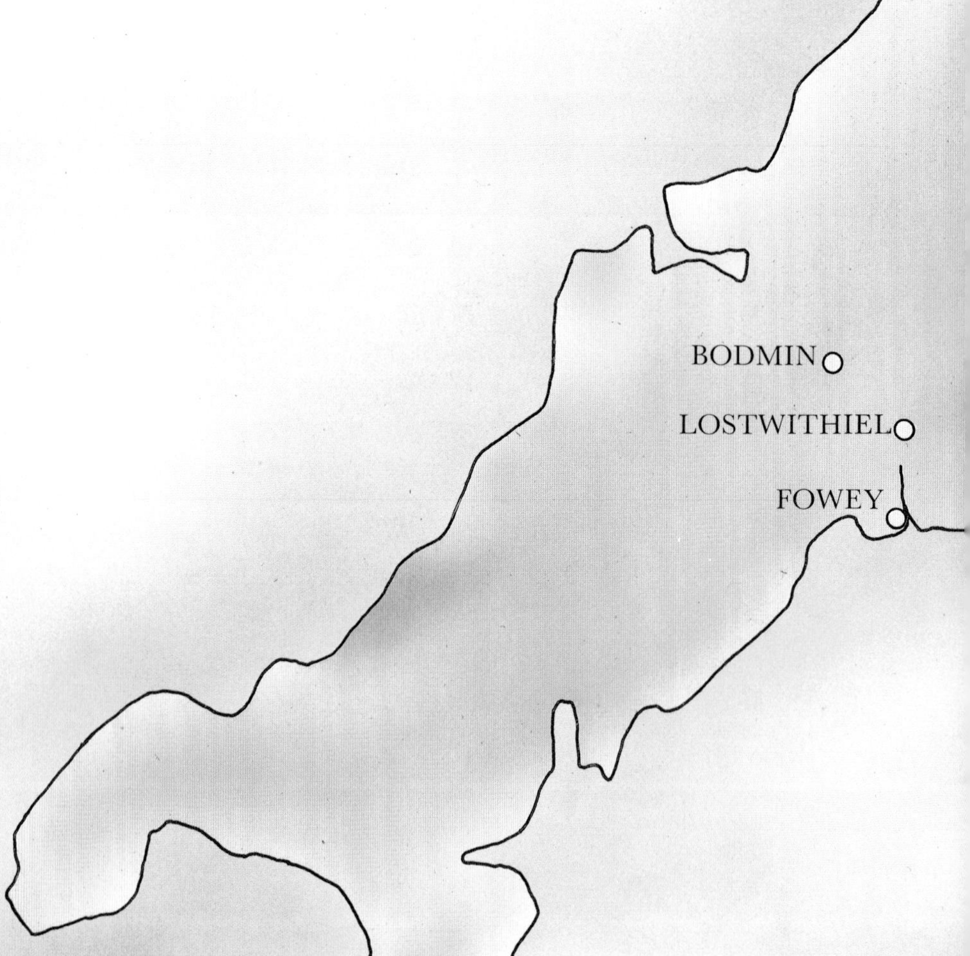

BODMIN○

LOSTWITHIEL○

FOWEY○

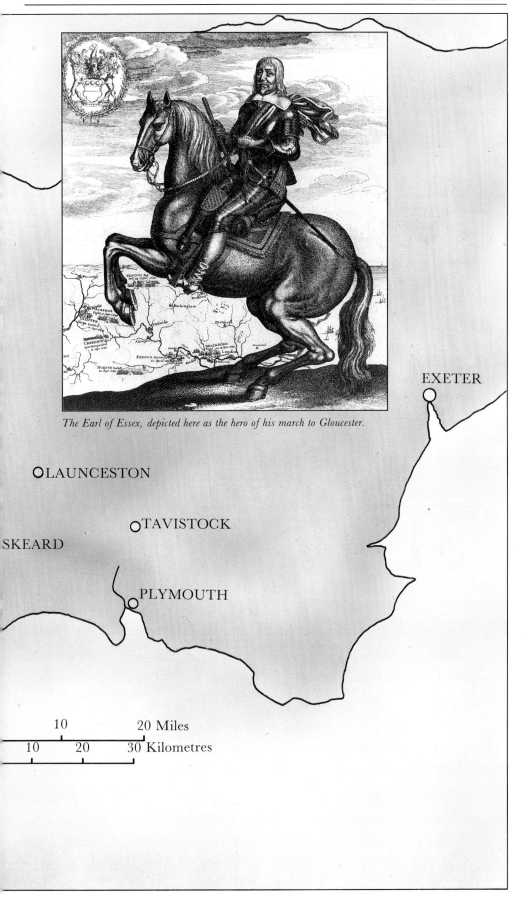

The Earl of Essex, depicted here as the hero of his march to Gloucester.

EXETER

○LAUNCESTON

○TAVISTOCK

SKEARD

PLYMOUTH

10   20 Miles

10   20   30 Kilometres

WAR IN THE SOUTH-WEST

PRINCE MAURICE had remained in Devon over the winter of 1644, in the Tavistock area. He had with him an army of around 6,000 men. By April he had invested Lyme (now Lyme Regis), where the Parliamentarian garrison had consistently disturbed the running of the local Royalist war effort in West Dorset and East Devon. It was expected that Lyme would fall within a week. As Waller and Essex closed on Oxford, Maurice was still there in May!

Essex set off towards the West, after arguing with Waller, with the aim of relieving Lyme from Maurice, who even by June had still failed to take the small town. By 14 June the Earl had reached Blandford and then he took possession of Weymouth, without a fight, on the next day. The Earl of Essex and his army were treated well on their march: the army was well behaved and he was personally very popular. On the other hand, he did not find many recruits. This had been one of his aims; he had been led to believe that he would be able to raise more men in an area which was, supposedly, fed up with Royalist rule. This had little foundation in truth. There was a world of difference between welcoming a well-behaved army and wanting to side with its political aims. Maurice drew off from Lyme as the Earl approached and Essex followed him to Exeter. Maurice continued to Barnstaple, and the Queen, who had given birth to a daughter, went on into Cornwall before going to France. But Essex did not besiege Exeter; instead he passed through Devon into Cornwall.

After the Battle of Cropredy Bridge, the King turned west after Essex. Behind him, Waller's army had collapsed and posed no threat. So fast did the King pursue Essex that as the Earl reached Tavistock on 23 July, forcing Sir Richard Grenville to abandon the siege of Plymouth, the

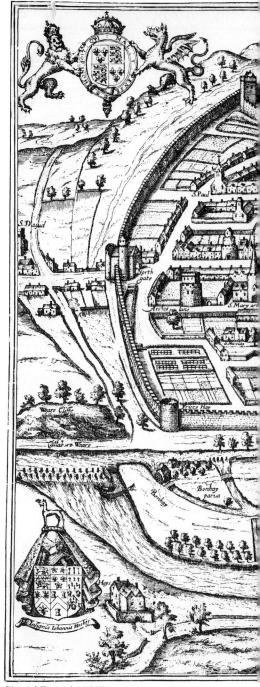

Plan of Exeter in 1618.

King was approaching Exeter. By 26 July, the King had reached Exeter and was only 30 miles (48 kilometres) away.

Essex found himself increasingly in a tight corner, as the King reached Launceston. The King now had an army of 16,000 after joining Maurice; Essex had only 10,000 after having left garrisons around Devon. It seems clear that the Earl had been seriously misled. The Royalist historian Edward Hyde, Earl of Clarendon, at that time a

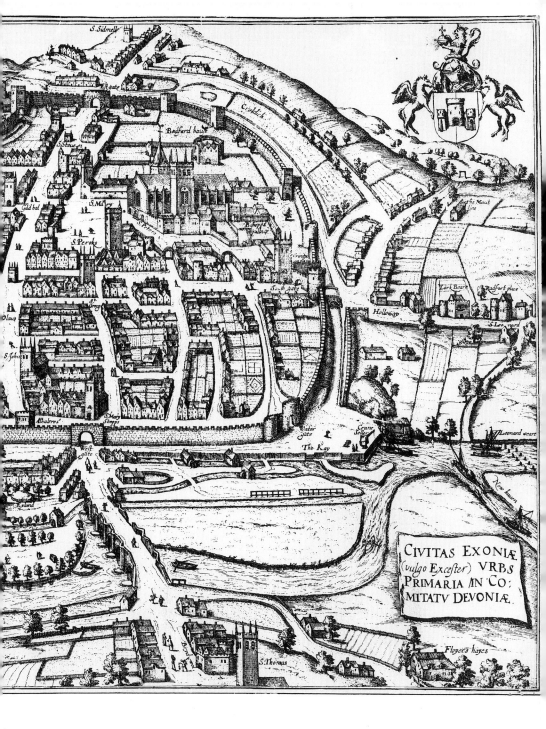

Labels on the map (as visible):
S. Sidwell · Eft gate · Bedford haule · S. Steuen · Gild hal · S. Mary · S. Peroks · S. George · S. John · Albabroc · S. Mary Stepps · Weft gate · yland · S. Olaue · South gate · The Cathedrall · Biffhope pallace · French · Crolditch · the Maut line · Lork Beare · Radfort place · S. Leonard · Hollway · Water gate · The Kay · Crane feller · S. Leonard scare · New haven · S. Thomas · Flayers hayes

CIVITAS EXONIÆ (vulgo Exceſter) VRBS PRIMARIA IN CO: MITATV DEVONIÆ.

councillor in Oxford, asserted that Lord Robartes had assured Essex of being able to gain a great number of recruits. Robartes was in position to know: he was a Cornishman, Braddock Down was fought very close to his estates, and indeed Essex's army was actually camped on Robartes's estates in July. Robartes was a friend of Sir Henry Vane, one of Essex's severest critics, and it was suggested that Essex was deliberately sent on a fool's errand as part of an attempt to discredit him. Although Robartes was no friend of Essex, it is unlikely that he did send Essex into a trap. It is more probable that Robartes and the Cornish MPs wished to have the Earl rescue their estates from Royalist sequestration. Nevertheless, they played a large part in getting the Earl cornered in the far west with the only Parliamentarian army in the south of England.

Lostwithiel from Beacon Hill.

The town itself, the starting point for the battle, lies on the A390. Minor roads lead from there to Fowey. The B3269 passes by Castle Dore, which lies to the east of the road just before the turning to Golant. The A390 is the line of Balfour's flight with the Parliamentarian horse and it can be used to reach Braddock Down (Chapter Two).

LOSTWITHIEL

Essex moved on to Bodmin at the end of July. There he hoped to resupply his tired army at the largest market in Cornwall. On 2 August Charles was only 20 miles (32 kilometres) away at Liskeard. As Essex moved on to Lostwithiel, the King closed on him from the east and Sir Richard Grenville moved in from the north. The King then tried to buy Essex's support and proposed that they might turn on the Scottish army in the north of England together. After all, Essex had been Captain-General in the English army during the war with Scotland. Essex was approached by his nephew, Lord Beauchamp, who gave him the King's letter, preliminary, it was hoped, to further discussions. But Essex, quite rightly, would go no further. Parliament might be in the pro-

cess of ditching him, but the Earl could not betray the trust placed in him. At the same time Lord Wilmot, Commander of the King's horse, in lieu of Prince Rupert, made unilateral overtures to Essex about imposing peace on the leadership of both sides by force of arms. Wilmot was probably the most vocal of many discontented officers in the King's army; and these had their counterparts in the Parliamentarian armies too, and the grumbling grew louder as the year progressed. But in this case, Wilmot was arrested at the head of his brigade, which prompted near mutiny. Charles himself had to ride amongst the horse to quell the disturbances. Rupert was the obvious man to take charge of the horse, as he was Commander, but he was still trying to limit the damage done by the disaster in the North. Instead, Lord Goring was sent down; he arrived on 7 August and took over Wilmot's

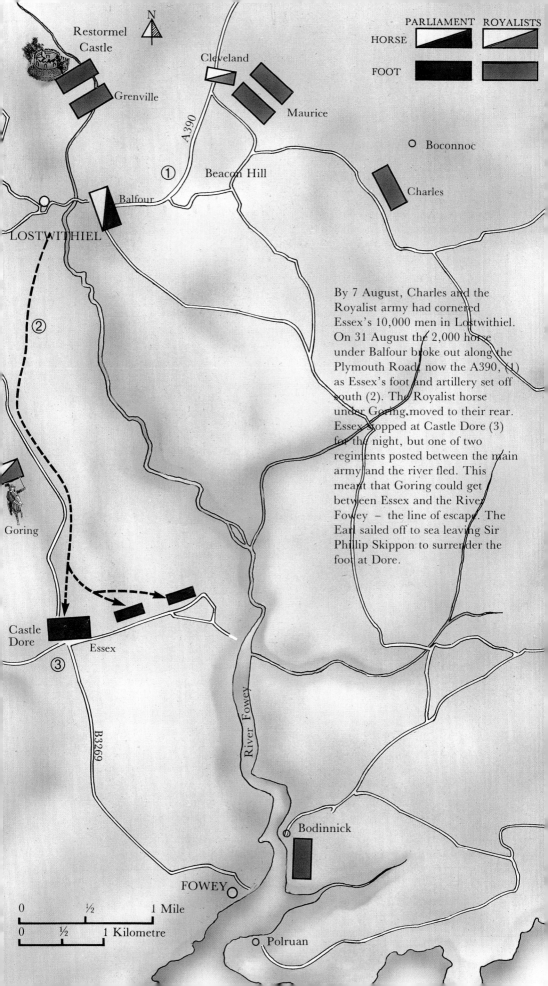

N

PARLIAMENT ROYALISTS

HORSE

FOOT

Restormel
Castle

Cleveland

Grenville

Maurice

A390

Boconnoc

①

Beacon Hill

Charles

Balfour

LOSTWITHIEL

②

Goring

By 7 August, Charles and the
Royalist army had cornered
Essex's 10,000 men in Lostwithiel.
On 31 August the 2,000 horse
under Balfour broke out along the
Plymouth Road, now the A390, (1)
as Essex's foot and artillery set off
south (2). The Royalist horse
under Goring, moved to their rear.
Essex stopped at Castle Dore (3)
for the night, but one of two
regiments posted between the main
army and the river fled. This
meant that Goring could get
between Essex and the River
Fowey – the line of escape. The
Earl sailed off to sea leaving Sir
Phillip Skippon to surrender the
foot at Dore.

Castle
Dore

Essex

③

B3269

River Fowey

Bodinnick

FOWEY

0   ½   1 Mile

0   ½   1 Kilometre

Polruan

command. Wilmot himself was confined in Exeter and then allowed to cross the Channel to France. Charles then allowed eighty or so officers from the Royalist horse, led by Prince Maurice and Lord Forth, to petition Essex with proposals for peace. Again Essex's loyalty to Parliament remained steadfast.

Negotiations over, Charles set about caging further the Earl of Essex and his army as the Earl tried to get Parliament to send Waller to his aid. All they sent, because Waller's army had fallen apart, was Lieutenant-General Middleton and a couple of thousand horse and dragoons. Money to cover arrears of pay and provisions were sent to Plymouth to fortify the bodies of Essex's armies. Their souls were taken care of with a day of prayers in the capital.

On 11 August Grenville moved into Bodmin, preventing Essex from travelling northwards. The King took up position at Breconnoc near the battlefield of Braddock Down. On 12 August Grenville moved even closer, crossing the bridge over the Fowey at Respyn, and occupied Lord Robartes's house at Lanhydrock near the present B3269. By 15 August Sir Jacob Astley and Lord Goring had occupied Polruan

and controlled the Bodinnick Ferry on the east bank of the river, opposite the town of Fowey. Essex, in the town, himself implored Parliament for succour but the force under Middleton had already been defeated in Somerset by Sir Francis Doddington. The Earl was not entirely cut off: by holding Fowey he had direct access to the sea via the river. At sea his cousin, the Earl of Warwick, dominated the coast with Parliament's navy. Indeed, Warwick had just captured five Royalist ships which had attempted to blockade Fowey. Warwick's presence ensured communications with Plymouth, the nearest Parliamentarian garrison, but there was very little help there. Almost continuous siege had reduced food stocks and, because of the dire situation of the Earl of Essex, there was fear of yet another siege. There was no chance of the town sending soldiers to his aid or mounting a relief expedition: there were too few men even to guard the 4 miles (6½ kilometres) of defences.

Essex's friends in the House of Lords sought to help. They resolved to send Waller with an army financed with a grant of £10,000 from the income from excise. The Commons however settled for holding a fast day and began to dis-

The earthworks of Castle Dore.

mantle Essex's command by appointing Waller to be commander of all horse under Essex, without consulting the absent Earl. However they thanked the Earl of Essex for his good works and eventually asked the Earl of Manchester, at that time dithering around Lincoln, to go to the Earl's aid.

Meanwhile in Cornwall eight days passed with little event. The King had decided by 21 August, however, that Waller or someone must be on their way to help Essex, and the whole army moved forward. As Essex withdrew his outer posts, Royalists occupied Beacon Hill to the west of Lostwithiel and Grenville moved to Restormel Castle to the north. On 24 August Lord Goring and the Royalist horse established themselves at St Blazey, pushing Essex's own horse onto ever decreasing pasture.

Essex instructed Sir William Balfour to prepare to lead a break-out with the horse, whilst the Earl attempted to get south along the river with the intention of shipping the foot to Plymouth. The capture of Restormel marked another hiatus, but Charles was aware of the possibility of the Parliamentarian horse escaping and a night guard was posted from then on. The Earl of Cleveland was positioned on the road to Liskeard and Plymouth (A390) which seemed the most obvious route. Nevertheless the task of encircling 10,000 men was difficult and the lines around the area were thin in places. It also stretched the logistical ability of the King's army. This meant that large numbers of soldiers who should have been on duty were out looking for food. When Cleveland called out his men only 250 came under arms.

Balfour set off at three o'clock on the morning of 31 August with 2,000 horse. As Cleveland attempted to find more men, Balfour passed down the road with little trouble. By the time Cleveland could follow, it was too late: the horse had bolted. At Saltash, Cleveland was finally left behind and

Sir Phillip Skippon.

Balfour galloped off down the Liskeard road. He crossed the Tamar and entered Plymouth with the loss of only a hundred men.

Back at Lostwithiel the evacuation of the foot began. The wet and stormy night which had been such a help to Balfour only hindered the poor foot soldiers slogging along in the mud. Four of the cannon were left behind on the boggy road. The Royalist horse attempted to harass the retreat but they were hampered by the enclosed fields which bordered the road between Lostwithiel and Fowey. Major-General Phillip Skippon was in charge of the rearguard on a hill just south of Lostwithiel and from here he held off any further attacks on the Parliamentarian army. On 1 September in the afternoon, Essex marshalled his men in the ancient earthwork fort, Castle Dore. Between the fort and the Fowey, the Earl had stationed two regiments in order to prevent there being any chance of Royalists getting between him and Fowey. So far he had been lucky. The Royalist horse had not been able to

Fowey Habour.

concentrate their forces; Lord Goring had only arrived with the bulk of the horse at four o'clock; furthermore the enclosures had proved a great hindrance to them.

But the Earl's luck ran out. Under the strain of constant attack, worn out by tiredness and hunger, one of the two flanking regiments broke and ran. The other returned to the main army at Castle Dore. Royalist forces now got between Essex and the river and threatened the Fowey road. Essex's army was now cut off from Fowey and the position at Castle Dore would not be safe for long. Essex decided to cut his losses and escape possible imprisonment. He abandoned the army, took a fishing boat and made for Plymouth. Skippon was left in charge to make what terms he could. There was no chance of evacuation: Warwick had not been able to bring any boats to Fowey anyway, and besides, there was little chance of getting down the Fowey road. Even so, left to his own devices, Skippon thought of marching to Menabilly and making a break-out from there. His council of war thought otherwise, for the foot were incapable of making the same kind of dash as Balfour had managed. Moreover the Royalists were much closer, so that if the foot tried to get away they would be attacked every step of the way. Skippon surrendered.

Five thousand muskets and pistols and forty-two pieces of artillery complete with ammunition were handed to the King. It was a humiliating affair, but the soldiers were soon released. Skippon led the remaining 6,000 men to the east on the promise that they would not fight until after they had reached Southampton. Within eight weeks they fought against the King's army again, and later went on to form the bulk of the New Model Army, but at Fowey the King could not foresee that. Charles was hardly able to feed his own army let alone 6,000 prisoners. A longer term of parole might have been a better decision and could have resulted in more of them laying down their arms for good but, as it was, a whole army had been ruined.

On 2 September as Skippon surrendered, Essex arrived at Plymouth to find Balfour already there. Reluctantly, as they had shown him so little concern, Essex sought to explain his actions to Parliament. Actually his case was not that bad. Despite the fact that the foot had been disarmed, it was intact and the horse was complete with arms. Indeed, he had got his men out of a tight corner! In Parliament Essex's enemies concentrated on the disastrous loss of so many weapons, and the demands for his dismissal grew. For the Royalists it appeared to be a tremendous victory. Coupled with Cropredy and the disintegration of Waller's army, it all seemed to overshadow the loss of the North.

The High House, Stafford.

PRISONERS

It was very inconvenient to take prisoners. Since it was difficult enough to feed his own army, a general did not wish to encumber his resources with more mouths to feed.

The solution was to try to recruit rank-and-file soldiers for your side from the prisoners. The ones who could not be lured were paroled and were supposed to swear not to take up arms again for their own side. Sometimes, as at Lostwithiel, a time or geographical limit was placed on this parole.

Officers were often imprisoned. Even then they may have been paroled and allowed to track down a prisoner with whom they could be exchanged. These paroles were harder to break and were consequently more effective. Quite important officers like George Lord Goring were also swopped; but some men who were considered dangerous were not allowed this sort of bargaining and had to remain in prison for the duration of the war.

Each garrison would have its own prison, utilizing a county lock-up if appropriate or using the empty houses of enemy supporters. The High House at Stafford was one such place. The Parliamentarian garrison used it to house Royalist prisoners.

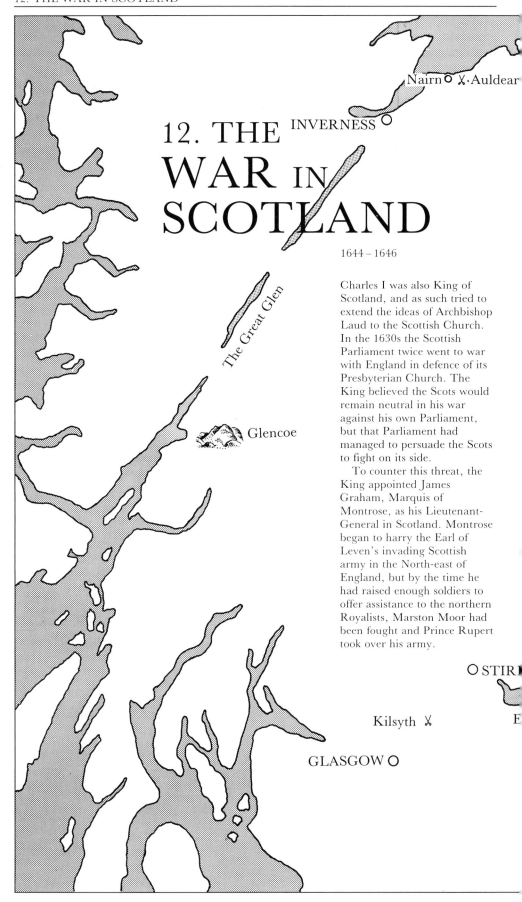

12. THE WAR IN SCOTLAND

1644 – 1646

Charles I was also King of Scotland, and as such tried to extend the ideas of Archbishop Laud to the Scottish Church. In the 1630s the Scottish Parliament twice went to war with England in defence of its Presbyterian Church. The King believed the Scots would remain neutral in his war against his own Parliament, but that Parliament had managed to persuade the Scots to fight on its side.

To counter this threat, the King appointed James Graham, Marquis of Montrose, as his Lieutenant-General in Scotland. Montrose began to harry the Earl of Leven's invading Scottish army in the North-east of England, but by the time he had raised enough soldiers to offer assistance to the northern Royalists, Marston Moor had been fought and Prince Rupert took over his army.

Nairn ○ ✗ •Auldear

INVERNESS ○

The Great Glen

Glencoe

○ STIR

Kilsyth ✗   E

GLASGOW ○

Alford ✗

ABERDEEN ○

Brechin ○

Arbroath ○

DUNDEE ○

TH ○

A Highland soldier as seen by a German artist
in the 1630s. Most Scottish soldiers in the
Civil Wars would have looked more like the
musketeer on page 117.

BURGH ○

Berwick ○

○ Kelso

Philliphaugh ○

Glencoe.

AFTER MARSTON MOOR, Montrose accompanied Lord Goring to Carlisle. From there he went back into Scotland with just two companions, Colonel Sibbald and William Rollo. At Blair Atholl he met up with a force of MacDonalds who had at last made it over from Ireland, under the leadership of Alasdair MacDonald. To these 1,100 men he added local volunteers and raised the King's standard on 28 August 1644. With this total of barely 2,000 men he launched the most astounding campaign of the whole of the three Civil Wars. On 1 September he routed a larger force of Scottish Covenanters at Tippemuir as he made his way to Perth. Less than a fortnight later he defeated another little army which had been sent to stop him reaching Aberdeen.

The Earl of Argyll, his old rival, was now his chief enemy. But as Montrose developed a form of guerrilla war, the Earl was left ineffective. When Montrose attacked Inverary, Argyll was firmly put on the retreat. Even in England old Leven could see that there was a serious threat to the stability of the Scottish regime. In Edinburgh itself this was more apparent. As Argyll attempted to get two regiments of clansmen over from Ireland, General Baillie was sent out to deal with Montrose.

The attack on Inverary was part of a campaign against the Campbell country, but after wreaking havoc there

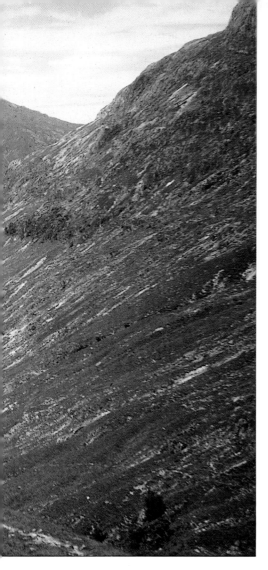

Inverlochy. The Earl thought that the information received after several night-time skirmishes suggested that he had found some stragglers from Montrose's army. Accordingly he and his second-in-command, Auchinbreck, drew their men into a large square to fend off any attack and to destroy these scattered MacDonalds. Instead as day broke, Montrose led his hitherto concealed army in a wild charge down the hill. The 4,000 men in the square were devastated by the surprise attack. As Montrose's men crashed through the first two lines, Argyll set his men an example to follow. He set off across the sea loch in his personal galley. Over 1,500 of the Campbells were killed in the fighting.

The fury in Edinburgh was intense. Montrose was declared a traitor, he was excommunicated, his coat of arms in Parliament was defaced and henceforth he was to be referred to only as James Graham. The Edinburgh government naturally played down the importance of the defeat at Inverlochy when it communicated with the English Parliament but to the Earl of Leven it sent urgent messages for help.

Baillie was now firmly on the defensive as Montrose marched down the Great Glen and slipped through the Cairngorms to attack Dundee in early April. This served the dual purpose of gaining him supplies whilst frightening the government at Edinburgh. A Covenanter army approached Dundee from the south, whilst Montrose lay in the town. They thought they had him trapped, because he had only about 1,000 men with him, whereas they had 3,000. Montrose went north along the coast road as Baillie shadowed him along the Arbroath to Brechin road (A933), attempting to hold him away from any inland route. Montrose doubled back along the road, which is now replaced by the A92, slipped between Baillie and the new garrison in Dundee and made off into the Highlands.

for a while, Montrose was forced into going north as Baillie came in from the east and Argyll with his new regiments advanced from the south. Montrose went through Glencoe and into the Great Glen. Here Baillie and Argyll sought to trap him. The former entered the Glen from the Inverlochy end and Baillie came down from the Inverness end. Montrose outwitted them by crossing over the mountains around Ben Nevis using passes almost lost amongst the deep snows. When Baillie's advance party under Seaforth of the Mackenzies and Argyll's scouts met in the middle of the Great Glen, their prey had already flown. On 2 February Montrose concentrated his men for an attack on Argyll's forces at

Colonel Urry, now fighting for the Covenanters, served under Baillie and showed an imaginative streak by attempting to separate Montrose from his Highland base as the latter marched out into the Moray region to meet reinforcements under Lord Gordon. Urry tempted Montrose north into a trap. Coming to join Urry were more members of the Campbells' allies, the Frasers and the Mackenzies. Montrose realized his plight and drew back only to be caught at Auldearn by Urry.

AULDEARN

AULDEARN is on the A96 between Nairn and the Laiken Forest. It stands on a slight ridge running north to south, which borders a small boggy area either side of a burn. On 9 May, Montrose turned at bay and positioned his horse on the rear slope of the ridge. His foot he placed in and near Auldearn and Alasdair MacDonald was posi-tioned on a slight eminence to the north and west of the village just above the road leading across the burn. In the village, Montrose had posted mus-keteers who were to fire constantly upon Urry's army to give the impres-sion that the main Royalist force was in the town.

Urry marched east along the route of the A96 with his horse flanking his foot. Convinced that Montrose had actually placed all his army in the village he made straight for it. Once across the burn his army shifted to the right so that only his left flank lay astride the road. This probably had something to do with the difficulties of crossing the boggy ground leading up to Auldearn. MacDonald and his 500 men attacked the left of Urry's army as it waded along the roadsides. Although he caught Urry off-guard, very little damage could be done as Urry had over 3,500 men and could easily hold the MacDonalds in check.

Three regiments, under Colonels

Auldearn battlefield.

Laver, Lothian and Buchanan pushed the MacDonalds back towards the higher and drier ground. Montrose's plan had failed. Urry was no longer content to continue towards the village; instead he wanted to destroy the MacDonalds. However, this presented Montrose with an opportunity he could not miss. Urry had turned his right wing from its earlier objective, and into this flank Montrose launched his horse. Although he had only 250 men, Montrose was able to rout Major Drummond's regiments. These then fled to their left and collided with the foot regiments beside them. The ensuing confusion communicated itself to the left flank fighting Alasdair MacDonald. Heartened by the success of Montrose's horse, the MacDonalds gave an extra push and Urry's army collapsed. It is sadly possible that about 2,000 men were killed in the battle, the overwhelming majority being from Urry's army. Scottish battles, or rather the pursuit of defeated armies, were much bloodier than their English counterparts.

The next two months saw the deadly game of hide-and-seek continue as

Auldearn is on the A96, just over 2 miles (3 kilometres) east of Nairn. The battlefield is more or less in the triangle formed by the B9101 and the minor road from Acharedgin to Auldearn. This latter road probably marks Montrose's line of hidden men. The Covenanters attacked along the line of the A96, heading east towards the village itself.

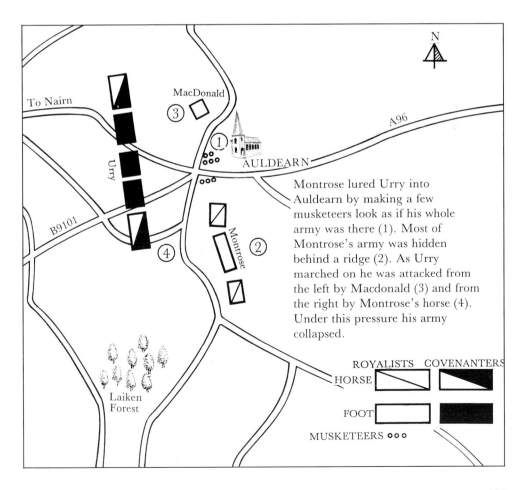

Montrose lured Urry into Auldearn by making a few musketeers look as if his whole army was there (1). Most of Montrose's army was hidden behind a ridge (2). As Urry marched on he was attacked from the left by Macdonald (3) and from the right by Montrose's horse (4). Under this pressure his army collapsed.

Asloun Castle, where Montrose spent the night before the battle of Alford.

Alford's bridge is on the A944 where it crosses the Don. It was along the forerunner of this road that the Covenanters marched. The battle took place between the river and the A944 and the A980. Thus the whole field can be seen from these two roads.

Montrose traversed the Cairngorms and the glens between them and the coastal plain. He was constantly trying to lure General Baillie into a trap. Baillie was likewise determined to catch Montrose on open ground where he was sure he could defeat him.

ALFORD

BAILLIE moved out of his base at Strathbogie in June 1645 when he saw a chance of cutting Montrose off from the Highland refuges. He crossed the River Don at Alford, having followed its valley inland. On 2 July Montrose moved on Baillie as he reached the south side of the Don. Baillie's army stood between the river and its marshes and the road which later provided the route for the A944. The Royalist army was, on this occasion, drawn up in conventional pattern with horse on the flanks. The right wing was composed of Lord Gordon with 200 horse and on the left under Gordon's brother, Lord Aboyne, were a further 200. In the centre were 1,800 foot in four foot regiments under Drummond of Balloch, MacDonnel of Glengary, Colonel O'Kean and Nathaniel Gordon.

Baillie's army had 800 horse which were concentrated on the left under Lord Balcarres. The 1,800 foot in the Covenanter army formed the right and centre. It was on Balcarres's flank that the fighting began. Lord Gordon attacked him with such ferocity that for a while the Royalists were able to overcome their lack of numbers. But the advantage did not last long, and Gordon was forced back until he drew level with Nathaniel Gordon's foot, which opened fire on Balcarres's horse and turned them back. It was this which panicked all of Baillie's horse and they ran off. In the centre the foot had met. Aboyne and O'Kean attacked first, followed by Balloch and Glengarry. Under this pressure Baillie's men

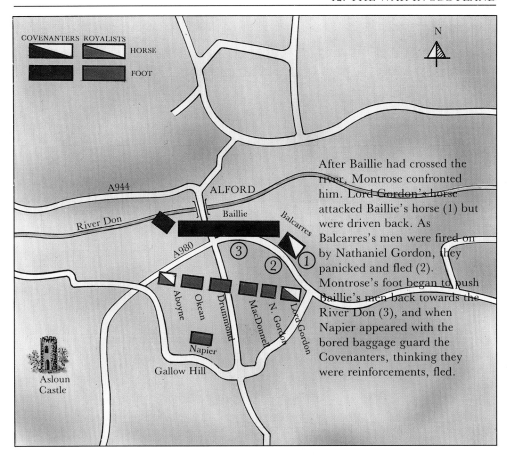

COVENANTERS ROYALISTS

HORSE

FOOT

N

A944   ALFORD

River Don

A980

Baillie

Balcarres

Aboyne   Okean   Drummond   MacDonnell   N. Gordon   Lord Gordon

Napier

Gallow Hill

Asloun Castle

After Baillie had crossed the river, Montrose confronted him. Lord Gordon's horse attacked Baillie's horse (1) but were driven back. As Balcarres's men were fired on by Nathaniel Gordon, they panicked and fled (2). Montrose's foot began to push Baillie's men back towards the River Don (3), and when Napier appeared with the bored baggage guard the Covenanters, thinking they were reinforcements, fled.

slowly gave ground. Suddenly, Montrose's eighteen-year-old nephew, Archie Napier, appeared with the baggage guard. They had become bored with their mundane duties and had wanted to join in the action. Their appearance, rather than their weight of numbers, decided the day. The withdrawal turned into a rout and the high casualties of Auldearn were matched in the pursuit across the Don. Lord Gordon himself was killed in the later stages of the battle. He and Montrose had been cultural bosom companions, as Gordon too was a scholar. It is a great stain on the character of the two nations that Gordon, Montrose, and Falkland in England, should be chiefly remembered for their contribution to the destructive elements in society, rather than for the civilizing influence that their talents could have brought in peace.

KILSYTH

AFTER ALFORD it was time for a reappraisal. Montrose's campaigns had been spectacular, but they were no more than a sideline in the great conflict engulfing the nations of the British Isles. Two weeks before the battle at Alford, the King's army had rushed headlong to destruction at Naseby; it was now imperative that Montrose should link up with the Royalists in England. With this in mind he began his descent upon the lowlands.

By August 1645 Montrose had an army of 4,500 foot and 500 horse. He made straight for Glasgow with Baillie at his heels, and Argyll also on his trail. Baillie aimed for no more than to turn Montrose from Glasgow but Argyll wanted to destroy him. The Royalists turned to face the Covenanters at Kilsyth somewhere to the north of the present A803, in flat fields at the foot of

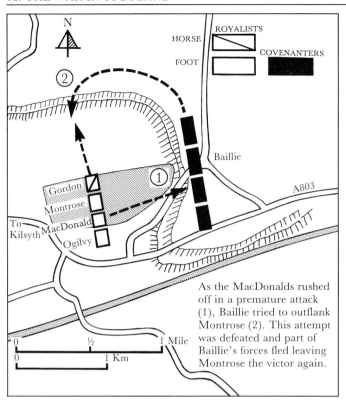

N

HORSE
FOOT

ROYALISTS
COVENANTERS

(2)

Gordon
Montrose
To
Kilsyth MacDonald
Ogilvy

(1)

Baillie

A803

0   ½   1 Mile
0   1 Km

As the MacDonalds rushed off in a premature attack (1), Baillie tried to outflank Montrose (2). This attempt was defeated and part of Baillie's forces fled leaving Montrose the victor again.

Kilsyth battlefield is north-east of Glasgow on the A803. Most of the field is now under the waters of the Townshead reservoir. The road to the north of this is roughly the route used by the Covenanter horse as it tried to outflank Montrose's men. By taking this road eastwards the remains of the battlefield can be seen. By continuing up the hill towards Low Banton, the traveller is brought to the position held by Baillie's and Argyll's forces as they looked down on Montrose's men standing in their shirt-sleeves in the hot August sun.

the encircling Campie Hills. Much of this field now lies under a reservoir so is inaccessible to the traveller, but on 15 August 1645 Montrose used the walls of the small enclosed fields as defence works. To his front he placed a small body of men in a collection of outbuildings at the foot of the hills. All of the Royalist horse was on the left flank under Nathaniel Gordon and Lord Aboyne. The foot was grouped in three bodies under Lord Airlie and Alisdair MacDonald. As it was a sweleringly hot day the Royalists had stripped to their shirts.

Baillie was not keen on attacking Montrose, as he had so much experience of defeat at the Royalist's hands and did not want to go through it again. Argyll, however, was single-minded in his desire to crush Montrose now. The Parliamentary committee which accompanied Baillie's army agreed with the Earl. Baillie had experienced their contribution to military sense before: they had forced him to do battle at Alford! Even worse, on this occasion they insisted on interfering with Baillie's dispositions on the field. Much to the delight of the watching Montrose they forced Baillie's horse into undertaking a flanking march around the edge of the hills, to the Royalists' north and left flank.

As the Covenanter army pressed forwards and skirmishing broke out around the outbuildings, the MacDonalds became over-excited and rushed off on a wild charge without orders. This disrupted Montrose's plan and in any case they were soon in trouble as they had inadvertently taken on the bulk of Baillie's army.

On his left Montrose's horse were also in trouble as Baillie's men came at them from the hillside. The Gordon horse were unable to defeat the flanking movement. Timely help from the aged but dogged Lord Airlie changed matters and the Covenanters were chased off. Baillie looked now to his reserves, the Fifeshire levies, to stop the rot on his right. The centre of his army was now becoming increasingly embroiled in the fight around the outhouses. But to his dismay, the

Fifeshire boys, unhappy about being dragged from the harvest, were nowhere to be seen. With uncommon good sense they had decided that the harvest was more important than getting mauled by Montrose's Royalists. The Earl of Argyll too found his determination to destroy Montrose sapped, turned tail again, setting thereby an example for the others to follow, as half-hearted generals have so often done. Baillie's horse concurred with his action and too left the field. The last Covenanter army in Scotland had been destroyed.

TO THE WAR'S END

FOLLOWING THE VICTORY at Kilsyth, Montrose captured Glasgow and became dominant in Scotland. The country was his and he acted with the utmost humanity. All who would pledge allegiance to Charles I were welcomed in, and the tax burdens he imposed were fairly mild. Armed with a commission from the King, he prepared to call a new Parliament at Glasgow. Charles I seriously consid-

ered going north to link up with Montrose, but had only reached Doncaster before his route was blocked by Lord Fairfax and Lord Leven.

By 6 September, parts of the Scottish army in England had marched homeward under David Leslie and were at Berwick. Montrose's own forces were scattered and undertaking a series of recruitment drives. At Bothwell Castle, the army headquarters, Montrose had only 700 men. Even so, he set off towards Leslie, assured of 2,000 recruits from the estates of Lords Roxburgh and Home. At Kelso he was informed that the Lords and their men had changed sides, and Montrose pulled back towards Philliphaugh to join Alisdair MacDonald. It was all part of an elaborate trap. Lord Traquair had lent him a hundred horse and promised to inform him of all Leslie's movements. But although Traquair convinced Montrose that Leslie was still at Berwick, in reality the Covenanter army was already at Philliphaugh. Montrose awoke to the sound of horses moving. It was Traquair's men leaving the camp. Despite a rapid march to join

Glasgow circa *1680.*

them, the 600 foot at Philliphaugh were defeated before Montrose could reach them. Most of them surrendered to Leslie in good faith, but he was overruled by the Parliamentary committee which now accompanied him. The disarmed MacDonalds were murdered where they stood.

Glasgow fell again and many of the officers from Montrose's army were brutally executed by the Covenanters intent on revenge. 'This work', as one of their 'holy men' claimed, 'gangs bonnily on.' Yet Montrose, with an important crop of prisoners, refused to join in the primitive blood-letting. 'If the meanest corporal in my army had given quarter to their general, I would abide by it.' But the aura about him had faded. Petty jealousies, submerged by the successes, now reappeared. It took five months to overcome them and build a new army. By March 1646 he had 5,000 under arms. Leslie was no longer in the country and Urry had changed sides again, to be welcomed into Montrose's camp. As Montrose prepared to take the country again, the King surrendered at Newark. The Monarch demonstrated one of his characteristic defects – he ditched Montrose, again turning to the almost imbecilic Hamilton in order to win over the vile Argyll.

Thus ended the fantastic campaigns in Scotland under the best of all Royalist generals. He was not the only talent to be carelessly thrown aside by the Stuarts, but perhaps he was the most unnecessary.

Bothwell Castle, Montrose's headquarters.

James Graham, Marquis of Montrose (1612 – 1650)

Having studied at Glasgow and St Andrews, the young James Graham succeeded to the Earldom of Montrose in 1626. During the 1630s he toured Europe and on his return was swept up in the crisis over the attempted imposition of Laudian innovations in the Scottish Church. He signed the Covenant in defence of Presbyterianism but in the Edinburgh Parliament opposed the leadership of the Earls of Hamilton and Argyll, reaffirming his loyalty to Charles I. Nevertheless, in the Second War against the English, he led his regiment across the Tweed ahead of the rest of the Scots army and vigorously fought the King's forces. Again, once the war was over, he opened up negotiations with Charles I but was found out and arrested by the Earl of Argyll. He remained in prison until November 1641 when Charles and his Scottish Parliament were apparently reconciled.

When Henrietta Maria arrived in York in 1643 Montrose joined her there to discuss a Royalist rising in Scotland. But in Oxford the King did not believe that Scotland would drop its neutral stance. The now Marquis of Hamilton had convinced the King that he was the man to trust and Scotland could be kept neutral. This had the effect of making the King contemptuous of the Scottish representatives at court despite Henrietta's warnings based on the more astute Montrose's advice. As for Montrose's Scottish rising, it was seen to be unnecessary and was brushed aside.

Belatedly then, as Leven's army marched down the east coast, Montrose was created Lieutenant-General of the King's forces in Scotland. He went on to fight the most dramatic campaign of the war, which he continued until 1646. In 1649 he offered his services to Charles II. He tried again to raise the Highlands, only to be repudiated by his new King. He was captured and executed in 1650 by the very people who were now Charles II's supporters.

13. THE SECOND BATTLE OF NEWBURY

Despite the victory at Marston Moor, the Lostwithiel disaster had chastened Parliament; it, too, felt that the King was in a strong position. It perceived a very real threat to London, and set to work accordingly.

SEPTEMBER – NOVEMBER 1644

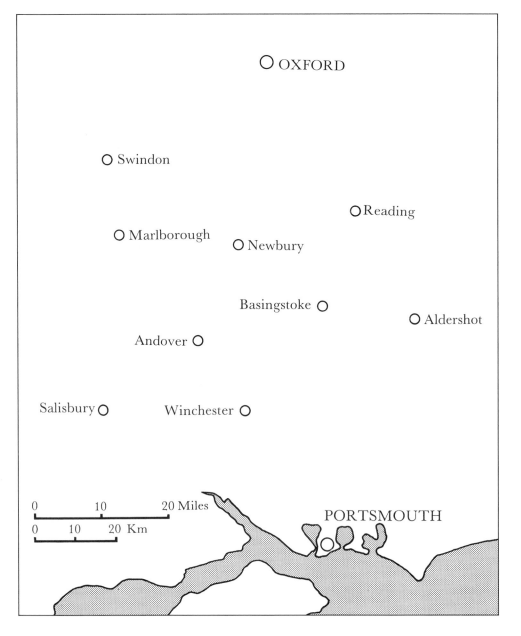

O OXFORD

O Swindon

O Reading

O Marlborough

O Newbury

Basingstoke O

O Aldershot

Andover O

Salisbury O

Winchester O

```
0          10          20 Miles
0     10    20 Km
```

PORTSMOUTH

A. THE OLDE HOVSE. B. THE NEW. C. THE TOVER THAT IS HALFE BAT FERED DOVNE. D. THE KINGES BREAST WORKS. E. THE PARLIAMENTS BREAST WORKS

THE THREAT TO LONDON

Basing House, a Royalist stronghold fortified within star-shaped earthworks by the Marquess of Winchester.

DESPITE THE VICTORY at Marston Moor, the Lostwithiel disaster had chastened Parliament: it, too, felt that the King was in a strong position. It perceived a very real threat to London, and set to work accordingly. There were three armies in the field: Manchester's at Reading, Waller's at Shaftesbury, and the Earl of Essex's sorry boys at Portsmouth. These were now to be united between the King and the capital. Essex was ordered to join up with Manchester at Basingstoke, if he could get away from Portsmouth by 16 October. On 17 October Manchester was already at the rendezvous and the Trained Bands from London were on their way to him. Waller was being pushed back from Shaftesbury and he too arrived at Basingstoke on 19 October. Essex arrived two days later. Together they had an army of 19,000.

The King's plans were much more mundane than Parliament imagined. He had with him an army of only 10,000, much less than accompanied him at Turnham Green in 1642. Instead of thinking about London, he was concerned to stabilize the safety of his own capital, Oxford. Ever since Essex and Waller had briefly threatened it the previous summer, Oxford had been on the defensive. The King therefore set out to relieve three of the outposts which were currently under siege: Basing House, Donnington Castle and Banbury. Basing was actually the most urgent: supplies had been rushed in during September, but there was a great shortage now. Accordingly the King moved towards Whitchurch on 20 October. He was unable to reach Basing; the unification of the three generals at Basingstoke had further isolated the garrison. On the other hand, Banbury was rescued on 25 October by the Earl of Northampton with some of the King's horse and sections of the Oxford garrison. The King now directed himself to dealing with Donnington Castle near Newbury.

PARLIAMENT had a new problem. In many ways the unification of the three generals had caused more trouble than it was worth. The vexed question of seniority came to the surface at Basingstoke. Essex, as the first Captain General, was certain that he was the premier commander. Manchester would not acquiesce and he had deliberately held back from going to Essex's aid in August, largely from a concern to retain his military independence. He had never wanted to work with Essex and in the summer this had been plainly shown. In short, Essex would serve under no one and no one would serve under him. To solve this, a committee was created – a council of war. On it sat the three generals, several of their lieutenants and two civilians. Essex was reduced really to being the mouthpiece of the committee: it was he who presented the results of its majority decisions to the army. Fortunately for all concerned he became ill, as much from a wounded pride as aught else, and he took to his bed throughout the following campaign. In his absence the committee found new drive and resolved to engage the King wherever they could force him to battle.

The King with his smaller army had reached Newbury as intended. His army now lay between Donnington Castle and Newbury in a strong position. One body was placed between the River Kennet and the River Lambourn to the north, just before the two rivers joined (probably near the present A4). To the north of the Lambourn lay Shaw House, fortified with prehistoric earthworks and garrisoned by Sir George Lisle. Donnington Castle and its guns dominated the left flank of the King's army which was to the north. Over to the west or rear of the army lay Prince Maurice around Speen Hill and village. The Royalist centre was composed chiefly of the massed horse under Sir Humphrey Bennet. Along the

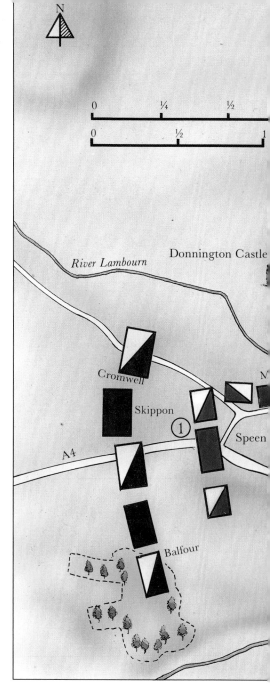

Lambourn's northern bank, between it and Shaw, were the rest of the foot under Sir Jacob, now Lord Astley.

The Parliamentarian leviathan arrived at Clay Hill to the north-east of Newbury, probably having travelled along the future route of the A3440 from Basingstoke to around Aldermaston and then on the line of the A4 to Thatcham. From there, on 26 October, the King's positions could clearly be seen. It was an almost impregnable situation, with Maurice

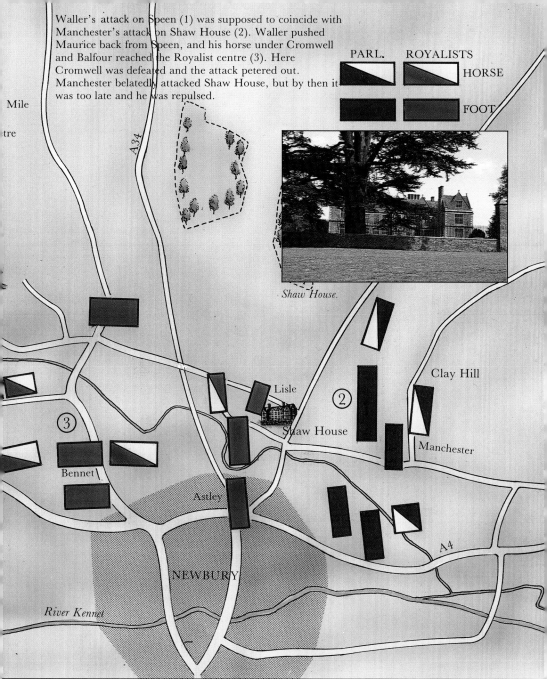

Waller's attack on Speen (1) was supposed to coincide with Manchester's attack on Shaw House (2). Waller pushed Maurice back from Speen, and his horse under Cromwell and Balfour reached the Royalist centre (3). Here Cromwell was defeated and the attack petered out. Manchester belatedly attacked Shaw House, but by then it was too late and he was repulsed.

Mile
tre

PARL. ROYALISTS

HORSE

FOOT

Shaw House.

Lisle
Shaw House
②
Clay Hill
Manchester

③
Bennet
Astley
A4

NEWBURY

River Kennet

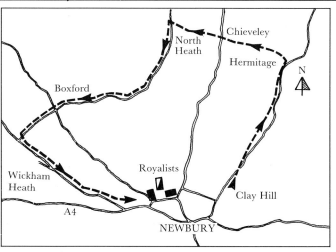

The once-majestic Donnington Castle is situated about 2 miles (3 kilometres) north of Newbury, to the west of the A34 to Oxford. From Donnington, a minor road to the east leads to Shaw House. Further along this road the traveller can take the B4009 which marks the first part of Waller's great march (*right*). To the east of this latter road is Clay Hill – the position held by the Earl of Manchester.

Chieveley
North Heath
Hermitage
N
Boxford
Wickham Heath
Royalists
Clay Hill
A4
NEWBURY

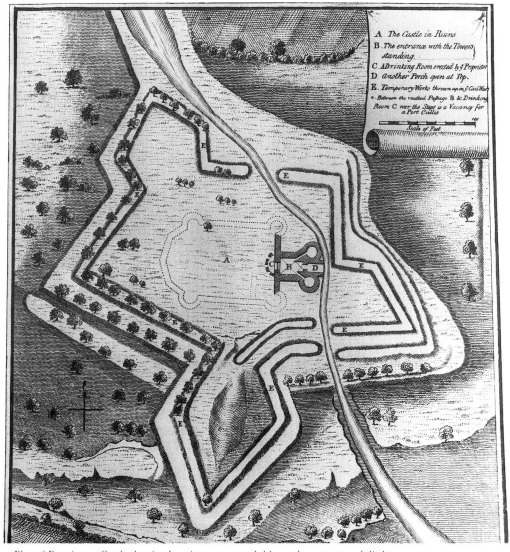

A. The Castle in Ruins
B. The entrance with the Towers standing.
C. A Drinking Room erected by $ Proprietor
D. Another Porch open at Top.
E. Temporary Works thrown up in $ Civil War
* Between the vaulted Passage B & Drinking Room C. over the Steps is a Vacancy for a Port Cullis

Scale of Feet

Plan of Donnington Castle showing how it was surrounded by earth ramparts and ditches.

protecting the rear, the conflux of the Kennet and the Lambourn guarding the front and centre, Donnington covering the right and Shaw House out in front. A direct assault was out of the question. Nevertheless an attack was to be made. Manchester was to stay on Clay Hill, opposite Shaw House, but a considerable detachment was to be sent in a wide semi-circle around Donnington to come in from the west. Waller was given this task, with Essex's horse under Balfour, and Essex's foot under Skippon, his own horse, Manchester's horse under Cromwell and the London Trained Bands. This section was drawn

to the rear out of range and out of sight of the Royalist guns during 26 October. In the evening they set off, towards Hermitage, then Chieveley which lay on the Oxford road (A34) and on to North Heath where they camped.

It remains possible that the Royalists suspected that something of this nature was afoot. Perhaps they detected the sudden disappearance of a major portion of the Parliamentarian army; at any rate Maurice began to face his forces about and dug in on Speen Hill. He had time to do so: Waller's rest at North Heath meant that it was early morning before his army crossed the

Lambourn at Boxford. By this time he was in full view of the Donnington garrison. The suspected threat to the rear of the Royalist army had materialized; nevertheless Maurice had already constructed earthworks and was ready for Waller's attack.

Manchester's attack that morning on Shaw House was supposed to be a diversionary attack to draw attention from the west. But the attack was pressed with far too much vigour and the army was tired out by trying to storm Lisle's strong defences. Too many lives were lost in what was supposed to be just a sideshow. In any case the Royalists were not misled. Waller was attacked as he made his way across the Lambourn at Boxford and then harassed all the way to Wickham Heath. It was at least two o'clock before Skippon and Balfour arrived on the heath just to the north of the road from Newbury to Marlborough (A4). From there they had to approach Speen through a maze of enclosed fields and narrow lanes, which took up about a ¼ of a mile (½ kilometre). Thus it was another hour or so before they were in a position to attack. But once within striking distance of Speen, they were left with little choice. Maurice had five guns planted behind his fortifications, and the fire from these and the cannon in the castle made standing still impossible to contemplate. They pressed on. In the event it was only a short fight before Maurice's men lost heart and began to retreat down the eastern side of the hill. Once on this exposed ground, they continued to fall back to the village. Some of Skippon's men realized that the cannons they had just captured had actually been theirs, which had been lost at Lostwithiel. With joy they turned these on Maurice's regiments of foot. Indeed, Maurice's Cornishmen were pursued through the village by Skippon's boys and Waller's attack had now brought him within striking distance of the Royalist centre.

The Earl of Manchester.

It was now that Manchester's silence became ominous. He had been supposed to co-ordinate an attack on the Royalist front with Waller's attack from the rear. So far Waller had been left on his own. It is possible that the fight in the morning had been so exhausting that the Earl considered it unwise to launch another so soon. It may also have been true that the low cloud impaired his view of the situation in the west. Whatever the cause, it remains that Manchester did not launch his attack at the right time or for some time after.

Meanwhile, Balfour and Cromwell began to order their horse preparatory to attacking the King's horse some 400 yards (370 metres) distant. Whilst the latter stood in the open fields of Newbury, Cromwell and Balfour had to traverse enclosures to reach them. This made keeping order in the ranks and files very difficult. Balfour had the additional difficulty of having to traverse marsh land to his right which followed the edge of the River Kennet. As he cleared the last hedge, Bennet charged. It was an opportune moment for the Royalist. He was attacking disordered horse with an ordered force travelling over open fields. Thus Bennet went through the stages of the charge, walk, trot, gallop and headlong charge, with little difficulty. As Balfour had no such chance, his men were most likely caught at a standstill and they were probably still divided by the hedges anyway. As a result, Bennet drove him off at first attempt. On the left Cromwell, too, was beset by problems. The Earl of Cleveland attacked him as he extricated himself from the hedge line. Despite Cleveland's capture, the Royalist horse were successful here too. Lord Goring, who completed the process, was no doubt glad to pay off the debt incurred at Marston Moor. After that, Waller's attack crumbled. His foot came to a halt around Speen and his horse were defeated and inactive under the fire of Donnington's guns.

Only now did Manchester attack, but it was already dark. The sun would have set at about half-past four. At Shaw House Lisle rushed about in his shirt sleeves, so he could be seen easily, in the gathering dark, encouraging his men. It was a desperate fight, for all its being an unnecessary one. As the night got deeper and colder, the firing died down.

The King's strong position had held out against what was one of the more imaginative strategies of the whole war. But it was still necessary for him to get out. His army was still only about half the size of that led by his opponents. As the moon sank the Royalists moved off along the Oxford road (A34) depositing the artillery and supply carts at Donnington Castle. It was dawn before the Parliamentarians knew they had gone.

DONNINGTON REVISITED

WALLER and Cromwell set off after the King's army on the morning of 28 October, only to be recalled by Manchester. The King and his army reached Oxford safely on 30 October, and were joined there by Hopton and Rupert, who brought reserves from Bristol.

Manchester, against the advice of many of the officers, declined to take anything more adventurous than an attack on Donnington Castle. This failed and on 2 November, the army set off towards Oxford. Piqued by the other officers having got their own way, Manchester mumbled about removing his army back to East Anglia. This brought the army to a halt and then they all turned about and returned to Newbury.

Charles I now made Rupert Commander-in-Chief of the whole army, thereby retiring Lord Forth, and set out to return to Donnington. Manchester ordered Cromwell to attack, but it was obvious that the horse were exhausted and underfed and, besides, the optimum time had now gone (but Manchester had secured grounds of complaint against Cromwell). On 9 November, the King arrived at Donnington, took the guns out and put supplies in. He then drew his army up in battle formation on the Shaw and Newbury open fields at right angles to his former front. His position, behind the Lambourn and the Kennet, was even stronger than it had been a fortnight before. In response the Parliamentarian commanders decided not to attack until the King began to retreat. As the Royalist army began to pull out on 10 November, indecision again set in across the Kennet. Parliament's army was underfed, its clothing was old and rotten and the autumn bit coldly. Nothing was done.

Four days later the Committee of Both Kingdoms ordered its army to stay in the field and not to go into winter quarters whilst the King was active and

Donnington Castle.

capable of relieving Basing House. This order had to be disobeyed – the army was too weak to undertake staying out of quarters. As a result, Charles got supplies into Basing House. His return to Oxford was greeted as a great triumph.

Something had to be done. The great gains of the summer seemed to stand as nought. This was largely an illusion: the loss of the North was a mortal wound to the Royalist cause, only yet its seriousness was not fully realized; but to Parliament and its supporters the end of 1644 appeared very bleak indeed. In this atmosphere negotiations were opened at Uxbridge between the two sides, and Manchester began to claim that Cromwell was a man of unsound principles. At the same time the first actions were taken to remodel the army.

THE SELF-DENYING ORDINANCE

THE CONFUSION caused at the battle of Newbury by the absence of an overall commander epitomized the problems of the Parliamentarian army leadership. Three separate armies had fought for Parliament in the battle and the commanders of each, Essex, Waller and Manchester, were intensely jealous of each other's position. Out of the ensuing *post mortem* came the resolution to create a new army. Before that took place, the leadership of Parliament's military effort was changed, almost by accident.

The Earl of Manchester opened the hornet's nest by attacking his second-in-command's integrity in Parliament during November 1644. Cromwell and he differed greatly in religion and politics. Whereas the Earl favoured the

Cromwell at the Storming of Basing House by Ernest Crofts. After a siege by local forces lasting some weeks, Cromwell arrived with further troops in October 1645. The house was destroyed, most of its occupants slaughtered and its treasures plundered.

establishment of a Presbyterian church to fill the hiatus in England's religious affairs, Cromwell wanted a series of decentralized (Independent) Protestant congregations. Manchester, disillusioned by the continuing failure to defeat the King, saw negotiations as the only solution. Cromwell was for outright victory.

Manchester openly questioned Cromwell's leadership of the horse at Newbury, implying that his negligence allowed the King to win. This was a cover for the Earl's attempt to remove Cromwell from his army and he went further, claiming that Cromwell was filling the officer corps of the Eastern Association army with Independents like himself. It was claimed that these men not only opposed the proposal that the Scottish army should be brought south, but also that they were against the establishment of a Presbyterian church system, which was what Pym had promised the Scots. Such was their opposition that it was asserted that Cromwell and his colleagues were prepared to fight the Scots. Additional charges of promoting social revolution and levying unwarrantable taxes, ensured that the matter would be referred to a committee under Zouch Tate MP.

Cromwell was clearly on the defensive, and the charges were important and had some foundation, not the least of these being ineptitude at Newbury. On 5 December Cromwell admitted before the committee that he was guilty of causing the present rift in Parliament. He went further and, in a spirit of humility, went on to urge that everyone should deny their private ambitions and work only for the public good. In specific terms this was soon turned into a piece of legislation, the Self-Denying Ordinance, which prohibited men like Cromwell and (say) Brereton, from simultaneously holding military office and a seat in Parliament. One or other had to be relinquished. The real catch in this was that a Lord

Oliver Cromwell by Robert Walker.

could not relinquish a seat in the Upper House and thus would have to give up military command. At one stroke the English peerage lost its control over the armed forces.

In effect the change was really one of personality rather than class. The new army was commanded by Sir Thomas, later Lord, Fairfax, and Cromwell and some others held onto both seats and office by the granting of special commissions. Parliament's executive, the Committee of Both Kingdoms at Derby House, which embraced both commoners and nobility, kept a firm grip on the army at least for the time being. Nevertheless a new spirit was present in Parliament's war effort, and this was to be crucial.

14. THE BATTLE OF NASEBY

The second battle of Newbury had taught Parliament important lessons about the leadership and composition of its army. The army that faced the King the following year at Naseby was the beginning of the modern professional British Army.

MAY – JULY 1645

Officer of the New Model Army.

THE NEW MODEL ARMY

OVER the dismal winter of 1644–5 Parliament dealt with two issues. The question of denying ambitions and working single-mindedly for the cause had turned from a statement of commitment into a fierce debate on who should hold military office. The creation of one single army, breaking down regional loyalties, was a major achievement.

This newly modelled army looked very fine on paper. The foot was to be 12,000 strong and would consist of twelve regiments. The horse would have 6,000 men, again in twelve regiments. There was also to be one dragoon regiment a thousand strong and an artillery train. Within each foot regiment the ratio of pike to musket would be the same and the horse troops would also remain the same size. On the other hand, the multiplicity of colours went. A standard coat in Venice red – the origin of the British redcoat – was introduced for both horse and foot. The colonel's colour, which had formed the background or field to the ensign or cornet and had once determined the colour of the uniform, was to be used as a lining. This would be displayed on the turned-back collars and cuffs of the soldiers. Regiments would still be referred to by the colonel's name and there was no standardization of the regimental ensign or cornet.

But as Lord Eythin had said of the dispositions on de Gomme's map of

Marston Moor, was there such a thing in the field? The horse was soon up to full strength, much of it being Eastern Association regiments reordered, likewise the dragoons under Colonel Okey. The foot was a different matter. Many desertions after Newbury had left Parliament able to muster only around 7,000 men. The next six months saw the wide use of conscription to fill the empty ranks. Even by Naseby, half-way through the year, it was not up to full strength. It was not viewed with much trepidation by its enemies. The Royalists mocked 'the new noddle' and this partly explains their over-confidence on the morning of 14 June 1645.

The New Model Army has often been portrayed as a politically astute army dedicated to religious and political change. True, within it were men who were aware early on of the problems of trying to negotiate with the King after the war was won. When discontent about arrears of pay and conditions of service in the planned campaign in Ireland pushed the army into alliance with the political radicals, the Levellers, there seemed for a while great potential for some social change. But even in the heady days at the close of 1647 its willingness to challenge the high command was limited. The army was not politically homogeneous and, like most armies, it served as a prop to the social and political status quo, not as an agent for sweeping change.

Naseby battlefield. The ridge in the centre is where Fairfax's foot stood, with Ireton's horse to the right on the ploughed field.

THE SIEGES OF LEICESTER AND OXFORD

T HESE two concurrent sieges offer a very great contrast. On the one hand that which occurred at Oxford was not pressed closely whilst that at Leicester was a short affair involving an assault by the besieging forces.

As Charles moved out of Oxford on 7 May to rendezvous with Maurice and Rupert and launch an attack on Sir William Brereton who was besieging Chester, Sir Thomas Fairfax moved on the King's capital. Fairfax had been appointed to command the New Model Army. Oliver Cromwell, technically debarred from military office by virtue of the Self-Denying Ordinance, was his Lieutenant-General of horse by virtue of special temporary commissions. Phillip Skippon, as Major-General, was in command of the foot and Henry Ireton was Commissary-General. The New Model settled down outside Oxford intent upon a slow siege. Fairfax used the time to train his new recruits and to get the diverse elements of the army used to working with each other. It was unlikely that he would be able to starve Oxford into surrender unless the King were to be away for some considerable time.

As the King's army marched northwards, news was brought to him of Brereton's retreat into Lancashire on 25 May. He was also informed of the Oxford siege. Brereton's retreat changed things considerably. Despite Rupert's and others' eagerness to undo Marston Moor by defeating the Scots in the North, a target was chosen for a demonstration of military power. The target was Leicester. Like all four of the major county towns in the region under Lord Loughborough's command it had long been a Parliamentarian garrison. It was not particularly strong or significant. Until mid-1644 Loughborough had been able to control the rest of the county despite the Parliamentarian interference from the

Leicester Guildhall.

town. This interference had been more effective of late as Loughborough's power had diminished after the fall of the Royalist North. More pertinent to the Royalist council of war which decided its fate was the fact that it was badly defended. The defensive walls which, because of the River Soar, only needed to cover three sides of the town, were over 3 miles (5 kilometres) long. The county committee and the council had built them to encompass the homes of their members who lived outside the medieval town walls. Normally these houses should have been pulled down and the earthworks built closer to the old town. The garrison was just too small to hold such a large area. In the town were only 1,770 regular Leicester troops, a detachment of dragoons under Major Innes, who had been bribed to help out, and the evacuees from the

garrison of Kirkby Bellars who fled to the town as the Royalists approached, making a total of around 2,000. The King's army of around 10,000 passed through Ashby de la Zouch, collecting parts of Lord Loughborough's remaining forces on 26 May. On the following day it went through Loughborough town. The King slept at Cotes Hall that night, the site of the small battle in 1644. On 28 May the horse appeared outside Leicester and two days later the town was surrounded. Rupert constructed gun batteries opposite the Newarke – the fourteenth-century addition to the town defences which was the weakest section of walling.

The town refused Rupert's demands that they surrender and on the afternoon of 30 May the bombardment began. It took just three hours to smash through the wall. At midnight the town was stormed at four points, the breach made at the Rawdykes, Horsefair Leas, Belgrave gate and St Margaret's parish in the north-east. It was a hard fight. The garrison was supported by the men and women from the town who loaded guns and built barricades. They all fought desperately to keep the Royalists out but to no avail. By two o'clock the market place had been reached and fighting came to an end. Possibly as many as 500 members of the garrison and the brave townsfolk were killed. The Parliamentarian press turned it into a massacre and this was later dredged up in the King's trial where it was asserted that the King had ridden through Leicester denying quarter. It was tragedy enough without any embellishment.

Lord Loughborough was given the town as a base for the reconstruction of his war effort which had lain in tatters

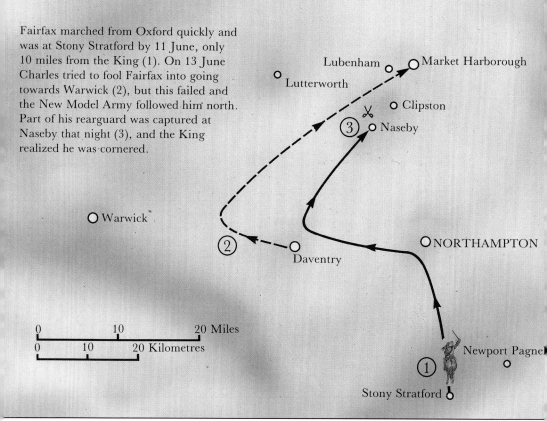

LEICESTER O

N

Fairfax marched from Oxford quickly and was at Stony Stratford by 11 June, only 10 miles from the King (1). On 13 June Charles tried to fool Fairfax into going towards Warwick (2), but this failed and the New Model Army followed him north. Part of his rearguard was captured at Naseby that night (3), and the King realized he was cornered.

Lubenham o o Market Harborough
Lutterworth o

Clipston o

③ o Naseby

O Warwick

② O
Daventry

O NORTHAMPTON

0   10   20 Miles
0   10   20 Kilometres

Newport Pagnell

①

Stony Stratford

since 1644. He began to rebuild the defences on a more practical scale and recruit a new army.

The King now turned his attention to Oxford. Fairfax had begun to attack the outposts by the end of May. Gaunt House fell on 31 May, but Boarstall House withstood many assaults. The Royalists had abandoned and burned down Godstow House and set fire to the suburbs of Wolvercote and North Hinksey. The meadow lands around the town had been flooded. Fairfax, based at Headington, ordered the construction of earthworks on the eastern side of the Cherwell and probably aimed to attack the north side of the town. After the fall of Leicester he determined to go north to seek out the King, but the New Model was in effect controlled by the Committee of Both Kingdoms and Fairfax sought their permission. On 3 June he was given a free hand and the siege of Oxford was abandoned.

Naseby field can be reached from the M1 by using Junction 20 and the A427 towards Theddingworth. From Sibbertoft there is a minor road direct to Naseby. The modern disregard for the past will soon be more manifest here than at any other battlefield in this book. Arguably the most important of the Civil War battlefields, Naseby is soon to be ruined by the building of a link road, between the M1 and A1, right across it. The field is, at present, beautiful countryside and is unusually integral. From the monument just to the west of the Sibbertoft road and reached by a footpath, the traveller can see the majority of the field. To the north is Broadmoor, from where the Royalists advanced. Immediately to the front of the monument are the slopes of Red Hill where the action took place. The Sibbertoft road was then a track leading to enclosed fields on the moor. To the left of the monument is the line of Rupert's charge and the attack on the baggage wagons. It is over this line of attack that the new road will run.

154

THE BATTLE

As FAIRFAX moved north from Oxford, the King began to move south. The council of war in Leicester had decided to go to the rescue of Oxford. It was not a popular decision. Some, including Rupert, had preferred a march north. The Northern horse, the remnants of Newcastle's army, now under Marmaduke Langdale, were also angry for they had wanted to go into Yorkshire and fight Lord Fairfax and the Scots. Langdale and the King remonstrated with them. Charles promised to go north once Oxford was secured. Unimpressed even by the word of a king, they set off homewards anyway. The Royalist plan was to go to Market Harborough in south Leicestershire and wait for Lord Goring to join them with the forces which he had been ordered to bring out of the South-west. But Goring was too involved in the siege of Taunton to be drawn northwards until he had won. There was also promise of men from Wales under Gerrard but they were still marching to join the King.

Fairfax, too, was looking for support. Cromwell was in East Anglia getting in recruits. Colonel Vermuyden was in the North Midlands where he had been shadowing the King with a brigade of horse. On 8 June he turned up at Newport Pagnell and three days later Fairfax arrived at Stony Stratford where he waited for Cromwell. Further north the King dithered about. Instead of going north or moving nearer to sources of support, he had gathered a herd of cattle, moved on Daventry and dispatched them to Oxford under escort. He certainly knew that Fairfax had left off the siege by this time and the town could well look after itself. By waiting at Daventry for the return of the escort they succeeded in getting close to the New Model. It would now be difficult for the Royalist army to shake off Fairfax if it did try to go north. It was 11 June, when Fairfax arrived at

Stony Stratford before the escort returned to the King's army. Fairfax was only 10 miles (16 kilometres) away but it was not until the afternoon of the following day that this was realized, when a scouting party ran into the New Model south of Daventry. The Royalists moved east onto Borough Hill, but they were not attacked. They stayed on the hill until 13 June and then moved north, followed by the New Model which Cromwell had now rejoined. The King was heading back to Leicestershire where he hoped to gather reinforcements from Lord Loughborough's garrisons and other parts of the Midlands. It had been belatedly realized that Goring was staying put and Gerrard was nowhere near; and the search for troops was frantic. The Royalists tried a diversionary march towards Warwick to lose the New Model before it set off to Market Harborough, but Fairfax was too close to be shaken off. The feint west was entirely wasted as Cromwell and the horse dogged their every step. On that night the Royalist army camped in the Lubbenham and Market Harborough area. A shoddy rearguard was left at a small village called Naseby to look out for the enemy. The King and Rupert were unaware how close Fairfax was until Ireton arrived at Naseby and captured some of the slumbering rearguards.

There was an emergency council of war at Harborough that night, where it was realized that it was too dangerous to continue to withdraw. But Rupert was opposed to the idea of taking on the New Model which had around 13,000 men to the King's 8–9,000 men. He was overruled. The idiot factor on the council, Lord Digby, was in favour of attacking; both he and the King disparaged the New Model, repeating ridiculous gossip about quarrels among its regiments. This combined to create a gung-ho attitude fortified by self-confidence after taking Leicester. Sensible counsel was overridden.

A contemporary plan of the battle of Naseby.

As Fairfax brought his army up to the Naseby area in the early hours of 14 June, he selected a strong position on a ridge east of the village about 1½ miles (2½ kilometres) south of Clipston. From here the Royalist army over in Leicestershire could be clearly seen. It was an admirable position: the front was protected by boggy ground and the ridge was quite high. Actually, it was too good a position: Cromwell and his commander decided to move off it and shift west, as no army would have attacked them had they remained on that ridge. They moved back towards Naseby and drew up the army on the

156

Red Hill and Mill Hill ridge, directly north of the village. On the right Cromwell commanded the majority of the old Eastern Association horse – 3,500 men in all, in three lines. The first of these consisted mainly of his own regiment, Fairfax's and Edmund Whalley's; the second of Sheffield's, Pyre's and part of Fiennes's; the rear consisted of the rest of Fiennes's, Rossiter's Lincolnshire horse and the East Anglian horse Cromwell had brought with him. In the centre Skippon led the 6,000 or so foot. Five regiments were placed in the front line and three behind, with the final

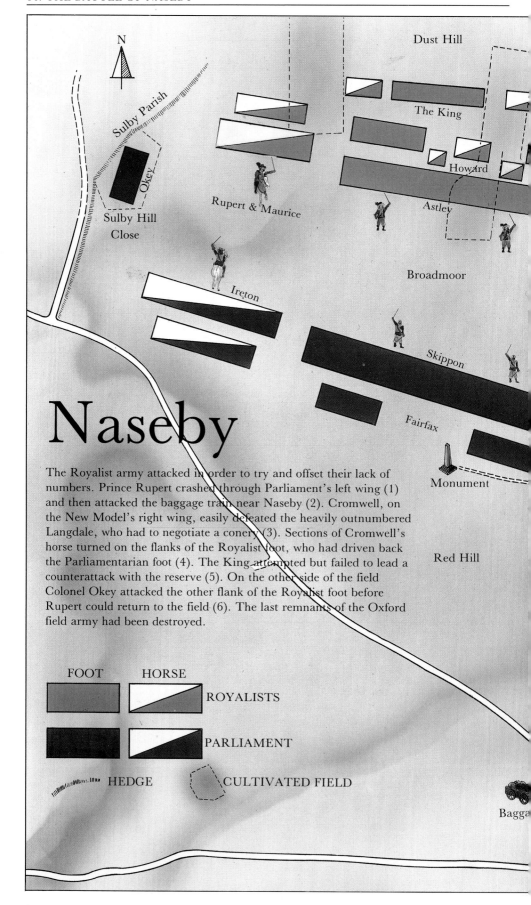

N

Dust Hill

Sulby Parish

The King

Okey

Howard

Sulby Hill
Close

Rupert & Maurice

Astley

Broadmoor

Ireton

Skippon

Fairfax

Naseby

Monument

The Royalist army attacked in order to try and offset their lack of
numbers. Prince Rupert crashed through Parliament's left wing (1)
and then attacked the baggage train near Naseby (2). Cromwell, on
the New Model's right wing, easily defeated the heavily outnumbered
Langdale, who had to negotiate a conery (3). Sections of Cromwell's
horse turned on the flanks of the Royalist foot, who had driven back
the Parliamentarian foot (4). The King attempted but failed to lead a
counterattack with the reserve (5). On the other side of the field
Colonel Okey attacked the other flank of the Royalist foot before
Rupert could return to the field (6). The last remnants of the Oxford
field army had been destroyed.

Red Hill

FOOT   HORSE

ROYALISTS

PARLIAMENT

HEDGE   CULTIVATED FIELD

Bagga

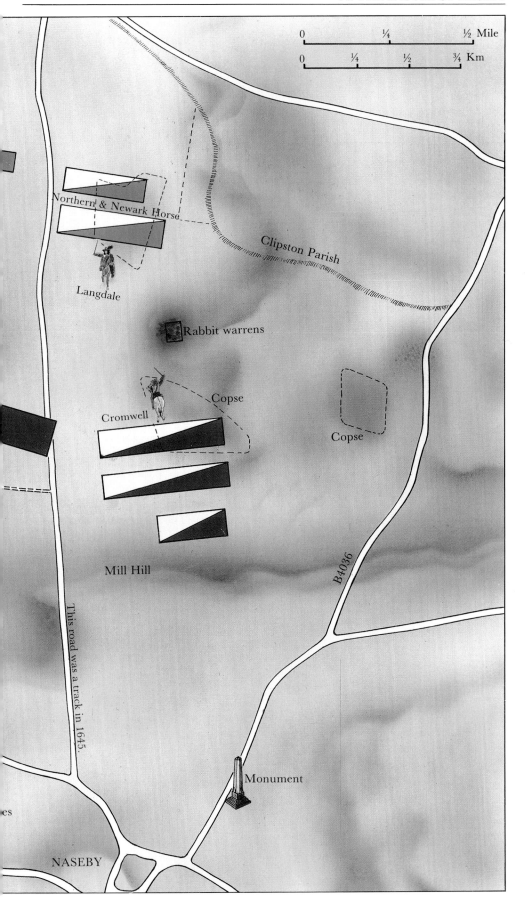

The monument to the battle of Naseby.

regiment under Colonel Pride in the rear. On the left Ireton had six regiments of horse in two lines including more of the horse Cromwell had recently led in.

Prince Rupert had observed the shift in position and hoped to exploit it. The Royalist army was brought up on to Dust Hill. He had not wanted this fight at all, but as Commander-in-Chief he had to find every advantage possible, especially as his army was so much the smaller. Between Dust Hill and Red Hill lay the Broad Moor which had several fields carved out of it and was used for growing cereal crops. To the west of Broad Moor was Sulby parish separated from Naseby by a large double-row hedge. To the east the

boundary with Clipston parish was most probably similarly marked. If so this created a sort of funnel, opening out in the direction of Naseby, through which the Royalist army had to travel. Other geographical features are important. To the right front of the King's forces abutting Sulby hedge seems to have been an enclosure called Sulby Close. To the left front of the Royalist line was a conery (a man-made series of rabbit warrens for keeping rabbits for meat) complete with a warren house.

As the Royalists made their appearance Fairfax withdrew his whole line about a hundred paces, back onto the reverse slope of the Red Hill/Mill Hill ridge. This hid them from any cannon fire and also kept his new recruits from seeing the frightening spectacle of an army in full battle array coming towards them. Furthermore, as the Royalist army approached them it would appear to grow as it emerged from the strictures of the funnel effect. As to gunfire, the Parliamentarian commander need not have worried: the Royalist artillery was struggling along well to the rear of Rupert's rapid march. At the same time as he withdrew the main army, Fairfax put Okey well to the front of Ireton's flank in Sulby Close from where they could fire upon any attack launched on his left.

The Royalist army had the foot in the centre led by Lord Astley. It was drawn up in two lines interspersed with some horse regiments brigaded under Sir Thomas Howard. On the right flank was Prince Maurice with the Oxford horse; his own and his brother's regiments along with the Queen's regiment formed his front rank. He had a rear rank of two regiments. On the left flank Marmaduke Langdale had the Newark horse and the recently returned Northern horse. Langdale however, had less than 2,000 to face Cromwell's 3,500.

At ten o'clock in the morning the King's army descended Dust Hill and hurried across the Broad Moor. Rupert had joined Maurice on the right wing and it was they who hit the enemy slightly ahead of the others. Some of Rupert's horse collided with Sulby Close and rode into the field where Okey's men stood. They were driven out or killed and the dragoons continued firing on the Royalist horse as it trotted and then cantered past. Just after Fairfax's forlorn hope pulled back out of the way, Rupert and Maurice crashed into Ireton's front line. Ireton at the head of his regiment drove straight through a gap between two regiments opposed to him and turned on the flank of the Royalist foot; but the rest of his line crumbled, the Royalists rode straight on unscathed by Ireton's

from an Original Painting.   M.Ld. Gucht. fecit.

Henry Ireton.

resistance and defeated his second line as well. Ireton's wing was wrecked. But here was a fatal flaw. Instead of stopping to deal with Skippon in the same way, Ireton had swept round upon Astley. In the mistaken belief that he had won the horse battle, Prince Rupert and the horse charged on and attacked the baggage wagon to the north-west of Naseby.

On the opposite flank where action was joined almost as quickly, a model lesson was taught. Cromwell counter-attacked Langdale at about the time the Royalist horse were negotiating the conery. The New Model horse swamped Langdale's front line and the first to break were those units which were assaulted by Whalley's regiment. They turned and hit the rear line and the rot began. Quite simply the Newark and Northern horse were overwhelmed as the right end of Cromwell's line attacked their flanks. A rout began. But Cromwell only sent a small portion of his wing after them. The rear two lines of his horse were undamaged and these he turned in on the Royalist foot.

In the centre of the field Astley and Skippon clashed after the horse on the flanks had collided. Astley, heavily outnumbered but far from outclassed, pushed up the hill and drove back the New Model's front line. This turned and ran into the second line. It remains an academic point as to whether this second line would have held Astley or not. The truth of it was that it did not have to. Cromwell's flank attack defeated the Royalist foot. For a brief moment there was the possibility of the King leading an attack on Cromwell's men as they turned on Astley. Indeed he prepared to fall on them with the remains of the Newark horse and his own footguards which formed a reserve, only to be held back by the Earl of Carnwrath. It may well have made little difference: Cromwell still had men to spare and would probably have been able to deal with the attack without turning from destroying Astley's left flank.

Rupert was repulsed from the baggage train and returned to the field. It was too late: all he could do was make his way to the King and join in the retreat. In the last stages of the battle Okey led his dragoons into Astley's right flank. There was nothing to do but surrender. Only one regiment fought on – Prince Rupert's regiment of foot which had been a part of the reserve and carried on either bravely trying to give the others time to get away or foolishly failing to admit defeat. Fairfax himself led this final attack on them.

Parliament's new army lost a couple of hundred dead and the King's old one over a thousand. Once a retreat began the casualties started to mount. On the Royalist forces ran, on to Leicester where Lord Loughborough had only

had a fortnight to undertake repairs, and on. The King stayed at Ashby that night and went west the next day. With him went a portion of the horse. Many more stayed in Leicester, too tired to go any further.

In that far-too-often-excused flush of violence after a hard-won fight, the King's pursuers killed, cut and maimed the women found with the King's baggage wagon. In the cold light of day, the New Model soldiers claimed that they thought they were being attacked by popish witches uttering curses and waving swords. It was pure cant. They were 'assailed' by the terrified wives and lovers of the Royalist soldiers defending themselves from the brutalities of male aggression.

Apart from this perpetual stain, it was a notable victory. The King's only experienced field army was wrecked; it was likely that the foot were lost for ever. Lord Loughborough's new capital was attacked two days later and the guns which had battered down the Newarke in May were, in the hands of new owners, turned again on the town walls. Loughborough, by his judicious surrender, saved the survivors of Naseby within the town from certain captivity. He also smuggled five hundred valuable horses out of the town under cover of darkness. All of this would be necessary if there was to be any new military effort.

GORING AT LANGPORT

ONE of the only hopes the King had left was to build a new army centred upon Lord Goring's army of 7,000 in the South-west. Fairfax knew this too and he marched southwards to deal with the problem. As the New Model approached via Stonehenge, Dorchester and on towards the River Yeo, Goring crossed the river near Yeovil. Fairfax followed Goring towards Langport. The Royalists were intending to retreat towards the King via Bridgwater. If he had reached the West Midlands, then the King would have been able to create an army of the same size as the New Model.

To try to lure Fairfax away from the route to Bridgwater, Goring sent the buffoon George Porter towards Taunton. It worked. Fairfax, now supported by Edward Massey and the forces out of Gloucestershire, sent 5,000 men after Porter. It had been foolhardy of Goring to trust him. Porter was caught at Ilchester and defeated. Goring was left alone at Langport. On 10 July Fairfax moved through Somerton on the road to Langport and Goring dug in.

His position was a strong one. There was only one crossing over the brook, Wagg Ryhne, and the marshland bordering it. He placed musketeers and cannon on his side of the brook to defend the road. His problem was one of numbers, for the New Model was by far the larger force and Fairfax easily out-gunned him. Within a short time Goring's guns were silenced. 1,500 musketeers were massed against his centre and the Royalist musketeers were overwhelmed. Cromwell's regiment of horse crossed the brook and drove back Goring's horse, giving more of the New Model horse time to get over Wagg Rhyne. Goring's small army was defeated and retreated to Bridgwater.

Goring continued into Devon; his casualties had been light but desertions were increasing and his army dwindled. He was amongst a population which was increasingly reluctant to hand provisions to a defeated army. Goring's men became less and less patient and violence escalated. The pacifist movement which sprang up in this region as well as elsewhere – the clubmen – actually favoured neither side. However, when faced with what was rapidly becoming an unruly mob and the New Model, whose men were still at this point being regularly paid and maintained good order, it is not surprising that they took to helping General Fairfax. With an efficient Parliamentarian army and a populace increasingly fed up with the war, the Royalist cause was well and truly on the wane.

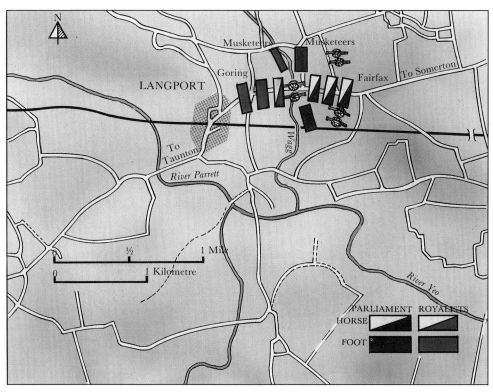

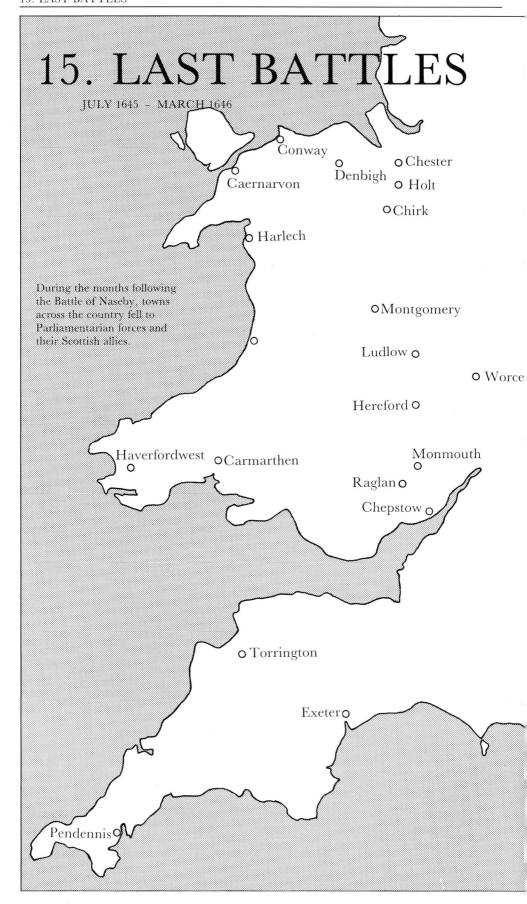

15. LAST BATTLES

JULY 1645 – MARCH 1646

Conway

Caernarvon

Denbigh

Chester

Holt

Chirk

Harlech

During the months following the Battle of Naseby, towns across the country fell to Parliamentarian forces and their Scottish allies.

Montgomery

Ludlow

Worce

Hereford

Haverfordwest

Carmarthen

Monmouth

Raglan

Chepstow

Torrington

Exeter

Pendennis

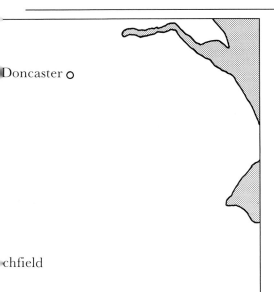

Doncaster o

chfield

w-on-the-Wold

o Oxford

LONDON
o

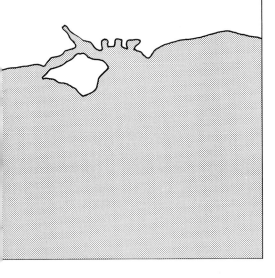

ROWTON HEATH

A FTER NASEBY Charles I sought to create a new army. It was not long before he had a collection of some surviving horse, about 3,000 men, but this was insufficient to tackle the New Model. The King toyed with several notions. He hoped at one point to go north into Scotland and join Montrose. He marched as far as Doncaster before turning back in the face of the Scots and the northern Parliamentarians. In September Rupert surrendered Bristol to Fairfax and the New Model. This left the King with no base in the West. Charles again looked north. He marched to Chester which was again under siege from the indomitable Brereton. On 18 September Charles had left Raglan Castle. By 22 September he was at Chirk and the decision to go to Chester had been made. With his lifeguard, the King pressed on into the town, whilst Langdale and the horse attacked Colonel Michael Jones's small besieging force. Jones had at this point reached the city suburbs by the time the King arrived at Chirk. The day after, Langdale crossed the River Dee at Holt with 2–3,000 horse in Jones's rear.

Once over the river, Langdale pressed on to Rowton Heath which was then open land to the south-east of Chester; much of it is now built over. General Sydenham Pointz had been shadowing the King since the opening of the campaign and now he followed Langdale. He marched to Hatton Heath from Whitchurch on the same evening as the Royalists arrived on neighbouring Rowton Heath. Pointz hoped to evade Langdale and link up with Jones and then to bottle the King in the city, but his intentions were discovered. Langdale turned his back on Jones and Chester, and faced Pointz. The Parliamentarians were in enclosed fields adjoining Rowton Heath and Langdale hoped to lure them out and attack them as they came.

Naturally Pointz was reluctant to do so. Nevertheless, the Parliamentarian horse did leave the protection of the hedges and either attacked Langdale or attempted to pass down the road to Chester (A41). Either way they were defeated by Langdale and pushed back.

It proved only a temporary setback. Jones sent a few horse and some musketeers from the Chester suburbs. As both Langdale and Pointz only had horse, the fire-power of the musketeers proved valuable. With supporting fire-power Pointz attacked the Royalist horse and this time he won. Langdale began a retreat towards Chester.

The King sent reinforcements out of the city under Lord Lichfield, but they were caged in the suburbs by Jones. Langdale's retreat was carried on into the same suburbs. It was now a disaster. In the narrow lanes to the south of Chester's walls Langdale's men became lost in a maze. Jones's musketeers could pick them off one by one as Pointz's horse pushed them further into Swan Lane, Strickland Lane and Firkin Lane. Although the heath has now gone, the traveller can still wander around these dreadful lanes and imagine the panic of horse and man. Fortunately many of the Royalists were able to surrender.

The King's small force had been badly mauled and whilst the ever-stupid Lord Digby attempted to make light of the disaster, the King fled into Wales. Chester fell under a far stricter, and in the end successful, siege. Charles' vain hopes of joining Montrose came to an end. In the same month the greatest of all Royalists also succumbed at Philliphaugh.

The war was now lost and wise men like Rupert knew it and grudgingly accepted it. Others, of course, could not and would not. Lord Digby and Langdale set off into the North to raise the area for the King. They took with them the remains of the Northern horse. At Sherburn in Elmet they too were defeated.

The King still hoped to create a new army and he again turned at the end of the year to Wales and the Marcher counties. Lord Astley was commissioned to create a new army and supply 2,000 men to Oxford and relieve Chester. He was to keep the port open to receive the expected reserves from Ireland once a treaty was signed with the Catholic Confederation. Astley was to work with Lord Loughborough who still clung on to several garrisons in the North Midlands. But Loughborough was having serious arguments with some of his subordinates, particularly Harvey Bagot at Lichfield. Astley refused to support Loughborough yet he demoted Bagot to deputy governor and made Thomas Tyldesley governor of the town and close. Furthermore he

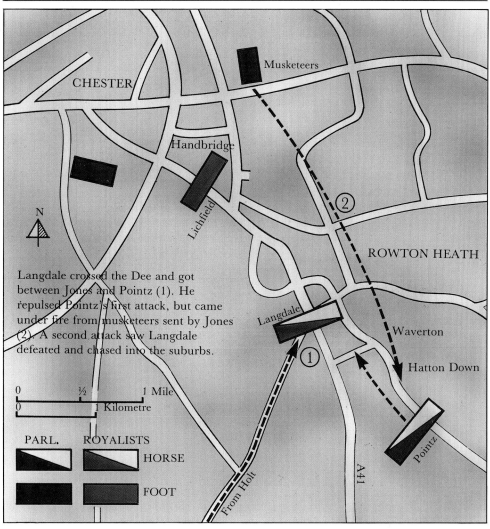

CHESTER

Musketeers

Handbridge

Lichfield

N

ROWTON HEATH

②

Langdale crossed the Dee and got
between Jones and Pointz (1). He
repulsed Pointz's first attack, but came
under fire from musketeers sent by Jones
(2). A second attack saw Langdale
defeated and chased into the suburbs.

Langdale

Waverton

①

Hatton Down

0   ½   1 Mile

0   1 Kilometre

PARL.   ROYALISTS

HORSE

FOOT

From Holt

A41

Pointz

*(Left) A model of King Charles watching the battle of
Rowton Heath from King Charles Tower, Chester.*

replaced Loughborough's Sir Andrew
Kniveton, governor of Tutbury with
Sir William Blakiston of the old North
Army. This seems to have been too
much for Loughborough to bear. He
had been the chief Royalist in the
region: now superseded, he surrendered his large garrison at Ashby
and went into exile. He gave up this
important garrison at a good time, for
he managed to free both his own and his
brother's estate from sequestration and
saved many of his loyal subordinates
from the same fate. Nevertheless
sections of what had once been
Loughborough's army joined up with
Astley and secured a large part of the
West Midlands.

The only other Royalist force, the
remains of Lord Goring's army, in

Rowton Heath can be reached on the
A41 and is about 3 miles (4¾
kilometres) out of Chester. Most of
the action took place on the line of
this road. Pointz had marched
towards the city from Whitchurch,
and Langdale crossed the River Dee
at Holt on the A534/B5130. Indeed
Langdale's route would have been
along the line of the latter road out of
Holt to Aldford, where a minor road
branches off to Rowton. The first
part of the battle would have been in
the Rowton/Hatton area. Much of
this is now built over. The final
scenes of the day took place under
Chester's walls and some of them are
still traced by the suburbs to the
south-east.

Cornwall, now under the great Lord Hopton, came to grief in February. He and his army were caught at Torrington by the greater Sir Thomas Fairfax and defeated. Only Astley was left now as Hopton surrendered himself and disbanded his forces. Astley had gathered 2,000 horse and 1,500 foot. Some of these were placed in garrisons during January and February, but by March 1646 Astley prepared to take 3,000 men to Oxford. After he left Worcester he was trailed by Sir William Brereton. On 21 March Astley was caught at Stow-on-the-Wold and defeated. The last battle of the first Civil War did not last long. As the old Astley sat on a drum head amongst his captors he advised them to 'Go and play boys lest you fall out amongst yourselves'. It proved to be a prophetic statement.

Stow Church, where Royalist prisoners were locked up after the battle.

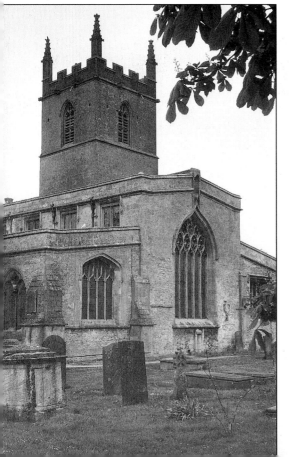

WALES AND ITS CASTLES

DURING 1645 the Royalists' hold on Wales weakened significantly, often because of their inability to work with each other. For example, the Archbishop of York was incapable of working productively with Sir John Owen (the two of them held Conway, castle and town). In the end Owen took over the castle and the Archbishop complained to the King, only to have Owen accuse him of treason. On 9 June the Royalist forces from Monmouth, Worcestershire and Herefordshire were defeated as they marched to Ludlow; two castles in west Shropshire fell to Parliament and the castle of Montgomery changed hands as Sir John Price changed sides, for the fourth time, and declared himself on the side of Parliament.

In July Charles was attempting to create a new army in Wales and the Scottish army marched south to deal with him. By 25 July the Scots besieged Hereford. The Welsh gentry gathered together a large number of soldiers but opposed the appointment of regular army officers to command them. They desired to control this army and also wished to appoint governors to the castles in the Principality. Within a few weeks Haverfordwest had fallen and the remains of Pembrokeshire fell into Parliamentarian hands.

After the battle of Rowton Heath the King was briefly based in North Wales. By now he had given in to the idea of the gentry's 'Peaceable Army' as there was no possibility of creating a new field army. The Peaceable Army was of questionable loyalty and, as Charles left the Principality, garrisons fell to Parliament's new ex-Royalist local leader, Sir Trevor Williams.

Chepstow and Monmouth fell in October and Carmarthen surrendered to Rowland Laughharne and his local Parliamentarian forces. By November only Aberystwyth Castle held out in all of South and Mid-Wales. Lord Byron

EVILS OF WAR

BATTLES and skirmishes were only one feature of the war in Britain. More than any other of the country's civil wars, these wars penetrated deep into society as a whole. It was once asserted that a ploughing labourer had to be removed from the field of Marston Moor before the battle began. The story further implied that the man was utterly unaware of the conflict then raging. The story is mere picturesque nonsense, a later society poking fun at the 'less intelligent' times which had preceded it.

Battles did not take place on every doorstep, but marching armies passed through many areas. Yet it was taxation which probably brought home to most people the reality of the war. Parliament and the King both imposed a series of levies on the counties to pay for it. The Royalist' 'Contribution' and the Parliamentarian 'Assessment' were property and income taxes which were supposed to pay for the everyday running of the armed forces. There were excises, which by 1645 had been extended to foods and would affect the vast majority of the population, even those without the wherewithal to pay Assessment or Contribution. The estates of both sides' enemies were sequestered. The profits from them – rents, money from produce or timber, etc. – were used to further the war.

When collection was impracticable, such as when the Royalists controlled large areas from which Parliamentarian garrisons had to eke out an existence, or at the end of the war when the Royalists were thrust into the same position, then plunder and theft were substituted. In some areas neither side had ever maintained absolute mastery and if villages were not constantly plundered then they were shared, often faced with

Cartoon of a plundering soldier.

paying double taxes because of their predicament. In the South-west, as Goring's forces were driven from pillar to post, the looting was dreadful and violence spread from the confines of the battlefield. Murder was committed in several areas and blamed upon the soldiers, and soldiers and civilians engaged in brawls in the towns and garrisons of Britain.

Sieges were perhaps the most distressing feature of the war. They were the seventeenth century's version of the bombing of civilian populations in the new barbarous age. The whole population of a garrison town under attack was bound up in the violence and deprivation. Starving a garrison out, as at Chester in 1646 and Colchester in 1648, meant also starving the inhabitants. All were rationed and all driven to eating horsemeat and sometimes rats just to survive. The Civil Wars were a grim lesson to the people of England, Scotland, Ireland and Wales.

Chepstow Castle.

intended to utilize North Wales if he was forced to surrender Chester. When he did so, to Sir William Brereton at the beginning of February 1646, he entered Wales, where he was treated as an interfering outsider and received little cooperation. Moreover, his mission to bring over troops from Ireland after the hoped-for treaty with the Catholic Confederation, filled the locals with horror. By the end of May Sir Thomas Middleton had blockaded Byron in Caernarvon and in June he surrendered. Raglan and Pendennis held out until August; Denbigh until October. Holt remained Royalist until January 1647 and Harlech only surrendered on 15 March 1647, over ten months after Charles had surrendered to the Scots.

PEACE AND UNCERTAINTY

WHEN CHARLES handed himself over to the Scots at Newark on 6 May 1646, he did not really intend thereby to end the war. He had intended to drive a wedge between the Scots and the English Parliament and enlist the former's help against the latter if possible. But it was not to be; yet. Newark surrendered within a couple of days, but Charles's circular which ordered the surrender of the other Royalist garrisons met with a limited response. The war dragged on into the summer and for Harlech it did not end until the following year. Charles failed to enlist the help of the Scots and they could not come to any

out of joint. Crops failed in the harsh and wet weather and Parliament's continued taxes, especially excise, bit hard into the finances of the people. Moreover the army was now unpaid; arrears stretched back over forty weeks for the foot by mid-1647. In response the soldiers turned for political help to the radical group, the Levellers. The joint army/Leveller programme embraced not only the question of arrears, but also the question of service in the planned campaign in Ireland; it included pensions for widows; indemnity before the law for any act carried out in war time that could, in peace, be construed as illegal; and, most important, a new system of government. A broader franchise was envisaged producing a one-chamber assembly filled with representatives whose seats were distributed according to population size. There was no role for a monarch or a House of Lords. Whilst the rank and file and the junior officers pressed through their elected representatives (agitators for these ends), the high command, the grandees, were more conservative. In October 1647, frustrated at Parliament's inability to come to terms with the King, the grandees, Fairfax, Cromwell and Ireton in particular, presented the King with their own propositions – the Heads of the Proposals. These were perhaps the best offers Charles received but he rejected them. He had good hopes of winning the Scots over to his side this time. It was clear from the Putney Debates, where the grandees met the army Levellers, that these two groups were a mile apart in terms of their views of the new England. Nevertheless the escape of the King from Hampton Court and his flight to the Isle of Wight, threw the two sections of the army together. It was lucky for them that they were so, for England was again to fall into the ruin of war.

firm agreement with him either. In some despair they handed or rather sold him to the English in return for payment of arrears of soldiers' pay.

Needless to say, the peace was not stable. Charles still refused to enter into negotiations with any resolve. He kept an eye open for divisions amongst his enemies and for any chance of enlisting foreign or domestic aid. There were fundamental sticking-points in the attempt to come to terms. Charles would not surrender his friends to Parliament's justice. He could not give up his position as the head of a national church nor could he concede to any more emasculation of his kingly power.

In the country as a whole, times were

16. THE SECOND CIVIL WAR

MAY – AUGUST 1648

THERE WERE two distinct incitements which brought about this second war. The first and perhaps most predictable, was the King's alliance with the Scots. The second was frustration with Parliament's government coupled with personal dissatisfaction felt by some of its hitherto adherents.

Once the King had escaped from Hampton Court on 8 November he began to negotiate with the Scots. This time he acquiesced to a three-year period of Presbyterianism in England. By 28 December 1647 he had broken off discussions with the English Parliament and plans for a Scottish invasion were underway.

King Charles imprisoned in Carisbrooke Castle.

Pembroke

Berwick

This second war was more a collection of loosely related incidents resembling the latter days of the previous war rather than a full-scale conflict.

Carlisle

Kendal

Settle

Lancaster

Wetherby

Clitheroe

Pontefract

Preston

Wigan

Manchester

Warrington

Derby

Uttoxeter

Nottingham

Colchester

LONDON

Rochester

Canterbury

Maidstone

Carisbrooke

Pembroke Castle.

Yet it was not this which sparked off the actual renewal of war. Pembroke Castle's governor, Colonel Poyer, declared himself a Royalist, once sure of Charles's alliance with the Scots. He had hitherto been a supporter of Parliament and his change of heart was not really a political one. He had not been paid for some time and was about to be replaced. He did not like Parliamentarian rule in South Wales and was, like many others, jealous of the prestige of the New Model Army officers. He was not the only Welsh dissident; Rowland Laugharne, a prime mover in the destruction of the Royalist cause in Wales, also declared his support for the King.

In response Cromwell was sent with sections of the New Model Army to deal with the situation. Laugharne was soon dealt with and in May the siege of Pembroke was begun.

THE KENTISH REVOLT

O N 11 MAY as Cromwell marched into Wales the Kentish revolt began. Kent had always had a strong Royalist faction, but the county's proximity to London had long stifled any expression of this tendency. But by 1648 Parliamentarian rule as exhibited by Anthony Weldon and the county committee had become thoroughly odious. The abolition of Christmas provoked serious rioting in Canterbury on 25 December 1647. On 10 May 1648 the leading figures from these riots were brought before the Assizes. When the grand jury threw out the charges and then began to canvass a petition attacking the county committee, Weldon tried to suppress it. The reaction was immediate and by the end of the month as many as 10,000 people assembled near Rochester and appointed the Earl of Norwich, Lord Goring's father, to lead them.

Sir Thomas, now Lord, Fairfax had with him only a small section of the New Model, about 7,000 men, to deal with the escalating situation. However he was not dealing with a trained army and at Blackheath about a thousand rebels surrendered to him. Several of the coastal towns and forts had been occupied by Royalists. At Maidstone Fairfax defeated the garrison and drove them out. At this point Norwich's forces began to split up, some of them reinforcing the small coastal forts, and only 3,000 dashed upon London with the Earl. Canterbury was soon retaken by Fairfax and more would-be Royalists drifted away; some actually went to join the Royalist fleet under Prince Charles.

London did not fall to the rebels and when Phillip Skippon closed the gates of the city yet more of Norwich's men drifted away. A small group of more hardy spirits ferried themselves across the Thames and joined Royalists in Essex. These men included Sir George Lisle, Sir Charles Lucas, Lord

James, Marquis of Hamilton.

Loughborough and Lord Capel. With these men and their levies, the Earl of Norwich entered Colchester, hotly pursued by Fairfax and his small army. Once in the town the Royalists were soon bottled up. Cut off from the Royalist fleet the only hope these men had was that the Scottish invasion would either result in their relief or that Fairfax would be drawn away by it.

THE BATTLE OF PRESTON

A S EARLY AS APRIL, Marmaduke Langdale had crossed the border between England and Scotland and captured Berwick and Carlisle. After that nothing else happened until 8 July when the Marquis of Hamilton led the Scottish army into Carlisle. Again there was a great pause: for six days. Langdale joined Hamilton there and the combined forces came to around 12,000 men. Three quarters of them were Scots; some of them, like William Baillie and John Middleton, had fought against the King in the first Civil War. Hamilton and the army progressed very slowly. So slowly that General John Lambert, who had been awaiting his arrival on the east-coast route, was able to cross the Pennines and follow them with two regiments of foot and four of horse. At Penrith Hamilton was joined by a further contingent from Scotland: he now had 10,000 foot and 4,000 horse. More men were expected.

Pembroke Castle fell to Cromwell on 11 July and this freed him to go north. By 27 July his horse had arrived at Appleby. Lambert had pulled back over the Pennines, either to stop Hamilton heading for Pontefract Castle, now in Royalist hands, or because he wished to go north and recross the hills and get between Hamilton and Scotland. Hamilton still behaved as if there were no hurry. He stopped at Kendal for a whole week, where his army behaved so badly that potential support in the area faded away. As he reached Hornsby, Cromwell and Lambert joined forces at Wetherby. Hamilton again stayed put for two days, but his army was now much bigger, around 20,000. Cromwell and Lambert had under 9,000 and only 6,500 of these were seasoned troops. As the Scots pressed on to Manchester to join up with an already aborted rising under Lord Byron, Cromwell crossed the Pennines and marched to Clitheroe on 16 August: he was now at Hamilton's rear. The Scottish army was spread out over 20 miles (32 kilometres), with its horse in front at Wigan and the foot trailing at Preston, when Cromwell attacked Langdale on 17 August. Langdale was marching towards Preston on the road from Settle and Lancaster (A6). Langdale turned and placed his foot on the Longridge to Preston road (B6243) in the enclosed fields on either side. His front was protected by the boggy ground west of Ribble Moor. The lane turned into a quagmire as Cromwell's horse tried to push down it. The Parliamentarian foot were traversing the enclosures on either side of the road, attempting to push Langdale's men back from the road sides to let the horse through. It was a nasty, bloody fight with Cromwell's

The Battle of Preston by Charles Cattermole.

men at last bludgeoning their way through. As they cleared the road they turned on the flanks of Langdale's foot and drove them from the fields.

With Langdale out of the way, Cromwell fell upon the Scottish foot at Preston as they attempted to cross the Ribble. Hamilton himself was nearly cut off from the river. In the town itself there was a great deal of vicious fighting as Cromwell's men pressed in. Most of the Scottish foot got over the Ribble and Darwen over the respective bridges, but Hamilton had to cross by boat as the New Model got to the bridgehead. As the Marquis set off towards Wigan to fetch the horse, he left detachments to hold the bridges. This attempt to hold Cromwell back failed and 4,000 Scots and Royalists were captured and a further 4,000 died. Many of the latter were Langdale's men.

Were it not a tragedy of life and death the sequel would have made a farce.

Ribbleton Moor, where
Langdale attempted to hold
Cromwell back, is on the
B6243 as it goes north-east
from Preston, and just before it
reaches the M6. It is now a
built-up area. So is the line of
Langdale's retreat. The bridge
over which Hamilton
attempted to push the foot is
now replaced by that carrying
the A6. There is a monument
to the battle here. The traveller
can take either of the routes to
Wigan mentioned in the text,
but the skirmish at Winnick
took place just off the A49
before it crosses the M62. The
museum at Preston – the
Harris Museum and Art
Gallery – has a display
concerning the battle.

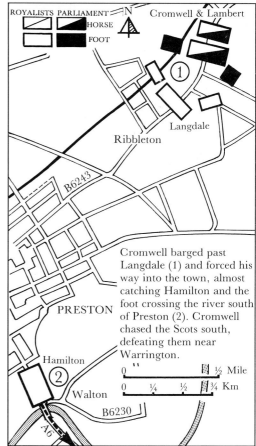

Cromwell barged past
Langdale (1) and forced his
way into the town, almost
catching Hamilton and the
foot crossing the river south
of Preston (2). Cromwell
chased the Scots south,
defeating them near
Warrington.

John Lambert.

There were two roads from Preston to Wigan. One went to the west via Standish (now the A49) and the other to the east via Chorley (probably a combination of what is now the A6 to the south of Chorley and the B5106 or the minor road from Scot Lane end). Hamilton took the Standish road and Middleton with the horse, who had realized that something was wrong, set off north via Chorley. Thus in the dismal rain of the night of 17 – 18 August the two groups missed each other. South of Preston, Middleton realized his mistake when he bumped into Cromwell's horse. He immediately turned south. Middleton and Hamilton met on Wigan Moor and the Scots continued on towards Warrington. Cromwell who had left 4,000 men at Preston to watch for Scots reinforcements coming from the north, was not far behind. At Winnick he was attacked by a small force which held him up for a few hours; another 2,000 men surrendered and a further 1,000 died. Hamilton still had 7,000 men with him but they were wet and hungry. The foot had lost most of its ammunition and when Baillie attempted to get his 4,000 men to hold the bridge over the Mersey at Warrington, about half laid down their arms. As most of the others had no ammunition there were only 250 men capable of holding the bridge. Baillie and the rest of the foot surrendered.

After this, Cromwell turned north to deal with the threat to his rear. Sir George Munroe and 3,000 Scottish soldiers returned from Ireland were marching down to join Hamilton. Lambert pursued the Marquis and the Scottish horse southwards. At Uttoxeter the retreating Royalist forces attempted to go north with the aim of giving Cromwell and Lambert a wide berth and returning to Scotland. But the troopers would not go on and Hamilton surrendered to Lambert. Lord Grey appeared and took the Marquis prisoner to Ashby de la Zouch Castle, over which he was governor, before sending him to Windsor. Langdale had left the Scottish army just before Uttoxeter with some of the Scots horse. At Ashbourne they refused to go on and Langdale set off with the few English horse left with him. These men were captured after a fight at Willoughby in Lincolnshire. The fighting in this war had been more vicious than that of the previous one and the harshness continued in the aftermath. Only Hamilton's conscripts were sent home, the volunteers being sent as virtual slaves to plantations in Virginia and Barbados.

At the end of August Cromwell and Lambert reunited. As they did so the Earl of Leven raised an army in West Scotland to overthrow the government which had sided with Charles I. After a brief period of fighting, Leven and the government attempted to unite in order to keep Cromwell at Berwick where he had been since 18 September. Eventually Cromwell was welcomed into Edinburgh as a 'saviour' and a treaty signed. By the terms of this treaty Berwick and Carlisle were handed back to the English, Sir George Munroe was sent home and both Leven's army and that of the government were disbanded.

THE SIEGES

AS THE EARL OF NORWICH and the other Royalist leaders hustled their forces into Colchester, Fairfax was close behind. One of the New Model regiments pushed right into the suburbs, in an attempt to cut off a number of Royalists from the gates. The ensuing fight lasted until midnight on 13 June and was a murderous one which cost Fairfax alone around 1,000 men. Fairfax had only around 4,000 with him after this as the volatile nature of Kent had forced him to leave behind several garrisons. On 14 June he sent for the siege train and for reinforcements. There was still some Royalist activity behind him. The Earl of Holland and the Duke of Buckingham led a small and ultimately unsuccessful rising at Kingston-upon-Thames. This tied down numerous regiments which Fairfax desperately needed.

Around the town, Fairfax began the construction of a series of earthworks, chiefly on the western or London side of the town. The river Colne – Colchester's link with the sea – was blockaded by a man-of-war in the estuary. The Royalists in the town were cut off from either renewed support from Kent or the Thames valley, or from the small royal fleet in the channel. To supplement his small army, Fairfax used the Essex and Suffolk Trained Bands, a further 5,500 men.

This was a hard siege unlike many of those in the previous war. Fairfax fired the suburbs, which was fairly standard practice. Usually the defenders did this to prevent their enemies using buildings outside the town as vantage points. Fairfax did it to drive the inhabitants into the town, to drain foodstocks and cause a rift between the townspeople and the garrison. He then refused to allow the women and children to leave the town. When the women marched out anyway, Fairfax ordered his

The siege of Colchester. This map shows the main siegeworks constructed around the town by Fairfax.

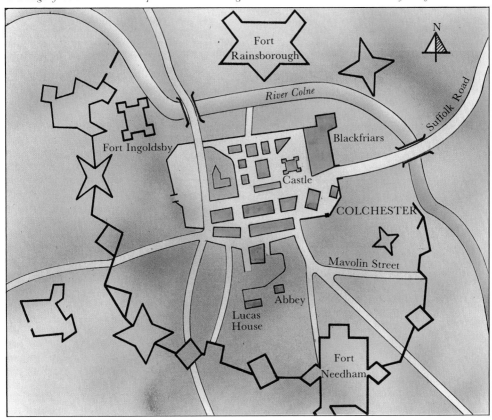

soldiers to strip them and drive them back with sticks. He was determined that the resources of Colchester should be used up as quickly as possible. The more mouths to feed in the town the quicker this would be. He also cut off the water supply.

Inside the town it was Lord Loughborough, as Commissary general, who had to deal with these problems. He issued horsemeat from the slaughtered mounts to both the garrison and the townspeople. With water he had an easier task. There were some wells in the town and the almost continuous rain which soaked and demoralized Hamilton's army in the North, was the very staff of life in Colchester. Nevertheless the Royalists were in an untenable position unless there was to be any hope of rescue by Hamilton. When on 23 August the garrison heard of Hamilton's defeat, they realized that they could not fight on. A break-out was planned but the soliders were on foot and ill-fed. Fairfax now had a much larger army around the town and there was little chance of getting away. On 27 August 1649 Colchester was surrendered. Norwich, Capel and Loughborough were dispatched to Windsor Castle. It was expected that they would be brought to trial later. Capel was executed the following year by order of the High Court of Justice. Norwich remained in prison, but Loughborough, who was considered too dangerous, faced execution too. He did not wait to find out. On the eve of the King's execution he escaped from Windsor and fled to Holland.

Fairfax was an angry man after the siege ended. He concocted a court martial and it found George Lisle, Charles Lucas and Bernard Gascoine guilty of having broken parole. The three were sentenced to death, but Gascoine was released when it was realized that he was an Italian citizen. Lucas and Lisle, Royalist heroes of the two Civil Wars, were shot.

Other sieges still continued. Berwick and Carlisle were still in Scottish hands and Pontefract, the great fortress of the first Civil War, had been captured by Royalists on 1 June. After Preston and after Cromwell had crossed the border and forced peace upon the Edinburgh government, attention was turned on Pontefract. Colonel Thomas Rainsborough, one of the Levellers' most significant army supporters, was murdered in a bungled kidnap attempt. Cromwell stayed besieging the castle after Rainsborough's death and hung on until the purge of Parliament was complete. Still Pontefract held out. Even after the King was dead, the castle still defied the besiegers, now led by John Lambert. It was not until the following March that the castle eventually surrendered, and the second Civil War came to an end.

THAT MAN OF BLOOD

THE SECOND CIVIL WAR hardened the attitudes of many men towards the King. Whilst the Presbyterian sections within the Commons and Lords expressed a willingness to continue to treat with him, the fundamental shift of attitude within the army high command was the prime mover. Whereas the high ranking officers had negotiated directly with the King in 1647, they were not prepared to join in the abortive Treaty of Newport. There was little theoretical republicanism in the country; instead it was fear of continued disorder which drove men like Cromwell and his son-in-law Ireton to demand that the King should be brought to trial. They were worried that any continuation of disorder would allow radical groups like the Levellers to grow in strength. This would pose a threat to the existing social order. Fairfax, Cromwell and Ireton were part of the higher echelons of that order and did not wish to see it challenged.

Whilst the King was alive there was always the chance of further war. This

Lady Fairfax calling out during the trial of the King.

drove the army to purge Parliament of the Presbyterian members who stood in their way. Lord Grey of Groby and Colonel Pride stood at the doors of the Commons on 6 December and barred entry to the House and arrested several Presbyterian members. The King was brought from the Isle of Wight and lodged in Westminster. The purged Parliament abandoned the Newport negotiations and set up the machinery to try the King. On 1 January 1649 the second Civil War was declared to have been a treasonable act and a High Court of Justice was proposed by the Commons. The Lords objected and refused to deal with the bill. In response the Commons declared that they were the supreme power in the country and passed the bill as an act.

Fairfax was named as one of the commissioners for the trial and although he sat at one of the preliminary sessions which established procedure, he took no role. He was no revolutionary: not even a reluctant one like Cromwell and the others. Lady Fairfax voiced her opposition with more courage than her husband, by shouting during the trial that the Commons had no mandate from the people to try the King. On 21 January 1649, before the commissioners and the Lord President, John Bradshaw, the first public session began. Bradshaw was a distinctly second-rate man – only picked because the High Court judges had absented themselves from the capital. For the first time in his life Charles found favour with his people. He did not stutter and he argued with reason. He refused to accept the jurisdiction of the illegal court on the grounds that it was not founded in known law; nor could it prove how it came to be legally created. He was able to run rings around the incompetent Bradshaw, but the result was a foregone conclusion. On 30 January the King was executed on a scaffold outside the Banqueting House in Whitehall. He played this role faultlessly, gaining a popular sympathy he had never enjoyed whilst in power. This ensured that what should have been a glorious beginning to a brave new world was fatally flawed.

17. IRELAND

1649 – 1650

Ireland was the scene of the most bitter fighting of the Givil War period. Here we are not concerned with the battles, which were often little more than murderous skirmishes, but with the sieges of two of the towns: Drogheda and Wexford.

IN MANY WAYS it was Ireland which provided the spark which caused the outbreak of war in England and Wales. When the Catholic Irish went into open revolt in October 1641 there were two major repercussions in England. Firstly, the Catholics' insistence that they were acting with the King's authority cast suspicion upon Charles I. Secondly, and related very much to the first point, the question of who would command the army (which it was proposed to raise to deal with the rebels) became a critical political issue. It was

largely to stop the King calling together an army and then using it on his refractory Parliament, that the Militia Ordinance was issued.

For Ireland it was the start of ten years of tragedy. The anger of the Catholics led, in a few instances, to ferocious fighting and several massacres, leaving between 3,000 and 8,000 dead. The paranoia of the Protestant new Irish led to the exaggeration of these incidents. The wanderings in England of the Protestants made homeless by the troubles, spread the stories of the atrocities across the country. Dependent as they were upon the charity of English communities, these poor wanderers dramatically passed on the tales of their sufferings to a readily shocked Protestant audience. To compound this, the abolition of the High Commission Court in 1641 left England with no censorship except the fear of transgressing the treason laws. This led to a massive upsurge in the amount of printed books and, moreover, the creation of a newspaper industry. In common with the tawdry newspapers of later centuries, the vilest of the newsbooks printed scandal and half-truths in an effort to maximize sales. They spread rumours, terror and lies. As a result there was created in England a great fear and loathing for the native Irish Catholics which lasted throughout the period and influenced the responses to the situation which Cromwell found there in 1649.

As war ripped England, Wales and Scotland apart in the 1640s, Ireland struggled with its own war. In April 1642 small English and Scottish armies landed and began to fight the Catholics. By October the Deputy Lieutenant, the Marquis of Ormond, had also raised an army in the King's name and began to fight against them as well. The Catholics had meanwhile formed the Confederacy of Kilkenny. However, the aims of groups within the confederation differed. Some members declared to support the King, but others aimed at independence from England.

Naturally the King attempted to capitalize upon the Royalist sympathies of Viscount Tara's followers, not of course with the intention of doing any good by Ireland. Nevertheless the Gaelic nationalists under Owen Roe O'Neill resisted all Charles's approaches. By 1647 the confederates had been defeated at Dublin by Michael Jones's English army which had been sent over to Ireland and had superseded Ormond's role. Furthermore, Lord Inchiquin had defeated a confederate

The Marquis of Ormond.

force at Knockanoss. However by 1648, when the second Civil War broke out, Inchiquin turned his coat and Ormond returned to lead a Royalist army.

CROMWELL IN IRELAND

WHEN CHARLES I was executed the Catholic Confederacy and Ormond managed to forge the agreement which had eluded them hitherto. Together they were able to dominate most of Ireland. Only Derry (now 'owned' and settled by London and renamed Londonderry) and Dublin held out against them. Ormond settled his army around the capital and began a siege. Cromwell and part of the New Model was sent out to help before Charles II could get there. Three regiments were sent ahead to Michael Jones in Dublin. With these he launched an attack on Ormond's forces and defeated them at Rathinies. The victory was remarkable: Ormond's army collapsed.

On 15 August 1649 Cromwell landed with a formidable army. He marched on Drogheda, 30 miles (48 kilometres) north of Dublin, and captured it on 11 September. He then took Dundalk 20 or so miles (32 kilometres) further north and Trim, some 27 miles (43½ kilometres) from Dublin. He had by this time joined up with Sir Charles Coote's Ulster Protestant new Irish and overran the North-east as Owen Roe O'Neill lay ill. Cromwell himself left Coote and turned south in late September and took Wexford on 3 October. The matter of the east coast appeared to be largely settled. In the South, Cork's English garrison declared its support for Parliament, New Ross surrendered and other garrisons across Munster changed sides or surrendered. Cromwell began to plan the inland campaign.

However, he fell ill with a fever from which Michael Jones, now his lieutenant, died and the great army began to waste away. By the time he attempted to besiege Waterford, he could only muster 3,000 men. There was no chance of forcing a surrender and the siege collapsed in early December. Even so, there were now only a few ports left to the Royalist Irish, and whilst in theory Ormond had an army of 20,000 men, it was demoralized and scattered. Central and West Ireland were still in their hands, but as the Ulstermen marched south and Cromwell and his son Henry brought reinforcements across the Irish Sea, it was clear that they would be attacked in the spring. On 22 March 1650, Cromwell called upon Kilkenny to surrender.

Inside the town was Ormond's cousin, Sir Walter Butler. His garrison was riddled with plague and he could only mount a brave defiance for a short time. Henry Cromwell defeated a relief force under Lord Inchiquin at Marcroom to the south-west of Kilkenny and as Oliver brought artillery into the outlying areas, Butler surrendered. The Parliamentarians next turned on Clonmel but were kept out by Hugh O'Neill's garrison.

The walls of Clonmel.

Several attacks failed and O'Neill managed to get his forces out of the town without any hindrance when Cromwell's ammunition ran out!

Cromwell's campaign came to this rather ragged end. The English Parliament wanted him to come home. There was a threat of an invasion by Scotland where Charles II was now accepted as King, and the Lord General Fairfax was expressing his unwillingness to lead the army. In Ireland, Ormond and O'Neill still held out, despite the fact that many of their juniors were giving up. The alliance of Irish Catholics and the Old English settlers fell apart. Despite this, resistance continued. Cromwell left his son-in-law Ireton behind to continue his work. Limerick surrendered in October 1651 and resistance in Galway ended the following year. Ireton died of a fever without ever returning home.

Retribution was severe; a policy of resettlement was being enacted. Clare and Connaught, to the west of the Shannon, were set aside for the native Irish and gentry families were transported there wholesale. The rest of the country was taken for Protestant use. The Act of Settlement placed an army of 20,000 in the country, each soldier and his family being given a portion of the ten million acres of forfeited Irish land. By these means Ireland was to be civilized, controlled and made Protestant. Attitudes formed in 1641 – 2 were made visible in the

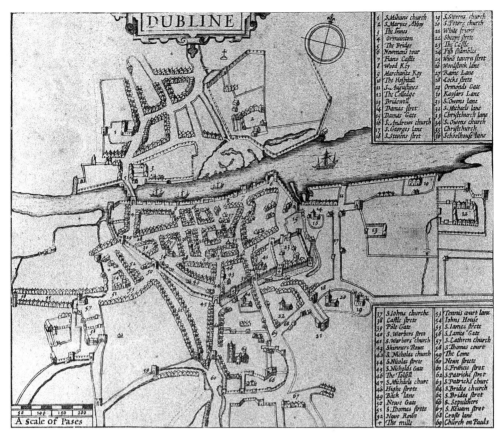

DUBLINE

1	S.Michans church	19	S.Stevens church
2	S.Maryes Abbey	20	S.Peters church
3	The Innes	21	White friers
4	Ormonton	22	Sheepe strete
5	The Bridge	23	The Castle
6	Newmans tour	24	Fish shambles
7	Hans Castle	25	Wine tavern stret
8	Wood Key	26	Woodstock lane
9	Marchants Key	27	Rame Lane
10	The Hospitall	28	Cocke strete
11	S. Augustines	29	Ormonds Gate
12	The Colledge	30	Kayfars Lane
13	Bridewell	31	S.Owens lane
14	Damas stret	32	S.Michaels Lane
15	Damas Gate	33	Christchurch Lane
16	S.Andrews church	34	S.Owens church
17	S.Georges Lane	35	Christchurch
18	S.Stevens stret	36	Schoolhouse lane

37	S.Iohns churche	53	Tennis court lane
38	Castle strete	54	Iohns Houfe
39	Pole Gate	55	S.Iames strete
40	S.Warbers stret	56	S.Iames Gate
41	S.Warbers church	57	S.Cathren church
42	Skinners Rowe	58	S.Thomas court
43	S.Nicholas church	59	The Come
44	S.Nicolas strete	60	Newe strete
45	S.Nicholas Gate	61	S.Francis stret
46	The Tolsell	62	S.Patricks stret
47	S.Michaels churc	63	S.Patricks churc
48	Highe strete	64	S.Brides church
49	Back lane	65	S.Brides stret
50	Newe Gate	66	S.Sepulchers
51	S.Thomas strete	67	S.Keuan stret
52	Newe Rowe	68	Croffe lane
+	The mills	69	Church on Pauls

A scale of Pases

Plan of Dublin (1610) by John Speed.

later years of the decade and the treatment of the defeated echoed this. Royalist soldiers captured in Ireland were shipped to Barbados and other colonies as bonded labourers.

DROGHEDA AND WEXFORD

IT was these two sieges which, if anything, were seen to epitomize the campaign of Oliver Cromwell in Ireland. They revealed the extent of bitterness felt by the English army towards the Royalists, who were still fighting after Charles's execution. They also revealed the contempt in which the Irish themselves were held.

Cromwell had landed in Dublin during August 1649 and began by declaring that no civilian would be harmed. He even opened a market in his army camp to encourage trade with the Irish and bring money into their hands through the sale of goods to the soldiers. To his north, Ormond strengthened Drogheda, placing Sir Arthur Aston, one-time Governor of Oxford, in command. By the end of the month the garrison was 2,871 men strong. Ormond himself was at Trecoghan in Meath, with 1,000 men and awaiting more from the North.

On 1 September Cromwell, with Michael Jones leading, set out. Two days later he arrived at Drogheda with 10,000 men and siege guns arrived by sea. The town was well fortified but Aston was low on ammunition. He implored Ormond to march to the bridge over the Boyne at Slane where he would be in a strong position, safe from attack yet able to threaten Cromwell's lines of communication. This he hoped might force Cromwell to retire. But Ormond still had only 1,000 men: O'Neill's promised 6,000 had not materialized.

On 10 September Aston was summoned to surrender. When he refused, Cromwell began to bombard the St Mary's area of the town. By the evening the steeple of the church had been wrecked and a breach had been made in the south wall. Aston knew that the situation was now hopeless, but Ormond sent him word that men were coming along the coast from Dundalk.

Inside the breach Aston constructed a triple line of earthworks behind the church; these formed a rough semi-circle linking the walls up in an effort to keep the attackers penned in. At five o'clock in the morning the attack was launched and the breach entered. After a tough fight Cromwell's men pushed over the earthworks. Aston and others withdrew and defended Mill Mount whilst the majority fled over the Boyne into the northern half of the town. As the Parliamentarians stormed in, the slaughter began. Aston and the defenders on the Mount were all killed: Aston was probably beaten to death with his own wooden leg. Those who managed to escape the murder on the Mount, like Sir Edmund Verney, son of the Standard bearer at Edgehill, were killed in cold blood the next day. Eighty others were massacred at St Peter's church when the steeple was set on fire. Two of the towers on the walls held out until 12 September. When they eventually surrendered, the officers were murdered in cold blood and every tenth soldier transported to Barbados. Every friar that the 'godly' Parliamentarians found was killed where he stood and several innocent citizens died too.

Cromwell sought to justify the unjustifiable. The English Parliamentarians were murderers at Drogheda and murder had, and has, no place in society, even under the cover of war-time expediency. Cromwell had an uneasy conscience. He suggested that the massacre was in accordance with the rules of war as they applied to a stormed town and that the citizens of Drogheda were guilty by association of the

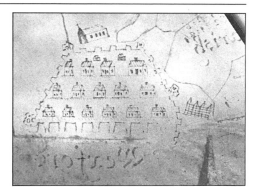

Detail from the Down Survey (circa 1656) *showing the town and castle of Wexford.*

murders of Protestants in 1641. It was an attitude which spared many lesser men any such pang of conscience.

Cromwell then went on to attack Dundalk and Trim. At the end of the month he turned south and marched on Wexford. The little port was a base for the small Royalist fleet and a convenient harbour for privateers who raided the coasts of the new Republic.

On 1 October Cromwell arrived at Wexford; by the following day he had 7,000 foot and 2,000 horse with him. The southern approach to Wexford was guarded by a castle and against this Cromwell erected a battery of siege guns. The emplacement lay alongside the (now trunk) road to Killinick and Rosslare. Inside Wexford itself the normal garrison had been supplemented by 1,500 men from Ulster. Cromwell was going to have to act quickly as his soldiers began to contract dysentery.

Michael Jones advanced along Rosslare Point to capture the fort at the entrance to Wexford Harbour. Once this was done Parliamentarian ships were able to use the bay to land supplies and ammunition. Meanwhile, Ormond advanced to Ross, west of Wexford. Going on across the River Slaney he marched to Castlebridge on the north side of the bay. Here was a ferry point connecting the shore with Wexford (there is a bridge now carrying the Wexford – Arklow road). The town governor, Colonel Synott, was summoned to Castlebridge; given Cromwell's concentration to the south of the town he was able to make the journey easily. Ormond intended to replace Synott with Sir Edmund Butler, who was at that moment heading towards them with a relief force.

On that same morning of 11 October Cromwell opened fire on the castle. Within a short time its governor Captain Stafford surrendered. The Parliamentarians then turned the castle guns on the town. Immediately large numbers of the garrison deserted and gave up their posts. Cromwell's soldiers poured into the town over the deserted south works. Only when they reached the market-place did they encounter serious resistance. Even here the fight was brief and the victorious Parliamentarians were soon free to embark on an orgy of murder. Priests and friars were the primary targets, but as many as 300 civilians and soldiers were drowned as they tried to escape from the town by sea. Naturally Cromwell again sought to shift blame which was clearly his to bear. This time he asserted that the massacre was God's will. The Lord had decided that this nest of vipers should be exterminated. Cromwell, his mere instrument, had actually tried to keep the town and its people from harm. It was God who directed the common soldiers to do otherwise.

Wexford Harbour.

Oliver Cromwell (1599 – 1661)

Cromwell was born into a middling Huntingdonshire-gentry family in 1599. He spent some time at Cambridge University, but like many of his contemporaries, he left without taking a degree. In the 1630s he opposed the enclosure and drainage of the fenlands. In 1640 he became a Member of Parliament and stuck with Parliament during the crisis of 1642, returning home in the summer to raise a troop of horse. He claimed that he picked men who knew what they were fighting for and loved what they knew. He also implied that he relied on talent rather than social rank, yet most of his men were of gentry or yeoman stock.

He and the troop arrived too late to participate at Edgehill but, it is suggested, he saw the way in which the Royalist horse lost all sense of order and discipline after a charge and decided to stop his men following the same manner. In 1643 he was chiefly in action in Lincolnshire and the Midlands and became Lieutenant-General to the Earl of Manchester's Eastern Association Army. At Marston Moor he led the attack on the Royalist right wing and defeated it. He was instrumental in the destruction of the two Royalist armies at the battle.

At the second battle of Newbury he did not perform as well and Manchester was able to claim that he was an ineffective and troublesome commander. Cromwell was saved from disgrace by the Self-Denying Ordinance and survived the proscription from military office by being granted a series of temporary commissions. In the New Model he served as Lieutenant-General and led the horse. At Naseby it was his wing which destroyed the Royalist left and turned on the flank of the foot. His victory here was the result of his overwhelming superiority of numbers as much as his superb control of his men.

In the second Civil War he led the campaign in Wales and then turned on and defeated the Scottish army. By the time Parliament had been purged, Cromwell was convinced of the need to execute the King and he participated fully in the trial. Later in 1649 he led the campaign against the Irish and in the year following he became commander of the army after Fairfax refused to lead a campaign against the Scots once they had made Charles II their King. In 1653 he expelled the Rump of Parliament from the Commons and accepted the role of Lord Protector of the Commonwealth.

In the succeeding years he attempted to create a 'godly' Parliament by a variety of electoral systems, but was never fully satisfied with the result. The great problem of the Commonwealth and Republic was that the conflicting sources of power within it, the Parliament and the army, could only be controlled by Cromwell and thus the fate of the nation was bound up with him. This was probably never his intention: but when he died the bold experiment came to a sad end as conflict came to the fore. With a characteristically English lack of imagination, the Rump Parliament turned up like a bad penny and brought about the restoration of the monarchy. God, for whom Cromwell and the 'saints' had fought, spat in the faces of the republicans like Colonel Harrison and paradise was lost.

18. DUNBAR AND WORCESTER

SEPTEMBER 1650 – SEPTEMBER 1651

These two actions were the major events of the third Civil War – the war fought for and by Charles II after the execution of his father.

Cartoon from a tract of 1651 suggesting the Scots intended to use the young Charles II for their own ends.

Jockey: I Jockey turne the stone of all your plots,
For none turnes faster then the turne-coat Scots.

Presbyter: We for our ends did make thee King be sure,
Not to rule us, we will not that endure.

King: You deep dissemblers I know what you doe,
And for revenges sake, I will dissemble too.

CHARLES II AND PRESBYTERIANISM

THE SCOTTISH PARLIAMENT was appalled by the execution of Charles I. Of course, he had also been the King of Scotland and yet they had not been consulted at all over the matter of his death. By 5 April 1649 the Committee of Estates (the executive arm of Scottish government) had recognized Charles II's right to the throne of Scotland. Charles II was of different mettle to his father: tall, fluent and for his age a man of maturity. He was only nineteen years old. Whilst Scotland attempted to woo him the young man toyed with joining Ormond in Ireland; but the disastrous campaign against Cromwell deflected him. Initially, Charles wished to work with Montrose, his father's brilliant Lieutenant-General. Charles knew that if he went into his northern kingdom without Montrose's expertise, then he might fall prey to the Estate's attempt to control him. Accordingly he reappointed Montrose to the rank of Lieutenant-General of Scotland and sent him to the Baltic States to recruit mercenary Protestant soldiers.

However, by April 1650 Charles had heard nothing from Montrose: it was not even certain that he was still alive. But he was, and he had landed in Orkney with 1,500 men. This news did not reach Charles and so he signed the covenant and made a promise to introduce the Presbyterian church system in England and Ireland.

Detachment of Cromwell's Cavalry Surprised in a Mountain Pass – a Victorian painting by Thomas Woodward

Furthermore, he repudiated Montrose who had already been arrested and barbarously executed. Perhaps there was something of the father in the son after all.

Once in Scotland, Charles was a captive of Presbyterianism and had to endure a series of four-hour long sermons! Meanwhile, David Leslie was raising an army of 26,000 men: but these were largely untrained and not comparable with the New Model Army. Scottish veterans of the 1648 campaign were not allowed to enlist. In England Fairfax refused to lead the New Model in the proposed campaign into Scotland, and Cromwell became its leader. The English army began its march up the Great North Road in July. By 15 July it was at Newcastle and eleven days later it was at Dunbar. On 29 July an attack on Edinburgh failed and the retreat was hounded by Leslie. Disease cost Cromwell several thousand men on top of those lost in action, as the whole campaign was dogged by dreadful weather. This made it difficult for the English to land supplies, and this was the only way that Cromwell's army could survive.

Charles II was not with his army. The Scottish government was still trying to turn him into a good Presbyterian. Moreover it was also trying to marry him into the Earl of Argyll's family. As for a coronation, this was constantly deferred for the very reason that, once crowned, Charles's power would increase. He knew this too and for this reason alone the young King was prepared to make a series of false promises regarding the establishment of Presbyterianism.

DUNBAR

LESLIE had the pleasant task of watching the English army disintegrate before his eyes in the dreadful weather of the late summer of 1650. The foolish New Model had not brought tents with it, and disease was rife. At the beginning of September,

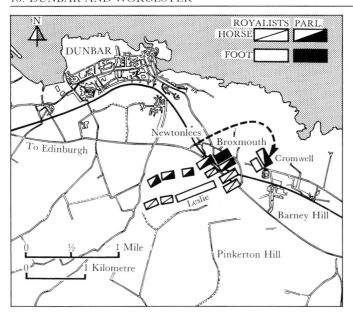

Dunbar Field is just south of the town and straddles the A1. There is a monument, near Portland Cement works entrance. By taking the lane to Pinkerton Hill the traveller can reach the place held by the Scottish centre.

Leslie's army moved to the south of Cromwell who was at Dunbar. It was soon realized that the Scots intended to block the route south at Cockburnspath.

Leslie moved up from the south-east and placed his army on Doon Hill, the seaward end of the Lammermuir Hills. His line stretched from Doon, to the east, towards the Great North Road (A1). Cromwell and the English army marched out of Dunbar to a position close by Broxmouth House and Newtonlecas.

On the night of 2 September Leslie moved down from the hill-top in order to bring Cromwell to battle. At the close of the manoeuvre he was still in a strong position. To his front lay Brox (or Spott) Burn which had carved a ravine for itself as it descended from the hillside. Over this there lay only one proper crossing: that of the Great North Road itself. Cromwell, Ireton and the one-time Royalist George Monck surveyed the situation and decided that Leslie's line was vulnerable. The resultant plan was very simple. There was to be a frontal attack right along the line to paralyse the Scots and prevent them making any quick response to the major part of the plan. This latter involved an attack on the left flank of the Scottish army across the burn at the road crossing. There, Leslie's army stood on open level ground without any protection from the ravine.

Leslie's army was over 22,000 strong and stretched over a front of some 3,000 yards (2,770 metres). On the opposite side of the ravine were perhaps less than half this number. In view of this the English had a very difficult task ahead of them. It took Cromwell some time to convince the officers of the likelihood of success. Nevertheless at four o'clock in the morning on 3 September General John Lambert and six regiments of horse, accompanied by General Monck with three of foot, crossed the burn by the road bridge. The Scots were caught by surprise in the early morning light: it took time for them to organize a defence. This gave Lambert the breathing-space he needed to establish a bridgehead.

Even so, when the Scots did pull themselves together, they were able to bring to bear their massive weight of numbers. Lambert and Monck were held firmly in place around the bridge. Leslie launched his horse in a counter-attack and they kept Lambert from venturing too far, but Monck was still able to get more and more foot over the burn. Soon the task of holding these ever-increasing numbers in check embroiled the whole of Leslie's centre. Cromwell with his own regiment of horse and a regiment of foot had crossed the burn at the lowlands area nearer to the sea and was approaching Leslie's right flank. Once in position, Cromwell's horse charged into Leslie's horse. Once the English foot had joined in the fight, the Scottish horse were defeated. A retreat was made across country to Haddington. A brave but pointless stand was made by the foot in Leslie's centre, but when the flanking regiments crumbled this came to an end. As many as 10,000 men were captured and a further 3,000 Scotsmen lay dead. This was probably Cromwell's greatest victory. Certainly it was a tactical success and the English had lost few casualties: Cromwell was to boast that only thirty Englishmen died. As for the Scots and Charles II, it was a disaster: their army had ceased to exist.

Straightaway Charles attempted to create a new army. The restrictions on the service of the veterans of 1648 were lifted in order to bring this about. But there were great problems: some Covenanters would not join forces with old Royalists and they attempted to go it alone. With near-inevitability, their tiny numbers were defeated. The disaster at Dunbar freed Charles from a lot of pressure. On 1 January 1651 he was crowned, but Edinburgh had now fallen. To offset this Cromwell had become ill. It was to be a full six months before he was well enough to take the field again.

ENGLAND INVADED

CHARLES II and General David Leslie managed to forge a new army out of Scots and English Royalists. The English contingent was led by Edward Massey, the one time Parliamentarian governor of Gloucester. The army was mustered around Stirling, well protected from attack. Lambert spent several months trying to entice Leslie out into the open, but with no effect. It was not until Cromwell's recovery in late June that any concerted effort could be made. Cromwell intended to cross the Forth at Queensferry and then to strike north and cut Leslie off from his supply bases in Fife. Coupled with this forces south of the border were to be brought north and east. This would leave a passage into England open. It was an invitation the ambitious young King would find hard to refuse. Naturally, it was not turned down. Leslie marched south as Cromwell occupied Perth on 2 August. It was Charles II who now called the tune. With an army of some 14,000 men he crossed the border. Immediately Lambert dashed south to join Colonels Harrison and Rich as they shadowed the King. Monck made sure that there was no going back for the Royalists by occupying Stirling. Cromwell followed behind the Royalists with the main portion of the army.

As Charles reached Wigan on 15 August, Lambert joined Harrison and Rich and crossed the Pennines. Soon he was at Warrington in front of the King. Charles was hoping to gather support as he progressed down the west of England; but the area had bitter memories of the campaign three years earlier. Moreover the Royalist gentry were financially ruined by years of war and heavy fines. The Protestants amongst them were mortified by the King's staying with prominent Catholic gentry families. Needless to say, this did nothing to encourage popular support either. On top of this, antipathy towards the Scots did not help nor did Charles's seeming acceptance, in England taken at face value, of Presbyterianism. By the time he arrived at Wigan, all he had picked up were a hundred or so men sent by the Earl of Derby from the Isle of Man.

The Commandery, Charles's headquarters for the battle of Worcester

WORCESTER

CHARLES'S projected march towards London was called off when it was realized that Cromwell's proximity would threaten the Royalists' flank, when they turned east towards the capital. As a result the army turned towards the Marcher counties, but Shrewsbury refused the King entry and Massey was quite unable to persuade Gloucester to open its gates. However, Worcester, with its now demolished defences, one of his father's most loyal cities, did allow him in. In the immediate area the new King raised 2,000 men: but these were quite inadequate to offset the losses through desertion and the army now stood at only 12,000 even with the new additions. On the other hand, Cromwell, with reserves from Yorkshire and East Anglia alongside garrison forces from the Midlands, had over 30,000 men. By 29 August he swung round from Warwick to the south of Worcester and prepared to attack.

The immediate task for the army of the Republic was to cross the rivers Severn and Teme. On 28 August Lambert had found that the bridge over the Severn was still passable despite Scottish atempts at demolition. By this means he was able to put men over the river and begin to approach Worcester from the south. Cromwell began to construct a boat bridge over the Teme near the point where it joined the Severn and at Timberdene on the Severn itself. These crossing-points would be necessary to prevent the attacking force from being split in two as it moved on Worcester.

The Scots under the new Duke of Hamilton attempted to prevent or at least delay the attempts to cross the rivers at these points and at Powick Bridge. Hamilton's men, south of Powick bridge in Powick itself, put up a strong resistance and were for some time successful. The battle really began on 3 September as Cromwell's engineers completed the bridge of boats. Via these two crossings the rear of the Scots at Powick was threatened and the latter had to withdraw. This left Colonel Fleetwood able to cross the bridge and approach Worcester from across the meadows on which the battle

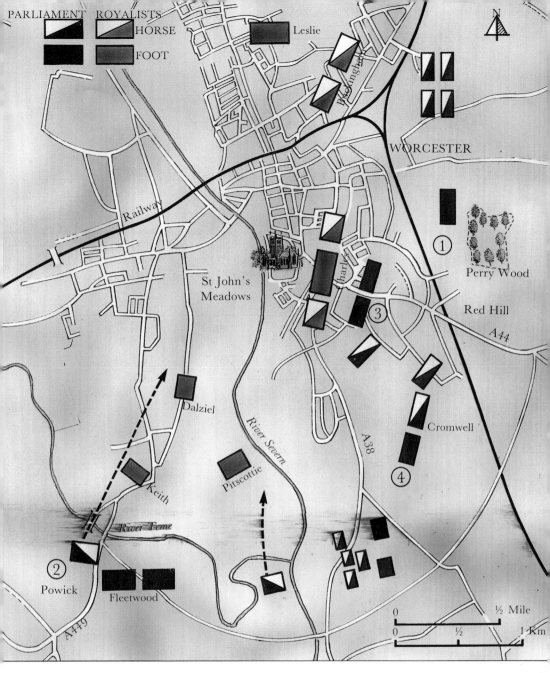

N

Leslie

WORCESTER

① Perry Wood

Red Hill

A44

St John's Meadows

Charles

③

Dalziel

River Severn

A38

Cromwell

④

Pitscottie

Keith

River Teme

② Powick

Fleetwood

A449

| 0 | | ½ Mile |

| 0 | ½ | 1 Km |

Cromwell pressed in on Charles II from the east (1) and from the south via Powick (2). At one point the young King defeated the Parliamentarian attack on the east of the city (3). However, Cromwell switched forces from the attack in the south and restored the situation (4). Once the Parliamentarians reached the walls to the east and west, there was little for the King to do but escape.

The site of the battle of Worcester is now largely built over. The line of the main Parliamentarian attack ran to the side of the A449 as it approaches Worcester from the south-west. Portions of the meadows still survive as open ground. Sections, too, of the old bridge over which Fleetwood pressed into the western part of the town can still be detected in the reconstructed bridge. To the east, the route of Charles II's counter-attack can be followed along the A44 through the East Gate, or Sidbury Gate, to the housing estates around Red Hill. The Commandery from where this attack was planned is on this road, as can be seen in the photograph overleaf.

of Powick Bridge had been fought nine years earlier. However, as the right wing advanced on the city it became separated from the right wing on the east of the Severn. Charles discerned this from the Cathedral tower, then led an attack on Cromwell's right wing. A large body of horse was gathered around the Commandery, the town house which was the headquarters of the defence force in the east of the city. Charles and the Duke of Hamilton, now back from the Powick area, led the attack themselves. The horse left the city at the East or Sidbury Gate and moved along the line of what is now the A44. Charles, leading the right wing, attacked the forces on Red Hill whilst Hamilton attacked those at Perry Wood. The attacks were successful and the Royalist horse established itself on Red Hill.

It was a difficult moment and one which demanded immediate action from Cromwell. In response he left Fleetwood to take charge of the attack over the meadows, whilst he led his own regiment back over the Severn. Gathering the fragments of the right wing about him, Cromwell counter-attacked. By sheer weight of numbers they were able to drive the Royalist horse off Red Hill and back into Worcester. Panic set in and the Royalists inside the East Gate became disordered despite Charles's efforts to control them.

Meanwhile, Fleetwood began to make headway over the meadows, and the Scottish forces were steadily pushed back towards Worcester's western approaches. Fleetwood pressed on to the bridge near the present cricket ground, and thereby cut off Charles's

View of the eastern side of Worcester. The Commandery is in the foreground; Sidbury Gate was close to where it abuts the A44. In the background is Red Hill, with Perry Wood on the left. In the centre is Fort Royal Park where traces of its fortifications are still visible.

escape route to Wales. Escape was now a major consideration. Cromwell's attack had reached the eastern walls of the town and large numbers of Royalists were laying down their arms. Only the English horse remained as an integral unit; to get their King out of the town, it charged down the High Street and along the route of the A44 as it leaves the city centre. Under cover of this desperate heroism, Charles got out through St Martin's gate in the gathering dusk. The English horse were driven back to the Town Hall where they made a last stand before being overwhelmed by the army of the English Republic. Charles's defeated army lost over 2,000 dead; Cromwell's as few as a couple of hundred. The last battle of the Civil Wars ended where the first war had begun.

Charles II escaping from Worcester.

ESCAPE

TRYING TO HIDE an unusually tall man with easily recognizable features was not an easy task: especially as there was a price on his head. For six weeks the King was on the run and, in all this time, he had to adopt a variety of disguises and undertake a number of masquerades. His first major helper was Charles Giffard, from one of the south Staffordshire Catholic families, which had supported the Royalist cause throughout. Giffard took the King to Boscobel House. On 4 September he hid in an oak tree with William Careless, another Catholic and one-time officer in Lord Loughborough's army. From there Charles was taken via Hobbal Grange to Mosely Hall on 8 September. There he was disguised as servant to Jane Lane whose brother John had been one of Lord Loughborough's colonels. They travelled to Bentley and on to Bromsgrove, Snitterfield, Stratford-upon-Avon, Stow-on-the-Wold and Cirencester to Abbots Leigh. Here on 12 September he was joined by Henry, Lord Wilmot, with whom he had escaped from Worcester. Three days later Charles and Jane Lane travelled to Trent near Sherborne. On 22 September he attempted to get a ship to France at Charmouth near Lyme. It did not turn up. Returning to Trent, he stayed there a week waiting to make new contacts. Eventually a passage was negotiated from Brighthelmstone (Brighton) with a certain Nicholas Tattershall. On 13 October a 50 mile (80 kilometre) trip via Heale, Hursley, Twyford and Hambledon (by which time he had rejoined Wilmot) was begun. The following day Charles lodged at the George Inn in Brighthelmstone. One day later he landed at Fécamp. The Restoration was now possible.

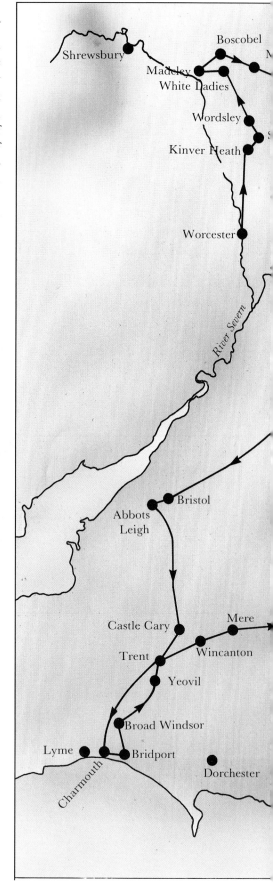

y Hall

entley

ridge

omsgrove

Wootten Wawen

ver Avon

Stratford-upon-Avon

Long Marston

Chipping Campden

Stow-on-the-Wold

Oxford

Cirencester

0   20   40 Miles

0   20   40   60 Km

Heale House

Mottisfont

sbury

Hambledon

Southampton

Brighton

Shoreham

oole

MUSEUMS
AND TOWN SITES

The museum is the birthplace of Robert Blake, MP for Bridgwater, who fought for Parliament in the South-west and in 1649 was given joint command of the fleet. The display consists of artefacts and documents belonging to Blake, also Civil War weapons and armour.

ASHBY-DE-LA-ZOUCH

Ashby-de-la-Zouch Museum, North Street, Ashby-de-la-Zouch, Leicestershire
Admission charge.
Open: Weekdays, 10.00a.m. – 12.00a.m., 2.00p.m. – 4.00p.m.; Saturday, 10.00a.m. – 5.00p.m.; Sunday 2.00p.m. – 5.00p.m.

The Civil War display includes a model of Ashby-de-la-Zouch Castle under siege with Civil War figures and a display board giving information about local events in the war.

BASING

Basing House, Basing, Basingstoke, Hampshire RG24 0HB
Admission charge except for disabled visitors.
Open: April to September, Wednesday to Sunday and Bank Holidays, 2.00p.m. – 6.00p.m.

The exhibition within the grounds of Basing House ruins displays archaeological material and pictures of the Civil War period. The ruins themselves show possibly the most extensive Civil War earthworks in England, and the Great Barn still bears the scars of Sir William Waller's siege of 1643. Costumed guided tours.

BRIDGWATER

Admiral Blake Museum, 6 Blake Street, Bridgwater, Somerset
Location: Off dual carriageway opposite the swimming-pool, through St Mary's Street, Dampirt Street, to Blake Street.
No admission charge.
Open: Monday to Saturday, 11.00a.m. – 5.00p.m.; Sunday, 2.00p.m. – 5.00p.m.

BRISTOL

Bristol City Museum, Queen's Road, Bristol BS8 1RL
No admission charge.
Open: Every day, 10.00a.m. – 5.00p.m.

There is no Civil War display in the museum, but very fine Civil War earthworks can be seen at Brandon Hill on the west side of the city. Westbury College, Prince Rupert's headquarters in 1643, can be see at nearby Westbury-on-Trym.

BUDE

Bude-Stratton Historical and Folk Exhibition, The Lower Wharf, Bude, Cornwall
Location: Near Bude Canal.
Admission charge.
Open: Easter to September, 10.30a.m. – 4.00p.m.

The museum, which is near the site of the battle of Stamford Hill, has minor artefacts from the Civil War period on display.

CHESTER

King Charles Tower (Branch Museum of The Grosvenor Museum, 27 Grosvenor Street, Chester CH1 2DD)
Location: In the city walls on the north-east side.
Admission charge.
Open: Easter to October, weekdays, 1.00p.m. – 5.00p.m.; Saturday, 10.00a.m. – 5.00p.m.; Sunday, 2.00p.m. – 5.30p.m. November to March, Saturday, 1.00p.m. – 4.30p.m. or dusk; Sunday, 2.00p.m. – 4.30p.m. or dusk.

Illustrated panels describe the Civil War in Cheshire and the siege of Chester. There are Civil War objects on display, plus replicas of a Royalist and a Parliamentarian in the upper chamber.

The tower was heavily damaged by the Parliamentary bombardment and subsequently rebuilt in its present form. Several sites in the city have connections with the war, particularly of course the city walls.

CLONMEL, EIRE

Tipperary S.R. County Museum, Parnell Street, Clonmel, Tipperary
Location: In the centre of Clonmel.
No admission charge.
Open: Tuesday to Saturday,
10.00a.m. – 1.00p.m.,
2.00p.m. – 5.00p.m.

The displays in the museum cover the history of the county, including the Cromwellian campaigns and the siege of Clonmel by Cromwell in April 1650.

COLCHESTER

Colchester and Essex Museum, 14 Ryegate Road, Colchester, Essex
Location: On the site of the castle, off the east end of the High Street.
Admission charge.
Open: April to September,
Monday to Saturday,
10.00a.m. – 5.00p.m.;
Sunday, 2.30p.m. – 5.00p.m.
October to March,
Monday to Friday,
10.00a.m. – 5.00p.m.;
Saturday, 10.00a.m. – 4.00p.m.

The museum contains a special display about the siege of Colchester in 1648, chronicling the main events, and has produced two booklets on the subject – one for adults and one for children.
Buildings in the town that were involved in the siege include Siege House, St John's Abbey Gateway and the tower of St Mary-of-the-Walls (now St Mary's Art Centre).

DEVIZES

Devizes Museum, 41 Long Street, Devizes, Wiltshire
Location: In the town centre near St John's Church.
Admission charge.
Open: Monday to Saturday,
10.00a.m. – 5.00p.m.
(4.00p.m. in winter).

The museum has a small display with a figure in Civil War armour and locally found Civil War swords and cannon balls. There is a brief account of the war in Wiltshire and of the battle of Roundway Down, which was fought about a mile from the town. Cannon ball and musket ball holes can be seen in the fabric of two churches in the town.

DUBLIN, EIRE

National Museum of Ireland, Kildare Street, Dublin 2
No admission charge.
Open: Tuesday to Saturday,
10.00a.m. – 6.00p.m.;
Sunday, 2.00p.m. – 5.00p.m.

The numismatic collection of the museum contains provincial and Civil War issues of the 1640s. The decorative arts collection includes glass, ceramics, costume etc. of the period, though not specifically related to personalities or events of the Civil War.

DUNBAR

Local History Centre, Newton Port, Haddington, East Lothian
Location: Above the branch library in Haddington, eleven miles west of Dunbar.
No admission charge.
Open: Monday, 2.00p.m. – 6.00p.m.;
Tuesday, 10.00a.m. – 1.00p.m.,
2.00p.m. – 7.00p.m.; Wednesday, closed all day;
Thursday, Friday,
2.00p.m. – 5.00p.m.

This is a reference library with background information on the battle of Dunbar.

EDGEHILL

Edgehill Battle Museum, The Estate Yard, Farnborough Hall, Farnborough, Banbury, Oxfordshire OX17 1DU
Location: Four miles north of Banbury on the A423.
Admission charge.
Open: April to September, Wednesdays and Saturdays,
2.00p.m. – 6.00p.m.

The museum displays a large diorama of the battle of Edgehill with 3,000 model soldiers, commentary and music. There are costumed dummies, maps, flags, armour, weapons, stocks and 'punishment horse'. Also available is a comprehensive guidebook giving a full tour of points of interest on the battlefield. Guided tours of the battlefield can be arranged for groups, and museum staff are able to visit schools and clubs throughout the year to give illustrated lectures.

EXETER

Royal Albert Museum, Queen Street, Exeter
No admission charge.
Open: Tuesday to Saturday
    (not Bank Holidays),
    10.00a.m. – 5.15p.m.

The museum houses a display of Civil War armour from Exeter Castle, and features contemporary architecture, ceramics, industries, town life and coins. Nearby Civil War sights include Exeter City walls and Powderham Castle. There is no specific war tour in the area, but the general City Trail draws attention to some Civil War features of interest.

GLOUCESTER

Gloucester Folk Museum, 99 – 103 Westgate Street, Gloucester GL1 1HP
Location: Close to city centre.
No admission charge.
Open: Monday to Saturday,
    10.00a.m. – 5.00p.m. including
    Bank Holiday Mondays.

Graphics and information panels describe the siege of Gloucester in 1643 by the Royalists, and the eventual relief by the Earl of Essex's Trained Bands. Items displayed include armour, ammunition and articles such as gauntlets, shoes, and horse harness typical of the period. The south gates of the city which were damaged in the siege are now displayed in the museum.
    Colonel Massey, the governor who took over the city's defences in 1642, lodged in what is now 26 Westgate Street; the impressive timber framing of this building can only be seen from the very narrow Maverdine Passage at its side. Matson House, Charles I's headquarters, may be seen in Matson Lane (now Selwyn School).

Gloucester City East Gate, Eastgate Street, Gloucester
Location: Close to city centre.
No admission charge.
Open: May to September, Wednesday
    and Friday, 2.00p.m. – 5.00p.m.;
    Saturday 10.00a.m. – 12.00noon
    and 2.00p.m. – 5.00p.m.

This monument was the scene of fighting during the siege of 1643 and this is described in exhibition panels, a guide and an audio commentary.

HEREFORD

The Old House, High Town, Hereford
Location: In the city centre.
Admission charge.
Open: Monday to Saturday,
    10.00a.m. – 5.30p.m. (closed
    1.00p.m. – 2.00p.m. and Monday
    and Saturday afternoons in
    winter).

The Old House dates from 1621 and displays of domestic items, fine furniture and Civil War armour are laid out on three floors to give visitors an insight into life in the seventeenth century. School visits are arranged with a Civil War theme at which reproduction armour and buff coats are used. There is also an annual twelfth night festivities afternoon in Civil War costume.

Churchill Gardens Museum, Venn's Lane, Aylestone Hill, Hereford
Location: Off the A465 Worcester Road, twenty minutes walk from the city centre.
Admission charge.
Open: Tuesday to Saturday,
    2.00p.m. – 5.00p.m., and also on
    Sunday during the summer.

A siege mortar, 'Roaring Meg', stands outside the museum. This was used in the siege of Goodrich Castle. A mortar ball is on display inside the museum.

HULL

Hull City Museums, c/o Town Docks Museum, Queen Victoria Square, Hull HU1 3DX
No admission charge.
Open: Monday to Saturday,
    10.00a.m. – 5.00p.m.; Sunday,
    1.30p.m. – 4.30p.m.

Seventeenth-century interiors are at Wilberforce House, where Charles I was entertained in 1639. Also to be seen in Hull are the Old White Harte (plotting chamber) and Beverly Gate, the site of the towns's refusal to admit Charles I in 1642.

HUNTINGDON

Cromwell Museum, Grammar School Walk, Huntingdon, Cambridgeshire
Location: In the town centre opposite the Market Place.
No admission charge.
Open: April to October, Tuesday to
      Friday, 11.00a.m. – 1.00p.m.,
      2.00p.m. – 5.00p.m.; Saturday,
      Sunday, 11.00a.m. – 1.00p.m.,
      2.00p.m. – 4.00p.m.
      November to March, Tuesday to
      Friday, 2.00p.m. – 5.00p.m.;
      Saturday, 11.00a.m. – 1.00p.m.,
      2.00p.m. – 4.00p.m.; Sunday,
      2.00p.m. – 4.00p.m.

The museum is mainly concerned with the life of Oliver Cromwell and contains paintings and manuscripts, armour, swords, etc.

LEICESTER

Newarke Houses Museum and Museum of the Royal Leicestershire Regiment, The Newarke, Leicester LE2 7BY
No admission charge.
Open: Monday to Saturday,
      10.00a.m. – 5.30p.m.;
      Sunday, 2.00p.m. – 5.30p.m.

The two museums are in historic buildings which were in the thick of the siege of Leicester. The Newarke Houses Museum is a general museum of local social history, but it includes a period room of the seventeenth century and some armour. The Regimental Museum is, in fact, a fortified gateway which linked the town of Leicester to the Newarke, now a historic district of the city containing Prince Rupert's Gateway and garden walls with evidence of bombardment.

LICHFIELD

St Mary's Centre, Market Square, Lichfield, Staffordshire WS13 6LG
Location: In the city centre next to Dr
      Johnson's Birthplace.

Admission charge.
Open: Monday to Saturday,
      10.00a.m. – 5.00p.m.;
      Sunday 10.30a.m. – 5.00p.m.

Three panels in the museum describe the three sieges of Lichfield during the Civil War. Nearby Civil War sights include the Cathedral Close and Dam Street.

LINCOLN

City and County Museum, Greyfriars, Broadgate, Lincoln LN2 1HQ
Location: Near the river, close to where the A46 enters the city.
Admission charge.
Open: Monday to Saturday,
      10.00a.m. – 5.00p.m.;
      Sunday, 2.30p.m. – 5.00p.m.

The display consist of pikeman's and harquebusier's (trooper's) armour, contemporary everyday objects and maps of the major actions in the county.
    There is a separate display in the Coin Room at the Usher Art Gallery, Lindum Hill, Lincoln.

LONDON

Museum of London, London Wall, London EC2Y 5HN
Location: Nearest Underground stations – St Paul's, Barbican, Moorgate.
No admission charge.
Open: Tuesday to Saturday,
      10.00a.m. – 6.00p.m.;
      Sunday, 2.00p.m. – 6.00p.m.

The Museum of London is concerned primarily with the social history of London. However, the early seventeenth-century gallery contains a small section on the Civil War, the Commonwealth and the Restoration. London's involvement in the war is outlined on information panels, and objects on display include weapons, coins, lockets featuring Charles I and a death mask of Cromwell.

NANTWICH

Nantwich Museum, Pillory Street, Nantwich, Cheshire
Location: Close to the town centre.
No admission charge.
Open: 10.30a.m. – 4.30p.m. (except
      Wednesday and Sunday).

As well as graphics and a description of the battle of Nantwich, the museum has a small display of Civil War armour and a letter written by Sir Thomas Fairfax.

NASEBY

Naseby Battle and Farm Museum, Purlieu Farm, Naseby, Northamptonshire
Location: In Naseby village.
Admission charge.
Open: Easter to September, Sundays, 2.00p.m. – 6.00p.m.; at other times for parties by arrangement.

The museum houses a miniature layout of the battlefield with 850 model soldiers. The display shows three stages of the battle, which is described in a ten-minute commentary. Relics from the field include swords, helmets, breast-plate, musket and cannon balls. Also on display are maps, letters, etc.

NEWARK

Newark Museum, Appletongate, Newark, Nottinghamshire NG24 1JY
Location: In the centre of the town.
No admission charge.
Open: Weekdays (except Thursday), 10.00a.m. – 5.00p.m. (closed 1.00p.m. – 2.00p.m.); Sundays (April to September) 2.00p.m. – 5.00p.m.

There are two cases in the museum devoted to the Civil War, displaying a coin hoard, siege pieces, pottery, siege map and cannon balls. There is also a model of the Queen's Sconce as it might have appeared. A Civil War information leaflet is available and the museum has also produced a booklet, *Newark in the Civil War*.

NEWBURY

Newbury District Museum, The Wharf, Newbury, Berkshire RG14 5AS
Location: Just off the A34 near the town centre.
No admission charge.
Open: October to March, Monday to Saturday, 10.00a.m. – 4.00p.m.; April to September, Monday to Saturday, 10.00a.m. – 6.00p.m.; Sundays and Bank Holidays, 2.00p.m. – 6.00p.m. (closed on Wednesday throughout the year).

An audio-visual presentation tells the story of the two battles of Newbury and the siege of Donnington Castle within the context of the reasons for the Civil War. Local objects connected with the battles, etc. are displayed in the museum, including a porcelain bowl used by Oliver Cromwell.

OXFORD

Museum of Oxford, St Aldate's, Oxford OX1 1DZ
Location: In the town hall in the centre of the city.
No admission charge.
Open: Tuesday to Saturday, 10.00a.m. – 5.00p.m.

The Civil War section of the museum describes the important position of Oxford during the war, and the display includes armour, map of actions in Oxfordshire, the 'Oxford Crown Piece' minted by Charles I and Jan de Wyck's 1689 painting of the siege of Oxford. There is a Civil War worksheet for school parties.

PRESTON

Harris Museum and Art Gallery, Market Square, Preston, Lancashire
Location: In the centre of the town.
No admission charge.
Open: Monday to Saturday, 10.00a.m. – 5.00p.m. (closed Sunday and Bank Holidays).

The Civil War displays in the museum are part of a large gallery covering the history of Preston. They contain relevant artefacts, some local and one or two from the Royal Armouries. The nearby site of the battle of Preston is now largely built up.

TAUNTON

Somerset County Museum, Taunton Castle, Taunton, Somerset TA1 4AA
Location: In the town centre.
Admission charge.
Open: Monday to Saturday, 10.00a.m. – 5.00p.m. (including spring and summer Bank Holidays).

Taunton Castle, which houses the museum, was Robert Blake's headquarters during the siege of Taunton in 1644–5. Inside is a small display on Taunton during the Civil War. The main exhibit is a hoard of 275 silver coins buried in 1643 or shortly after.

WOODSTOCK

Oxfordshire County Museum, Fletcher's House, Woodstock, Oxfordshire

Location: Fifty yards from the town hall, near the town gates to Blenheim Park.
No admission charge.
Open: May to September, Monday to
      Friday, 10.00a.m. – 5.00p.m.;
      Saturday, 10.00a.m. – 6.00p.m.;
      Sunday 2.00p.m. – 6.00p.m.
      October to April, Tuesday to
      Friday, 10.00a.m. – 4.00p.m.;
      Saturday, 10.00a.m. – 5.00p.m.;
      Sunday 2.00p.m. – 5.00p.m.

Explanatory maps with graphics and text describe the war in Oxfordshire, and there is a display of cavalry trooper's armour, swords, cannon balls, musket balls. The museum also houses a sites and monuments record with public access.

WORCESTER

Commandery Civil War Centre, Sidbury, Worcester

Location: By the canal along Sidbury, not far from the City Walls Road.
Admission charge.
Open: Monday to Saturday,
      10.30a.m. – 5.00p.m.;
      Sunday, 2.00p.m. – 5.00p.m.

The Commandery dates back to 1085, though most of the present building was constructed around 1500. During the Civil War it was the home of the Royalist Wylde family, and Charles II used it as his headquarters during the battle of Worcester in 1651. There is a fine display of weapons, armour, period rooms and an audio-visual programme re-enacting the events of the battle of Worcester.

The museum publishes a pamphlet, *Worcester Civil War Trail*, to guide visitors to Civil War sites in the city – the Cathedral, Sidbury Gate, Fort Royal, Nash's House, King Charles House, St Helen's Church and, two miles outside the city centre, Powick.

YORK

York Castle Museum, Eye of York, York YO1 1RY

Location: Centre of the city.
Admission charge.
Open: Summer, 9.30a.m. to 5.30p.m.;
      winter, 9.30a.m. to 4.00p.m.

An entire gallery is devoted to the Civil War in Yorkshire from 1642 to 1648, which tells the story by following the journal of a soldier who fought throughout the period. There is also an audio-visual display devoted to the causes of the war, plus a very large collection of armour, weapons and other items from the period. It is probably the most comprehensive Civil War gallery in the country.

Among the many Civil War sites nearby are the King's Manor (seat of the Council of the North), the walls of the city, which was besieged in 1644, and Clifford's Tower, which housed a garrison with cannon mounted on its roof. Marston Moor lies seven miles to the west of the city.

Index

*Italics indicate that the
entry is either illustrated or
appears on a map.*

206

208